BF
1021
P36

D0944254

BF 1021 P36

3 0450 00023 1705

PARAPSYCHOLOGY:

Its Relation to Physics, Biology,

Psychology, and Psychiatry

edited by

Gertrude R. Schmeidler

The Scarecrow Press, Inc.

Metuchen, N.J.   1976

John F. Kennedy Memorial
Library - CAL STATE L.A.

Library of Congress Cataloging in Publication Data
Main entry under title:

Parapsychology.

    Papers resulting from a symposium sponsored by
the American Society for Psychical Research, held
in New York City, May 18, 1974.
    Includes index.
    1. Psychical research--Congresses. I. Schmeid-
ler, Gertrude Raffel. II. American Society for
Psychical Research (Founded 1906) [DNLM: 1. Parapsychology. BF1031 P2235]
BF1021.P36   133.8'01'5   76-916
ISBN 0-8108-0909-5

Copyright © 1976 by The American Society
for Psychical Research, Inc.

Manufactured in the United States of America

John F. Kennedy Memorial
Library = CAL STATE L. A.

CONTENTS

iii

ACKNOWLEDGMENTS

Thanks are due to Miss Frances Kish, Dr. Lawrence LeShan, and Dr. Montague Ullman, who served with me on the Symposium Committee, and also to Mrs. Judith Skutch who, working in collaboration with members of the ASPR staff, was in charge of arrangements.

I am especially grateful to Mrs. Laura A. Dale, editor of the Society's Proceedings and Journal, for her expert editorial assistance from the first to the final steps in the production of this volume, and for making the Index.

G. R. S.

PARTICIPANTS

IRVIN L. CHILD is a professor in the Department of Psychology at Yale University, where he received his Ph. D. He is the author of Italian or American? The Second Generation in Conflict (1943), Child Training and Personality: A Cross-Cultural Study (1953, with J. W. M. Whiting), and Humanistic Psychology and the Research Tradition: Their Several Virtues (1973). Dr. Child has also published many articles in scholarly journals on personality, esthetics, and, most recently, parapsychology.

JAN EHRENWALD is a consulting psychiatrist at Roosevelt Hospital (New York City). He received his medical degree at the University of Prague and did postgraduate work at the University of Vienna. He has served on the ASPR Board of Trustees since 1956 and is a charter member of the Parapsychological Association. Dr. Ehrenwald's books include Telepathy and Medical Psychology (1948), New Dimensions of Deep Analysis (1954), From Medicine Man to Freud (1956), Neurosis in the Family and Patterns of Psychosocial Defense (1963), and Psychiatry: Myth and Method (1966). He has also published more than a hundred papers on neuropsychiatry, psychoanalysis, and parapsychology in the professional journals.

BERNARD R. GRAD is an associate professor in the Department of Psychiatry at McGill University, where he received his Ph. D. (magna cum laude in experimental morphology), and an associate scientist, Royal Victoria Hospital, Montreal. He has published more than 70 papers dealing with biology and related topics and a number of reports on his experiments in unorthodox healing.

S DAVID KAHN completed his medical studies at Harvard and was trained in psychoanalysis at Columbia University.

vi

Having completed five years of research in the psychophysiology of biofeedback while on the faculty of Emory University School of Medicine, he is now in the private practice of psychoanalysis. Dr. Kahn is a member of the ASPR Board of Trustees and has served as the Society's Secretary since 1964. He is the author of a number of papers on parapsychological topics, including "Studies in Extrasensory Perception: Experiments Utilizing an Electronic Scoring Device," published as Vol. 25 (1952) of Proceedings A. S. P. R.

LAWRENCE LESHAN received his doctorate (in psychology) at the University of Chicago. He taught at Roosevelt University and at the New School for Social Research, and has served as research consultant to the Union Theological Seminary (all in New York). Dr. LeShan, a member of the ASPR Board of Trustees since 1972, has made numerous contributions to the psychological and parapsychological journals and is the author of The Medium, the Mystic, and the Physicist: Toward a General Theory of the Paranormal (1974) and How to Meditate (1974).

ROBERT L. MORRIS received his doctorate (in biological psychology) from Duke University. Following two years of postdoctoral work in the Duke Medical Center, he became research coordinator for the Psychical Research Foundation (Durham, N. C.). He is now a full-time lecturer in parapsychology at the University of California (Santa Barbara). Dr. Morris, who has been active in parapsychology for more than a decade, has published a number of theoretical and experimental articles in the parapsychological journals. He served as president of the Parapsychological Association in 1974.

R. B. ROBERTS, a physicist, took his Ph. D. at Princeton and now is with the Carnegie Institution of Washington in the Department of Terrestrial Magnetism. His areas of research have been in nuclear physics, weapon development, biophysics, biosynthesis in bacteria, and biochemistry of memory in mice. He has served as president of the Biophysical Society (1964) and vice-president of A. A. A. S. (1967). Dr. Roberts, who is a member of the ASPR Board of Trustees, has been interested in parapsychology since his undergraduate days and has carried out occasional ESP experiments.

J. H. RUSH received his doctoral degree (in physics) from

Duke University. He has served as assistant professor of physics and astronomy at Denison University, research physicist in the High Altitude Observatory (Boulder, Colo.), and physicist in the National Center for Atmospheric Research (also in Boulder). He has contributed papers on astronomy and physics to the professional journals and is author of the book, The Dawn of Life. A charter member of the Parapsychological Association, Dr. Rush is also the author of the monograph, New Directions in Parapsychological Research (1964), and of many articles and reviews in the parapsychological journals.

GERTRUDE R. SCHMEIDLER completed her Ph. D. (in psychology) at Radcliffe College (Harvard University) and is a professor in the Department of Psychology, City College of the City University of New York. A charter member of the Parapsychological Association, she served as its president in 1959 and 1971. She has been a member of the ASPR Board of Trustees since 1964 and vice-president of the Society since 1971. Dr. Schmeidler has published many experimental and theoretical papers in psychology and parapsychology and is the author of ESP and Personality Patterns (1958, with R. A. McConnell) and the editor of Extrasensory Perception (1969).

BERTHOLD E. SCHWARZ is in the private practice of psychiatry. He obtained his medical degree at the New York University College of Medicine. Following a period of internship at Mary Hitchcock Memorial Hospital, he was a fellow in psychiatry at the Mayo Clinic and received the M. S. degree from the Mayo Graduate School of Medicine. He has contributed articles to various scientific journals on the psychiatric aspects of psi and is the author of Psycho-Dynamics (1965), The Jacques Romano Story (1968), and Parent-Child Telepathy (1971).

MANTAGUE ULLMAN is a graduate of the New York University College of Medicine and of the comprehensive course in psychoanalysis at the New York Medical College. He is an associate professor of psychiatry at the Downstate Medical Center, State University of New York, and director of the Division of Parapsychology and Psychophysics (formerly the Dream Laboratory) at Maimonides Medical Center. He has been on the ASPR Board of Trustees since 1948 and the Society's president since 1971. A charter member of the Parapsychological Association, he served as its president also in 1966. Dr. Ullman is author of numerous articles on psychiatry and psychotherapy. He has also published widely in the parapsychological journals and is the author of the monograph, Dream Studies and Telepathy: An Experimental Approach (1970, with S. Krippner), and the book, Dream Telepathy (1973), with S. Krippner and A. Vaughan).

ROBERT L. VAN DE CASTLE received his Ph. D. (in clinical psychology) at the University of North Carolina. Having served as a research associate in the Parapsychology Laboratory (Duke University), the associate director of the Institute of Dream Research (Miami), and an associate professor of psychology at the University of North Carolina, he is currently a professor of clinical psychology, School of Medicine, University of Virginia. A charter member of the Parapsychological Association, he was its president in 1970. Dr. Van de Castle has published many articles on dreams and projective tests as well as research reports in the parapsychological journals. He is the author of Content Analysis of Dreams (1966, with C. S. Hall) and The Psychology of Dreaming (1971).

FOREWORD

The papers presented in this volume are the outcome
of a symposium sponsored by the American Society for Psychical Research (ASPR), held in New York City on May 18,
1974. This meeting took place some nine years after a similar one, the "ASPR Forum on Extrasensory Perception,"
which represented an initial effort by the Society to present
a broad overview of the progress of scientific research in
parapsychology to the general public. At that time the key-
note speaker, Professor Henry Margenau of Yale, offered
some very sound advice: "Tolerate the strident critical voices
of hard-boiled, pragmatic, and satisfied scientists without too
much concern, and continue your own painstaking search for
an understanding of new kinds of experience, possibly in terms
of concepts which now appear strange" ("ESP in the Framework of Modern Science," Journal of the American Society
for Psychical Research, 60(1966), 227-8).

The ASPR, organized in 1885 under the leadership of
William James and with Simon Newcomb as its first president, has as one of its goals the collection of reliable information concerning paranormal phenomena and the presentation
of such information to the public. Events in this field have
been moving forward so rapidly since Professor Margenau's
words of advice quoted above that the Society felt it would be
timely to organize a second meeting which would again present authoritative accounts of research to a public whose
sources of information about parapsychology often contain
much that is unreliable.

Since most of the current ongoing research falls into
four major areas--physics, biology, psychology, and psychi-
atry--these were chosen as the main focal points for the
papers presented. Among the questions the symposium participants addressed themselves to were: What are the significant experimental findings? What are their implications?
What are their potential applications? What further research
is needed? As a consequence, the reader of this volume will

find himself exposed to a wide range of experimental and clinical concerns, strategies, and approaches; he will become familiar with studies carried out by some of the foremost experimentalists in parapsychology today, working in both academic and medical settings.

An explosion of concern with parapsychology has been generated both from below as a result of growing interest on the part of young people and from above as a result of the greater credibility extended to its findings by established scientific bodies (the acceptance in 1969 of the Parapsychological Association as an affiliate by the American Association for the Advancement of Science) and by national funding agencies (National Institute of Mental Health). The first has had important consequences in both education and research: college-level courses in parapsychology are becoming commonplace and research has been extended into numerous academic settings. The second has had a profound effect upon the temper of scientific criticism, transforming the belligerent hostility with which scientists responded to parapsychological claims in an earlier epoch to either suspended judgment or cautious acceptance. In a few instances, rather dramatic transformations have taken place, resulting in an active and courageous engagement with the field at the level either of research or of theory building.

The papers in this volume will, I think, convey to the reader a sense of movement in the field. Parapsychology is gathering both technology and talent on a broad enough scale to enable it to move beyond the fact-gathering, descriptive, and proof-oriented research phase into a phase where it can take for granted its own legitimacy and get on with the important business of redesigning a world view where the "para" can be dropped from a consideration of psi events. Parapsychology has suffered a long and awkward adolescence, and scientific interest in the field has had a painful and tenuous existence for close to a century. This delayed maturation is the result of an unfortunate circumstance related to the very factors making for the advance of science itself. As its forward thrust rescues certain phenomena from folklore, there is at the same time a backward push designed to prevent the contamination of the forward-moving enterprise by the unscientific conditions prevailing at the source of the folklore base. This is the nature of the tension which the understandable-- and, indeed, necessary--conservative stance of science has, in the past, rigidified into the hardened position of the orthodox establishment. Thus, parapsychologists have had an unnecessarily tough struggle on their hands, given the weight of the evidence, the number and qualifications of the investigators, and the seriousness of the undertaking. There is a growing feeling now, however, that the urge to accommodate is gaining ascendancy over the urge to reject.

I have ventured this optimistic forecast knowing full well that the history of psychical research should teach us that similar predictions have in the past been quite unreliable. Despite this, however, it seems to me that one cannot come away from the experimental work provided by the papers in this volume without sensing both the first stirrings of this change and the exciting things foreshadowed by them. Parapsychological data can no longer be swept under some consciously disowned, but nevertheless real ideological rug. The work of these experimentalists is slowly but surely finding its way into the mainstream of science. Once this comes about, all of man's ambitious encounters with nature through the application of scientific method will stand to benefit. Contradictions now so glaring and disturbing will eventually lead to a resolution at a higher level and result in greater common ground between what we now regard as scientifically valid data and what we now call paranormal data. This intermediate state of greater commonality, based on a growing recognition of the interrelationship between the two, will in turn breed its own contradiction, which will have to be resolved at a still higher level. When that point is reached, it will no longer make any sense to refer to the phenomena studied by parapsychology as paranormal; and by the same token it will no longer be possible to view the world in a way that leaves out and disregards the presence and significance of the psi dimensions of our existence.

Montague Ullman
President, American Society
for Psychical Research

INTRODUCTION

The articles that follow are both a survey and a sampler of parapsychology. Some emphasize an overview of research findings in a special sub-area and devote little space to theory. Some sketch the kind of theory that can unify laboratory findings and use little space for the data with which the theory must deal. Others are written from a more personal perspective. One psychiatrist, for example, offers jottings from his casebook which cover the range of psi from infancy to old age and suggests what these experiences mean for the life span. One psychologist, in order to tell us "what it feels like to be a parapsychologist," describes the ambivalence of our exhilaration at the challenge of psi's extraordinary implications and our timidity in developing new paradigms of classical science to admit them.

In spite of the variety of approaches, two themes emerge. One is the sober and critical way that the symposium participants, each a professional in a conventional scientific field, report the challenging facts that are parapsychology's subject matter. The other is their emphasis on integrating these facts into their own fields of expertise, from physics, biology, and psychology to psychiatric theory and practice. Though the tones of the articles range from factual to personal and the topics, from anthropology to nuclear physics, nevertheless they all seem to carry the same message. This message, as I read it, is that parapsychology relates to the conventional sciences in a way that extends their scope and will therefore extend and help to generalize their theories.

Gertrude R. Schmeidler
The City College
The City University of New York

Part I

PARAPSYCHOLOGY AND PHYSICS

Parapsychology has been a controversial topic for a long time. In science, this should not happen. Surely we have a right to expect that, once scientific methods are employed, controversy will quickly be resolved. Results should soon fall into one of two patterns. Either they will support the basic hypothesis so strongly that no reasonable person could deny it, or else they will be so inconsistent with the hypothesis that no reasonable person could continue to accept it.

Why then should parapsychological findings remain for so long on the borderline of scientific respectability? There may be many minor contributing factors, but probably the central answer lies in the topic of this section: the relation between physics and parapsychology. Classical physics could not cope with parapsychological findings, just as it could not reconcile the way light sometimes acts like a particle and sometimes like a wave. Though this latter difficulty troubled physicists, it left most laymen, such as psychologists, almost undisturbed. However, the conflict between classical physical laws and parapsychological data made many laymen feel that it was necessary to reject one or the other. Most opted for accepting physics.

Consider, for example, a recent statement by one eminent psychologist:

> Telepathy at short range is conceivable, barely ... but this becomes less conceivable when we are told that distance makes no difference to the transmission. And clairvoyance: where does the energy come from in that case? Or in psychokinesis? The parapsychologist ... is saying that there are big holes in physiology and physics. Set aside precognition, the very idea of which contains a con-

3

tradiction, and one must still have doubts, to say
the least, about parapsychology, as long as it maintains that bland disregard for the physical implications [D. O. Hebb, "What Psychology Is About,"
American Psychologist, 29 (1974), 78].

What Hebb writes here represents what many others
feel. It fits neatly into the picture that T. S. Kuhn has giv-
en us of scientific progress (The Structure of Scientific Revolutions; Chicago: University of Chicago Press, 1962). Kuhn's
argument in essence is that a science like physics will ordinarily present a general picture, or set of laws, or paradigm,
which is widely accepted. This is the base from which research is performed. As research advances knowledge, the
paradigm proves its usefulness. But during the same period,
some research is being performed which uncovers trouble-
some facts that do not fit into the basic, accepted laws.
When such facts loom large and give too much trouble, a
new paradigm is stated to include them. Such a new paradigm is a revolution in scientific thinking, like the Coper-
nican thesis that the earth revolves around the sun and Darwin's theory of evolution. A new paradigm demands so dras-
tic a turnabout, so clear a rejection of what "everyone" has
always assumed, that it is not to be accepted lightly. It
poses an intellectual threat to those who have found stability
in well-established, authoritative dicta, especially in fields
other than their own.

In the passage quoted above, Hebb is telling us that
he has made a prejudgment. He will accept physics' rules
for what can and cannot happen. ESP and PK are inconceiv-
able according to the physical laws he has learned; and he
will doubt the research findings rather than demand that physicists provide a new paradigm. Such an attitude, publicly
proclaimed by someone who is highly respected, seems to explain why the controversy about parapsychology has lingered
for so long. Authoritative individuals persist in denying the
facts. But the facts persist too. They are stubborn. They
will not go away.

What do physicists say? It is my impression that
they have been less likely to use this argument against
parapsychology. They seem to regard their own field as
a science in flux, with rewritable rather than immutable
"laws." Several of us, especially in the 1950s and 1960s,
who spoke on parapsychology to groups of psychologists or
physicists or engineers have remarked on this contrast: that

often some psychologists would argue emotionally that physical laws showed the data must be wrong, but that engineers or physicists almost never made such flat pronouncements. A question period following the talk would be more likely to find physicists inquiring (as of course many psychologists also did) about details of procedure or of data patterns that there had not been time to examine fully in the talk itself: to find what the facts were, rather than to express prejudgments about them.

Both of the physicists whose papers appear in this section deal with the point that Hebb raised. In the first paper, Dr. J. H. Rush presents some key parapsychological findings, examines their validity, and discusses the issues they pose. He asks, in effect, three questions. The first, which he answers in the affirmative, is: Are the findings clear enough, and well enough confirmed, to demand attention? The second, to which he gives a negative answer, is: Can these findings be brought into harmony with the paradigms of classical physics? And the third, where his answer is open but tends toward the affirmative, is: Can the findings be brought into harmony with the new paradigms which physicists are developing?

In the second paper, Dr. R. B. Roberts dismisses Hebb's point out of hand and proposes a theory which both organizes the facts we know and predicts some new ones. His theory is testable by research and it is stated so clearly that it can be disproved; it thus meets the two criteria that many of us use when we try to judge whether or not a theory is a good one. Once the research he outlines is performed, and the older experiments which bear on the theory are collated, the theory will be rejected or it will be supported. In either case we will know what to do next: follow out its implications if it is supported, or if it is rejected, develop an alternative.

J. H. Rush

PHYSICAL ASPECTS OF PSI PHENOMENA

> If "dead" matter has reared up this curious
> landscape of fiddling crickets, song sparrows,
> and wondering men, it must be plain even to
> the most devoted materialist that the matter
> of which he speaks contains amazing, if not
> dreadful, powers (Loren Eiseley, Harper's
> Magazine, October 1953).

1   THE VARIETIES OF PSI PHENOMENA: An Introduction

Prior to the experimental studies that were begun at the Parapsychology Laboratory of Duke University in about 1933, extrasensory perception (ESP) had been conceived rather loosely as "mental telepathy," meaning the communication of information from one mind directly to another without sensory means.   The idea of telepathy was audacious enough; apparently no investigator had seriously considered the possibility that a mind might somehow acquire extrasensory information that was not in anyone's mind.   Yet one of the earliest discoveries at Duke was that successful ESP subjects generally scored about equally well whether the target information was normally known to another person or not.

Nearly all of the fundamental ESP experiments at the Duke University Laboratory were designed around a very simple device, the ESP symbol cards.   For various reasons, these consisted of five symbols--the star, circle, square, cross, and wavy lines now familiar to many people--usually in a 25-card deck consisting of five cards of each symbol. The distinctive symbols were easy to remember, and the results of experiments were easy to evaluate statistically.

In a typical experiment, the cards were arranged in

approximately random order by shuffling in a simple machine. Later, randomization was done by reference to tables of random numbers. Then the experimenter presented the randomized sequence of symbols as ESP objectives, or targets, to a subject who tried to "guess" as many as possible of the symbols in order. The cards might be left stacked during the test, or the experimenter might lift one from the deck for each trial, either looking at it or not. The subject or the experimenter recorded each guess; and the experimenter also recorded the sequence of the target cards. The "hits," or coincidences between guesses and target symbols, were then tabulated and the statistical probability of the resulting score over a series of such runs of the deck was calculated. Parapsychologists generally consider a result significant only if the resulting probability is .01 or less, meaning that on average they could expect such a result only once in more than one hundred such experiments on the basis of chance alone. The ESP experiments to be mentioned here were done with the ESP cards unless otherwise stated.

Telepathy, Clairvoyance, and Precognition

The discovery of clairvoyant ability introduced the first theoretical complication into the parapsychological experiments. Previously, testing for telepathy had appeared quite simple in principle: I think of something and make a drawing or written record of it; you try to think of the same thing and record your impression; we compare our records. Now, it became apparent that such a test would be ambiguous. You might be getting information from my mind, or from my written record, or both (a situation called general ESP, or GESP). The remedy seemed obvious: I make no objective record of the mental target I am thinking of until you have recorded your response.

But another line of investigation had been developing, the experimental testing of precognition, which means the extrasensory perception of information not yet in existence and not rationally foreseeable. Experiments at Duke and elsewhere soon accumulated impressive evidence for the reality of this uncanny ability in GESP situations. Immediately, the evidence for telepathy was compromised. Instead of "reading the mind" of the sender, the receiver might be getting the information by clairvoyant precognition of the sender's later record of his thought-target. Absurd as it might seem, such a possibility could not be eliminated in the light of the evidence.

Apparently no rigorous test of telepathic ability is possible if any kind of objective record of the test targets is ever made. The sender must then record the target in terms of a random code known only to himself, and check the receiver's responses against this code. But it is highly desirable to have a second experimenter verify the target and response records. To meet this apparently impossible demand, at least two methods have been used to communicate the target code to the second experimenter without revealing it in any kind of objective expression. These will be detailed below in connection with specific experiments.

A similar difficulty appears in designing a test for pure clairvoyance. The scheme had seemed straightforward: in testing for clairvoyance, the experimenter must not look at the targets until the subject has called them. But just possibly the subject is getting his information not from the material targets, but by precognitive telepathy from the mind of the experimenter after he has viewed the target series. This possibility can be avoided by devising a machine that will generate a random series of targets, receive the subject's guesses, compare each with the corresponding target, and then destroy the target sequence, reporting out only the total score. This is equivalent to telepathy with a single experimenter; the difference is that we trust the accuracy and integrity of a well-designed machine, so that no independent check is necessary.

Details of many ESP experiments are given in Dr. Schmeidler's paper in this volume. Here we will examine only a few selected examples to illustrate the special features of the tests for telepathy and precognition.

McMahan (1946) reported an experiment for pure telepathy that yielded only marginally significant results, but which is notable as the first use of a procedure for excluding both clairvoyance and precognition. The experimenter worked with target cards bearing a number, 1 through 5. These cards were randomized and used as target decks, and the experimenter as sender looked at each card just as in a general ESP experiment. However, each subject was instructed to try to get the ESP card symbol of which the experimenter was thinking at each trial. The experimenter privately, before the experiment began, made up a mental code relating each symbol to one of the code numbers on the cards. Thus, if she turned up a "4" card for the next trial, she might think "cross" in accordance with her subjective code. Then, in checking the results, she had to make a mental translation of each subject response symbol into its corresponding number for comparison with the recorded sequence of target numbers.

The ingenious aspect of the experiment was the use of a scheme suggested earlier by J. B. Rhine. To permit an independent check of the scores, it was necessary to communicate the code relating symbols and numbers to a colleague; yet any objective expression of the code, even in spoken words, would open the experiment to the possibility of precognitive clairvoyance. McMahan communicated the code to another person on the staff, a close friend, by recalling to the other some inconsequential experience they had shared that involved a number that could not be deduced from the spoken reminiscence. The report mentions an example (not used in the experiment) in which the number 5 is communicated by recalling a private association of carnations with a certain family of five members.

This device, despite its ingenuity, is open to criticism because of its dependence on subjective judgments and possible misunderstandings. Birge (1948) proposed an entirely objective method for communicating the code privately, and carried out an exploratory experiment using it. The results were insignificant in terms of the direct score, but significant (P = .0015) when each response was scored relative to the target symbol for the next following trial. This is a rather common effect called displacement. Birge communicated his private symbol code to a colleague by means of a contingency table involving the ESP symbols, the corresponding target numbers, and the subject's responses. However, the method is too complex to present in detail here.

Further attempts to demonstrate pure telepathy have been conspicuous by their absence. Possibly the difficulties in experimental procedures, plus a trend toward the use of increasingly sophisticated instrumentation in parapsychological work, have discouraged definitive tests for telepathy. Other modes of ESP are more accessible. Yet we have the paradox that telepathy, the oldest and most popular and plausible ESP concept, is the least supported by firm experimental data. In fact, J. B. Rhine (1974) now considers telepathy an untestable hypothesis.

Precognition and Psychokinesis

Meanwhile, experimenters at Duke and elsewhere had been exploring another audacious hypothesis, that of psychokinesis (PK) or "mind over matter." Many reports of poltergeist manifestations and of experiments with rare individuals had indicated that movements of objects and other physical effects sometimes occurred apparently from no cause other than the influence of a certain person. To test this possibility under adequately controlled conditions, experiments were done with ordinary dice in which the subject "willed" a particular face or combination of faces to come up on each throw. Like the ESP cards, dice results are easy to evaluate statistically; and random selection of target faces, machine throwing, and photographic recording of the faces were soon adopted to insure the reliability of the results. Impressive statistical evidence accumulated, indicating that some subjects could indeed influence the falls of the dice. The degree of success was never spectacular, but over many trials the total effect was unmistakable.

We will come back to details of these experiments later. The immediate point is that the evidence for PK compromised the precognition experiments, much as the latter already had compromised the early tests for telepathy. If a test for precognition is to be valid, it must insure that neither subject nor experimenter takes any action to influence the predicted events. Extravagant as the possibility may be, the demonstration of PK opens up the possibility that either subject or experimenter may use PK, when the target deck is shuffled after the responses are recorded, to influence the card order in the direction of agreement with the prior responses.

To meet this difficulty, the Duke experimenters devised a procedure in which the order of the precognitive deck, after thorough machine shuffling, was finally determined objectively by a formula that depended on the maximum or minimum temperature published in a local paper on a previously specified date.   To influence the cut in his favor, the subject presumably would have to influence either the weather or the publication process.   Obviously this type of precaution is not absolute.   It depends on the assumption that in such circumstances precognition is more plausible than psychokinesis.

Such ambiguities are unavoidable in dealing with processes in which no causal mechanism can be traced.   They will be dealt with in more detail in the second section of this paper.

Some Precognition Experiments

Typical examples of the more sophisticated precognition tests that were developed at Duke University in the early phase were reported by J. B. Rhine (1942) and Humphrey and J. B. Rhine (1942).   The experimental procedure in each case was essentially that mentioned earlier, in which the target cards were mechanically shuffled at a time up to 10 days after the subject had made his predictions, and the deck cut at a level determined objectively by published local temperatures.   The gross scores in these tests did not significantly exceed chance expectations, but internal distributions of hits in the series differed consistently from random distribution to a statistically significant degree.

Schmeidler (1964) reported two series of tests designed to distinguish between precognitive general ESP and precognitive clairvoyance.   In these experiments, the ESP card symbols were translated into a numerical code and a computer was programmed to accept subjects' predictive calls, to generate random target sequences and compare them with the calls, and to tabulate the results.   In one-third of the tests both subject and experimenter received copies of the target sequences; in another third, only the experimenter saw the targets.   In the remaining third, the computer delivered only the scores, so that no one ever saw the target sequences.   This latter condition excluded any possibility of telepathy and was therefore a valid test for precognitive clairvoyance.

In the first series, the experimenter determined before the experiment which of the three conditions was to apply to each run. In the second series, the conditions were determined randomly after the subjects' predictions had been completed. As in the experiments by Rhine and Humphrey, the direct scores were generally insignificant. Only the score for precognitive clairvoyance in the first series was statistically impressive (P = .0006). However, detailed analyses of the results for individual subjects disclosed significant correlations between scores and feelings of success, individual ways of viewing time, and other personal characteristics.

Many experiments on precognition have been reported. One that is especially interesting because of the experimental design and the impressive results achieved was devised by Schmidt (1969a, 1969b). An electronic apparatus displayed to the subject a group of four small light bulbs, each with a pushbutton adjacent. Pushing any button would cause one of the lamps to light; which one was determined by a highly random physical process, the disintegration of an atom in a bit of radioactive strontium.

In a first series, the subject was asked to try to push the button next to the lamp that would then light, thus automatically registering a "hit." A total of 63,066 trials by three subjects in this series yielded highly significant results (P = 2×10^{-9}); i.e., one possibility in 500 million that the score was due to random events.

In a second series, each of three subjects was asked to choose whether to predict which lamp would light or to select one of the three that would not light, by pushing the adjacent button. Success in either mode was scored as a hit. A total of 20,000 trials (approximately 10,000 in each mode) yielded a probability of 6.55×10^{-10}--less than one in a billion.

It is worth noting that the subjects in these experiments had been selected from among a greater number in preliminary tests because of their superior scores. In the first series, two were professional "mediums" and the third an amateur psychic. In the second series, one of the mediums was replaced by a daughter of the other.

While the experimenter provisionally termed this procedure an experiment in precognition, he recognized that psychokinesis is an alternative possibility. In fact, detailed consideration of such experimental techniques as this raise serious questions as to whether such distinctions as precognition vs. psychokinesis have any fundamental meaning.

The possibility that animals as well as humans have precognitive ability has been the subject of several experiments. Duval and Montredon (1968) tested the possibility that mice might be able to avoid electric shocks by evasive action in advance of each shock. Four mice were put, one at a time, into a small cage with a floor divided by a low barrier. Either section of the wire grid floor could be electrically energized, shocking the mouse if it was in that side of the cage. An electronic device applied the voltage to one side or the other at short intervals, in a random order. Photoelectric detectors recorded which side the mouse was in when each shock was delivered and the results were electrically recorded.

It was found necessary to eliminate static or mechanical behavior by the mouse in order to isolate those trials in which relatively free or random activity allowed opportunity for ESP to influence its movements. Usually, after receiving a shock, the mouse would hop to the other side of the cage and remain there until shocked again; or it might simply remain in one side for some time. However, the elimination of these unsusceptible conditions was carried out by objective criteria unrelated to the results. The operation of the experiment was automatic, so that the experimenter was never present during a run.

In 612 trials under these conditions, the mice avoided the shock 53 times more than expected by chance (P less than .001). An interesting point is that the three wild mice that were used contributed 47 of the extrachance successes, the one domestic mouse only six.

Perhaps the most macabre experiment in parapsychology was reported by Craig and Treurniet (1974). Death is a common theme in popular accounts of precognitive experiences, suggesting that this event--especially the individual's own death--may be the most effective target for precognition. To explore this idea, an experiment was devised to discover any significant differences in the current behavior of two groups of rats if those of one group only were to be killed the next day.

A homogeneous lot of 72 individually identified rats were randomly assigned to two equal groups. One group immediately and the other 24 hours later were subjected to an "open-field test." Each rat was released at one corner of a large cage and its movements over the lines of a reference grid noted, as well as the time between release and its first movement. Shortly after the second day's tests, half of the members of each group, randomly selected at that time, were killed with chloroform. The survivors were kept alive for three weeks or longer.

Analysis of the records of individual activity revealed that the rats facing imminent death were on average more active than their luckier fellows, having crossed the reference grid lines at a mean rate of 15.7 times per minute versus 13.0 for the survivors-to-be. The difference was statistically significant (P less than .005). What mechanism might have made the rats more active if they sensed imminent death is obscure; but the results leave little room for doubt that the imminence of death was somehow reflected in their behavior. The authors note that this result has serious practical implications for any behavioral experiments involving rats or other animals.

Psychokinesis: The Decline Effect

Early in 1943, the Duke University Parapsychology Laboratory began publishing (Rhine and Rhine, 1943) a series of reports of more than 25 PK experiments that had been done during the preceding nine years. Publication had been delayed both to develop a strong body of confirmatory data for so implausible a phenomenon and to avoid compounding and confusing the controversy over ESP, which had been intense. These experiments, carried out with thrown dice as the targets, involved many detailed variations and gradual improvements in procedures. Hand throwing was soon supplanted by use of a cup and later by an automatic machine. Dice were thrown singly, in pairs for individual face targets or for a target sum, and sometimes in greater numbers per throw.

The cumulative effect of these data was to make a strong case for the validity of PK. Scores were never spectacularly high; but persistent evidence indicated that some subjects were indeed able to influence the falls of the dice consistently in favor of the designated faces, albeit by a small margin, piling up in some cases highly significant results.

These scores soon became a secondary consideration.
A decline tendency had been noticed from the beginning of
the PK experiments; i. e. , subjects generally tended to score
more successes in the early portion of a session.   But it
was not until 1942, after eight years of experimenting without much attention to the decline effect, that a thorough analysis of declines was undertaken.   The results of that
study (Rhine and Humphrey, 1944a, 1944b; Rhine, Humphrey,
and Pratt, 1945) constitute probably the strongest body of
evidence in existence for the occurrence of psychokinesis.

Results in PK tests usually had been recorded from
top to bottom of successive columns across a record page,
left to right.   To evaluate the decline effect, each record
page was divided into quarters: upper and lower left, upper
and lower right.   Only those record pages were used in
which the experiment had proceeded without a recess, change
of subjects, or other interruption.   The records of all known
PK tests that had been recorded in this manner were pooled
in the analysis because the purpose was particularly to isolate any decline or other internal scoring variation that
might be common to such experiments generally.

In 12 such experiments, the target had been a single
die face, even though the numbers of dice per throw had
ranged from one to 60.   The records of 11 of these series
revealed strong declines between the page totals for the
first and fourth quarters of the page.   The totals of all appropriate record pages from all 12 experiments (representing
nearly 300,000 individual die trials) exhibited a systematic
decline from first to second to third to fourth quarter, with
a critical ratio of the difference between first and fourth
quarters of 5.56.   The probability of such a distribution by
chance alone is approximately 2×10^{-8}, or one in 50 million
such bodies of data.

Similar analyses of six experiments in which two dice
per trial had been thrown for high-dice or other combination
targets showed a decline from first to fourth quarter-page
totals in five of the series.   The resulting critical ratio of
1.74 is only marginally significant because of the relatively
small numbers of trials involved.

Evaluation of the pooled quarter-distributions of all
18 experiments yielded a chi square of 69.25, implying a
probability of approximately 10^{-8}, or one in 100 million.
Further analyses based on quarter-distributions in elements

of less than a full record page yielded similarly impressive extrachance results.

It is important to note that this type of analysis was thought of only some years after most of the experiments had been done. The fact that no such analysis had been anticipated lends weight to the results. The systematic decline of scoring rate in the series evidently rules out any effects of biased dice as an explanation of the extrachance scores since any such effect would hardly change systematically through the course of every experiment. Similarly, recording errors, if they occurred in significant numbers, would be expected to increase with fatigue rather than decline.

Some Psychokinetic Experiments

In the years since the publications just mentioned, many types of PK experiments have been reported by investigators throughout the world. Most of these have involved mental influence on inanimate objects; but an increasing number are concerned with situations that simulate reported instances of psychic healing in which a human tries to influence the condition of a plant or animal. A few experiments have attempted to discover whether lower animals are able to exert PK influence on their environments.

A remarkable experiment based on a variation of the PK tests with dice was reported by Fisk and West (1958). Each day Fisk made a random selection of one of the die faces as the target for that day. The subject, in her home several miles distant, threw the dice without sensory knowledge of the target. Thus, the test presumably required both extrasensory awareness of the target and psychokinetic influence on the dice. Under these conditions, a series of 10,000 trials yielded a score with a probability of .0016. A further series of 15,032 trials also was significant, with a probability of .00017.

In recent years, fresh interest in PK experimentation has been manifested in connection with more varied and sophisticated apparatus and procedures. An intriguing example of this trend is an experiment by Schmeidler (1973), who arranged for a gifted subject to try to influence the air temperature recorded by an electronic thermometer. Several thermistors in various locations in the experimental room were connected to pens on a chart recorder and the subject was asked (in a predetermined, counterbalanced sequence) to raise and lower the temperature around a specified thermistor. He succeeded in doing so significantly in repeated trials.

Curiously, the records indicated that a drop in temperature at the target thermistor usually was accompanied by a rise in one or more nearby. This remarkable effect suggests that the temperature was lowered in one small region by somehow transferring heat energy into an adjacent region. This possibility justifies a further intensive investigation.

Schmidt (1970a) adapted his electronic random-number generator, mentioned earlier in connection with his precognition tests, to a novel PK experiment. The subject was confronted with a display panel bearing a circle of nine small lamps that were lighted in a random sequence as determined by the electronic circuit mentioned earlier. The circuitry was arranged to produce a "random walk" of the lights; i.e., one lamp at a time was lighted briefly; then it was turned off, and the one on either the clockwise or the counterclockwise side of the first lamp lighted, depending on the randomized signal from the circuit. Thus the lights would advance and retreat randomly, making little progress around the circle. Each subject was asked to influence the lights to advance consistently in one or the other direction. Success would of course imply the introduction of a non-random pattern into the impulses coming from the radioactive counter circuit.

After some exploratory sessions in which most subjects tended to score negatively (oppositely to their intention), a series of approximately 33,000 trials (lamp changes) by 15 subjects yielded a total score with a probability of less than .001. No reason for the negative direction of the score was evident.

PK Effects by Animals

Is psychokinetic ability limited to humans, or can other living organisms exhibit it? Schmidt (1970b) conducted an intriguing experiment to explore this question. A year-old female cat was put in a cold ($0°$ C) shack where she could cuddle up to the warmth of a 200-watt lamp. The power supply to the lamp was turned on or off at one-second intervals by binary signals from a random-number generator. Normally, the lamp would be on during very nearly one-half of any substantial time interval. It was expected that the cat would be highly motivated to keep the lamp on as much of the time as possible.

During five half-hour sessions involving 9000 individual "trials," the cat settled down near the lamp and apparently succeeded in turning the lamp on 115 more times than should have occurred by chance--a marginally significant deviation. During five succeeding sessions, however, the cat seemed to have developed a dislike of the lamp and avoided it. The score for these sessions was insignificantly below chance expectation.

Encouraged by these results, Schmidt (1970b) next devised a comparable experiment with cockroaches as subjects. Two, usually, were placed in a small cage with a metal grid floor that could be electrically charged. The insects normally avoid such a shock if given a choice. The charging voltage was turned on or off randomly at one-second intervals, as in the preceding experiment. In a series of 6400 preliminary trials, the shock was delivered 109 times more than chance expectation, a marginally significant level. A more extensive experiment was then carried out, involving a total of 25,600 trials with again a positive deviation of 309 (P less than .0001). When the data were broken down into 10 consecutive equal blocks, each block showed a substantial positive deviation.

These results indicate a very consistent and significant influence of the experiment on the randomness of a thoroughly tested generator. Possibly the experimenter rather than the cockroaches produced the deviations, but a later series that was run automatically in the absence of the experimenter produced similarly significant results. Why should the cockroaches (if they are the PK agents) influence the machine to give them more than the expected number of aversive shocks, rather than fewer? Schmidt suggests a "psi-missing" effect, a kind of confusion because the animals have had no evolutionary experience with electric shocks. Cats, on the contrary, have had millennia of experience of seeking warmth.

Healers

Another class of PK experiments is that in which a human subject tries to influence the condition or behavior of a plant or animal. The many popular accounts of "psychic healing" belong to this category, indicating that certain persons have ability to heal or cure certain disease conditions by personal influence. The inherent ambiguity of the parapsychological categories is evident again in these claims. Does the healer exert PK influence on the patient's body or telepathic influence on his mind?

A few attempts have been made to test such abilities under experimental conditions that somewhat simulate those of the healing situation. Grad, Cadoret, and Paul (1961) reported an experiment on wound healing in mice in which the rates of healing of artificially inflicted skin wounds were compared for mice handled by a reputed healer, others handled by persons who claimed no healing ability, and a group that were not handled at all. After 16 days, the difference between mean wound areas of mice that had been handled by the healer and of mice in the two control groups was significant ($P = .01$). Differences between the control groups were not significant. Healing was more rapid in mice handled by the healer.

Watkins and Watkins (1971) tested the ability of 12 human subjects, mostly persons of reputed psychic capabilities, to hasten the resuscitation of mice from ether anesthesia. Mice were anesthetized in pairs under as nearly as possible identical conditions. One of each pair was allowed to recover spontaneously as a control. The other was the object of the attempt to assist its recovery by mental influence; the mouse was not touched by subject or experimenter during the test.

One of the reputedly psychic subjects and the only three who had no such reputation produced no significant results. The eight remaining subjects (all reputedly psychic) produced consistently significant scores, with their mice awakening in 7/8 the mean time required by the controls (P less than 10^{-5}).

PK Effects on Plants

Are plants susceptible to PK influence? Grad (1967) tested the effect on germination and growth of seedlings of

saline solution that had been variously "treated. " A psychi-
atrically normal person and two seriously depressed persons
held in their hands for 30 minutes sealed pharmaceutical
vials of normal saline solution.   The vials were then opened
and used for the initial watering of barley seeds in soil.
Three separate plantings were watered with the three
"treated" vials, and a fourth with "untreated" saline as a
control.   Thereafter, the seedlings were watered with tap
water.   The experiment was conducted under multiple blind
conditions.

Throughout the experiment, the tallest plants were
those in the group initially watered by saline handled by the
normal subject.   Those related to one of the depressed subjects, a hospitalized neurotic, were next; then the control
group; last, exhibiting the least growth, were those related
to the depressed psychotic subject.   At the end of 15 days,
the difference between the first-mentioned group and the
other three was significant, but the differences among the
three were not significant.   (See Dr. Grad's paper in Part
II.)

Brier (1969) attached a polygraph recorder to a leaf
on a philodendron plant and studied the effects on the polygraph trace (recording the current through the leaf and thus
any changes in its electrical resistance) when a subject tried
to influence it.   Consistently positive results were obtained
through five series of tests.   The pooled results of three of
these that were comparable were significant (P less than
. 01).

Rare PK Talents

Nearly all of the PK experiments that have been mentioned made use of subjects who made no pretensions to
psychic ability.   In a somewhat different category are those
investigations that center about the effects produced by individuals who have developed "specialties" in psychokinetic
performance.

One of the most interesting and impressive of these
in recent years is Ted Serios, who has been investigated by
Eisenbud (1967) and by Stevenson and Pratt (1968, 1969).
Serios apparently was able by mental influence to cause abnormal exposures and sometimes recognizable pictures to
appear on film in a Polaroid camera instead of the scene in

the field of view of the camera. He demonstrated similar effects on television cameras. Any phenomenon that depends upon a unique individual is very difficult to establish convincingly because of the possibility of fraud and the impossibility of averaging out personal variables. Nevertheless, the evidence for the validity of Serios' phenomena is very strong.

A Soviet woman, Nina Kulagina, has established a reputation for her ability to move small objects psychokinetically and to produce certain other effects (Pratt and Keil, 1973; Ullman, 1971). A Maimonides Hospital technician, Felicia Parise, saw a film of Kulagina's feats and determined to try to develop such ability herself (Honorton, 1974). She succeeded in doing so, demonstrating repeatedly the ability to move small bottles across a counter top without contact and to influence the pointing of a compass needle.

It is noteworthy that each of these three persons, when attempting PK effects, deliberately develops a change of physiological as well as mental state, a condition of strong excitement or arousal that is attested by EEG records and other physiological criteria, besides being evident to ordinary observation. Apparently the mental state is one of intense concentration, a kind of identification with the object that is to be affected.

2 SOME PHYSICAL IMPLICATIONS OF PSI

The concept of parapsychology evolved out of a somewhat arbitrary preoccupation with the psychological aspects of psi phenomena. The field might just as well have been called paraphysics, because its implications for physics are fully as intriguing as they are for psychology.

Clairvoyance, telepathy, and other ESP experiences imply subtle but profound physical riddles. When information in a deck of cards or a drawing is replicated in the brain of a percipient without recognized sensory communication, or a person suddenly knows what is happening to another who is beyond sight or sound, the event must depend upon either a remarkably tricky physical process or something that transcends existing physical concepts.

The energetic alternative has not been adequately tested, and it deserves to be. Few experiments have been designed explicitly to test the possibility that ESP may be mediated by a physical agency analogous to radio, and those few have yielded inconclusive results. In the absence of definitive tests, however, the weight of evidence appears to exclude any explanation of psi in terms of current theoretical models. Many experiments have, incidentally, involved a great variety of distances and material barriers between "sender" and "receiver" or percipient and clairvoyance target; yet no unambiguous relations between these factors and ESP scoring rates have emerged. Psychological factors always appear to dominate the experimental situation, so far as any consistent influences on results can be identified. This impression is powerfully reinforced by the precognitive manifestations, a perennial stumbling block to any scientifically intelligible theory of psi.

Psychokinesis

The most obvious physical implications of psi are of course in the psychokinetic (PK) effects such as poltergeist disturbances, the physical phenomena of séances, and the much better-attested experiments with dice. As noted in Part I, Eisenbud's extensive experiments with Ted Serios and other remarkable developments in recent years have revived the lagging interest in PK. These, like the earlier PK investigations, indicate unknown relationships between purely subjective intentions and concurrent physical processes. In many instances these processes are by no means subtle. They involve gross changes in arrangements of material, with the implication of substantial transformations of energy somewhere in the process. We have some freedom to speculate on the role of energy in mental processes; but the physicist knows, as surely as he can know anything, that objects are not pushed about or tumbling dice manipulated or pictures imprinted on film except by expending energy. This assurance gives to such phenomena an impression of tangible reality that is lacking in the purely mental manifestations. They are therefore especially intriguing to the physicist, who can imagine experiments that may clarify the energetic process.

Yet, when he attempts such investigations he immediately encounters a causal hiatus. To cite an example mentioned earlier (Schmeidler, 1973), the experimenter arranges to record changes of temperature that may be induced by a PK psychic. Several thermistors (electrical thermometer elements) are placed at various locations in the experimental room, and a particular one is designated as the target for the PK effort. The thermistors are connected to a chart recorder and accessory circuitry, and of course to an electric power source. Eureka! The psychic does whatever a PK artist does, and the recorder indicates a change in temperature of the target thermistor, up or down as directed.

But what has happened? The air temperature at the target may have been altered; or the PK influence may have altered the composition of the thermistor or the voltage supply or the resistance of the wiring, or it may have pushed the recording pen directly. How is one to know? And, if one cannot know, how can he conduct any physically meaningful experiments with PK beyond establishing that an unaccountable effect occurs?

As Schmeidler (1973) noted, the thermistor experiment afforded some presumptive evidence that the PK action was directed to the vicinity of the target thermistor. When the target registered a drop in temperature, for example, one or more of the other thermistors some distance away showed a rise. This tendency suggests that the PK influence was producing a drop in air temperature at the target by transferring heat energy to another region. It would seem unlikely that, if the psychic were applying PK influence directly to the recorder pen, he would create such an artifact as was observed by influencing another pen oppositely.

Another interesting indication of such a localization of PK action on the ostensible target appears in an (unpublished) experiment carried out by Puthoff and Targ at the Stanford Research Institute: a torsion pendulum was arranged to give a very sensitive indication of its vibrations by shifting a laser beam; the movements were registered on a chart recorder. When the pendulum settled down, random vibrations in the room and supporting table kept it oscillating at a very low level, in both the torsion mode of about 10 seconds' period and in a rocking or swinging mode of much shorter period. When a psychic succeeded in stopping the long-period oscillation, as he intended, the short-period vibrations increased in magnitude. This effect, quite unanticipated, again suggests direct PK action on the pendulum rather than some other part of the apparatus, with a shift of vibrational energy from one mode to the other.

Nevertheless, in each of these experiments the presumption of localized PK influence on the ostensible target rests on plausibility and economy of concepts rather than analytical evidence. When the thermistor is used normally, for example, it is taken for granted that any temperature change it registers is a change in the temperature of the thermistor. This confidence rests on rather complete knowledge of the physical principles involved in the instrument, including the fact that all of its elements except the thermistor are not significantly sensitive to temperature changes. Since no such causal relations are known for PK effects, no such analytical approach is possible.

Statistical Peculiarities

It seems clear that quantum theory cannot now account for psi effects. Yet certain peculiarities of PK suggest a tantalizingly close relation to the statistical processes that are the basis of quantum physics. PK influence has been observed in many kinds of situations, involving both stationary objects and dynamic situations. These indicate that, at least in experiments, it is easier to influence a situation that already involves random or near-random motion than a static arrangement. Successful experiments have used tumbling dice or unmarked cubes, random electrical impulses derived from radioactive decay (Schmidt, 1969b), Puthoff and Targ's pendulum driven by random "noise" vibrations, and apparent changes of temperature in air in which molecules are in random motion (Schmeidler, 1973).

In each of these situations there is the suggestion that the PK perturbation is accomplished through an alteration of the probability describing the system rather than application or abstraction of energy directly. The effect suggests information more than energy. Clerk Maxwell fantasied a supernatural "demon" who could defeat the Second Law of Thermodynamics by operating a tiny door between two vessels of gas, admitting only fast molecules in one direction and only slow ones in the other. He would thus raise the temperature of the gas in the first vessel (full of more energetic molecules) at the expense of the second, which would become cooler.

We know now that Maxwell's demon is a fantasy: informing himself of the locations and velocities of the gas molecules would dissipate more energy than he could concentrate by this process. Yet the PK experiments mentioned above, as well as some others, inescapably suggest the intervention of a Maxwell demon that works. This observation is not intended to imply a breakdown of the Second Law of Thermodynamics; rather, it suggests that the PK practitioner may be able to intervene in somewhat the role of the demon, introducing information and order into the random situation, but at the expense of a compensating degradation of energy in his own system. In the case of Schmidt's random-number generator, the PK influence ostensibly interferes with the normally completely random process of radioactive decay that is described statistically by quantum theory. As Schmidt (1969a) remarks, "This [experiment] implies that quantum theory does not give, at least for systems that include human subjects, a complete description of nature" (p. 115).

The PK experiments with dice never have yielded extraordinarily high scores, in curious contrast to the comparable ESP card-guessing tests which sometimes have yielded scores of 100 per cent in a run. This observation suggests the possibility that PK is inherently a statistical phenomenon, whereas clairvoyance may be "all or nothing"; however, the observed difference may be an artifact of the experimental procedures. The concept of informed manipulation of energy already in the target situation finds some further support in Eisenbud's experiments (1967) with Serios' "thoughtography," in which the camera shutter was operated normally. Serios sometimes got abnormal exposures on film in an opaque package, but not pictures. The difference in performance could be psychologically motivated; but it suggests that manipulation of the light energy normally entering the camera is less difficult than directly influencing the film. Also, reports of paranormal voices on tape recordings usually indicate that the voices are barely distinguishable from the noise background--again suggesting, to the extent that such observations are valid, that the voices have been created by imposing some degree of order upon the random noise energy. The familiar reports of cool sensations during séance phenomena further support the impression of an intelligent ordering of randomly distributed energy.

Telepathy and Clairvoyance

Do any physical variables affect the level of success in ESP experiments? Almost all of the accumulated data indicate that neither distance nor material barriers nor any other factors have any influence on the scoring, except as they may affect the participants psychologically. However, more definitive experiments need to be done before the possibility of physical influences on ESP or PK mediation is dismissed. Osis (1965) and Osis and Fahler (1965) found some evidence of a decline of scoring with distance, though too many other variables were involved to permit of any firm conclusions. Forwald (1969) has reported remarkably consistent correlations between physical characteristics of tumbling cubes and magnitudes of the PK displacements. It is impossible, however, in Forwald's self-conducted experiments to distinguish between a lawful physical effect and the influence of the expectations of the engineer-experimenter.

Tests for possible effects of distance on ESP scoring are difficult. In any ordinary situation, distances of more than a few yards are complicated by walls and other material barriers which may exert some effect comparable to that of distance. Over very long distances, the bulk of the earth itself intervenes between subject and target. Discussions of possible distance effects on psi phenomena often mention the inverse-square law that applies in simple circumstances to propagation of light and other radiant energies. However, as was pointed out by Hoffman (1940), ESP scores measure information transfer, not power levels. To use a radio analogy, one does not note a decline in intelligibility of speech as he travels farther from a radio station until he is so far away that the signal begins to fade into the noise background. We should plausibly expect some such pattern if distance indeed has any effect on ESP performance. But the most difficult factor to eliminate from such tests is the psychological effect on performance of the participants' knowledge of the various test distances. One subject might be discouraged by increasing distance, while another might respond to it as a challenge. And, given the possibility of clairvoyant awareness of the distance itself, how can a blind experiment be designed?

Interplanetary spacecraft offer perhaps the best possibilities for definitive tests for any effects of distance or mass shielding upon psi communications (Osis, 1973; Rush, 1973; Schmidt, 1973). Such flights continue within radio range for two years or more, while the distance from earth continually changes. During this period, any practicable number of clairvoyants on earth could make repeated trials at ESP targets on the spacecraft. Sometimes the subject would be on the side of earth toward the spacecraft, sometimes on the opposite side, so that any effect of the earth's mass as a barrier to communication could be tested also.

A rudimentary experiment of this kind was carried out by one of the Apollo astronauts (Mitchell, 1971). Such an experiment on a manned flight is ambiguous, however, because it is open to the possibility that the percipient may precognize the records of the targets after they are returned to earth, thus circumventing the test of distance effects. For this reason, such tests can better be done using automatic equipment in the spacecraft. A random target generator and devices for receiving subjects' responses by radio from earth, comparing them with the target sequences, and reporting back the scores would present no great technological problems. There is some question, however, whether a clairvoyant could "find" a target that had no person associated with it. This point is crucial and must be settled by preliminary experiments on earth.

The Riddle of Precognition

Undoubtedly the most implacable challenge to physics in the realm of the paranormal is that posed by precognition. Despite the perennial frustration of attempts to find causal links in PK or other concurrent psi events, it is always possible to imagine such links and to continue to hope they may somehow be found. But nothing in our scientific world view allows for the emergence in the present of information about a future situation that is not rationally predictable.

It is true that relativity and quantum theory have introduced some perturbations into the former simple concepts of the causal sequence of events in time. Simultaneity is not an absolute relation, and causal relations among some events of atomic dimensions are ambiguous. Yet such anomalies are limited to practically insignificant magnitudes. They offer no solution to the enigma of detailed prevision of events that are days, weeks, or years in the future. Theorists who have given attention to this question (e.g., Chari, 1972) appear to agree that contemporary physical theory, bizarre and obscure as some of its concepts are, is nevertheless incapable of accommodating such precognitive events as are frequently reported in the parapsychological literature.

It is important to emphasize that this difference in the physical difficulties concerning precognition versus those relating to the other psi phenomena appears to be more than a difference in degree. A PK event concurrent with or following a subject's "willing" it, or clairvoyant cognition of an existing target, could be explained, hypothetically, on the assumption of an otherwise undiscovered physical agency--a radiation, force field, or whatever--without obviously contradicting fundamental principles. The hypothesis might be strained to account for the phenomena, as indeed such hypotheses are; but it would not in principle violate the fundamental concept of cause and effect.

The difficulty with precognition is at a more fundamental level, independent of specific mechanisms. The difference is crudely like that between trying to design a highly original type of heat engine and trying to design any kind of perpetual-motion machine. The former may present severe difficulties of detail; the latter is in principle impossible.

The conviction that neither a perpetual-motion machine nor precognition is physically possible arises from the fundamental irreversibility of processes in the physical world. The cascade of energy transformations that constitutes the world of events progresses relentlessly according to the Second Law of Thermodynamics and the direction in which it progresses is by definition from cause to effect, from past to future. From the standpoint of physics, precognition is a self-contradictory concept. Yet the dilemma cannot honestly be ignored. The evidence for precognition, both in experiments and in spontaneous experiences, is insistent.

3   AMBIGUITY OF PSI INTERACTIONS

Any attempt at physical rationalization of psi phenomena is further complicated by the ambiguity that is inherent in many, if not all, such cases. In precognition particularly, does one foresee an event that will occur independently of him, or does he influence events psychokinetically so as to fulfill his vision? Experiments at Duke University more than a generation ago demonstrated the possibility of the "psychic shuffle" in card experiments, in which ESP cards being impartially shuffled nevertheless were ordered so as to correspond significantly to a sequence of precognitive "guesses" previously recorded. Precautions were taken against such a self-fulfilling effect by keying the target sequence to some large, remotely objective event such as maximum temperature officially reported at a prescribed place and date. But such a precaution is based on plausibility, not principle.

Some investigators (e.g., Eisenbud, 1956; Tanagras, 1949) consider the PK alternative more credible and scientifically tenable, in most cases if not all, than that of precognition of independent events. They argue cogently enough that fulfillment of a glimpse of the future by PK on the part of the seer, however mysterious such a mechanism may be, does not do violence to fundamental concepts of time and causation, and that this interpretation is the more economical, since it is but an extension of contemporary PK, the occurrence of which is well demonstrated. Precognition, on the other hand, appears to require radical and paradoxical concepts, as mentioned.

At first sight, the concept of futuristic PK might appear to be ruled out on the basis of the inevitable conflicts among various individuals' attempts to manipulate the future. But precognition appears to be rare rather than universal and it is not infallible. Perhaps, as in other conflicts, some have their way and others do not. Perhaps in most cases significant conflicts of intention do not occur. The philosophical implications of the PK interpretation of precognition need to be developed in more detail. Bizarre as the PK alternative may appear in the large affairs of life, from the physicist's standpoint it is no more bizarre than the stark challenge of prevision of independently occurring events.

Another psi ambiguity occurs in the familiar dilemma of telepathy versus precognitive clairvoyance, the possibility that a "telepathy" subject is actually precognizing the later record of the target symbols in the "sender's" mind. The impression is strong that the familiar categories of psi manifestations are essentially meaningless; that they are diverse and ambivalent aspects of something that cannot be comprehended in terms of such familiar dichotomies as sender-and-receiver, subject-and-target, past-and-future.

4   PSI: A MANIFESTATION OF MIND

The preceding discussions point to an inexorable conclusion. Tentatively at least, we must admit that no convincing evidence exists for any influence of physical parameters on the psi communication channel. We are not even sure there is such a channel. The evidence for precognition raises formidable difficulties for the concept of a physical communication channel analogous to radio, or even the

concept of any physical constraints at all on the psi phenomena.

The most succinct comment one can make as to the
physical aspects of psi is that there are not any. We do
observe end effects--movements of objects in PK experiments,
expressions of responses in ESP tests--that are physical; but
nowhere between these targets and the interacting mind or
brain do we find any clear evidence of physical mediation,
or of any physical factor that influences the phenomena.
From the standpoint of physics, parapsychology is not a
science but a collection of miracles.

This is not to say that psi knows no laws. Rather,
such evidence of lawfulness as is observed relates almost
entirely to correlations between psi performance and various
psychological measurements of the participants in the experiments. We find consistent decline effects in scoring, correlations between scoring levels and subjects' attitudes
toward psi, positive or negative scoring according to the intention of the subject, and other more-or-less firmly established relationships. The essential point is that all of these
factors that appear to influence psi performance relate to
the mind of the subject, to his subjective psychological condition. Some of these conditions, such as a meditative state,
are correlated with measurable physiological variables;
and some may be induced by physiological influences, such
as certain drugs. But the significance of any such objective
influences clearly is in their effect upon the mental functioning of the subject, not upon any physical "communication
channel" between him and his target. To the extent that parapsychology is a science, it is an aspect of psychology and
psychophysiology.

Try as we may, we have not been able to isolate psi
phenomena from their intimate involvement with mind. Regardless of objective apparatus or conditions that we introduce into the experiment, the results always bring us back
disconcertingly to the person who produces them. They
carry more of the stamp of his individuality than of definable
physical law. Thus, for the present at least, the psi phenomena are truly parapsychological: they share the peculiar
inaccessibility of subjective mind.

Phenomena Analogous to Psi

It is important to note that in this respect psi is in the same class with all conscious, subjective experience. We can trace the transmission of light into an eye and the consequent chemical changes in the retina that evoke discharges in the optic nerve fibers, and correlate the quantum energy of the light with the perceived color and the energy flux with the brightness. But the process by which electromagnetic energy quanta evoke the experience of a rainbow, or pressure waves in the air a sensation of melodious sounds, is wholly occult. No causal chain bridges that chasm.

Even PK has its analog in ordinary experience. When Paul Revere watched for his friend's signal in the North Church belfry, his perception of one lantern or two evoked the decision that determined his subsequent course of action. In this as in every conscious decision, and probably in the unconscious ones also, physical events are altered by a process just as occult as PK.

Eisenbud (1956), in an excellent discussion of this and other such hiatuses or "disconnections" as he terms them, has pointed out several others in addition to the mind-body problem: the probability paradox, by which predictable statistical order emerges from large numbers of events that are individually independent and unpredictable; and the closely related quantum phenomena, in which inherently acausal, indeterministic small-scale processes somehow combine to produce the highly deterministic phenomena of large-scale physics.

Psi in Animals

Possible exceptions to the arguments linking psi with mind are those experiments involving simpler animals and even plants as subjects or agents. Instead of a human PK subject, a cat is used, then cockroaches (Schmidt, 1970b)-- and the PK effects continue! Rats (Craig and Treurniet, 1974) and mice (Duval and Montredon, 1968) foresee the future. One has the feeling of being in the presence of something either awesome or absurd. If the ostensible subjects are indeed producing the effects, then we may be a long step nearer to isolating a psi phenomenon from its confusing psychological impedimenta. But one cannot avoid an uneasy suspicion that the experimenter may be the agent, and that we are meeting ourselves in the mirror again.

Resolution of this ambiguity comes down to much the same considerations as resolution of the site of PK action on a complex apparatus, mentioned earlier. Since an experiment necessarily involves an experimenter, as designer if not as participant, it appears impossible in principle to exclude entirely the possibility of PK action by the experimenter. But if an extensive series of experiments with various relatively simple organisms yields similar results in different laboratories under the direction of various experimenters, then the presumption will be strengthened that the ostensible subjects are indeed the agents of the PK effects.

Despite this difficulty, such experiments may prove to be very important. Experiments with human subjects are plagued by the complex and devious interactions between experimenter and subject, and among multiple subjects. Provisionally, we may hope that such interactions will decrease as we go down the scale of biological complexity in choosing subjects. Any psi activity by a cockroach would, one assumes, be more self-centered and less sensitive to the mood or personality of the experimenter than would psi performance by a human subject. If that is true--and there is no real warrant for the assumption--then we may begin to approach a repeatable experiment, on the argument that performance of any kind by a simpler and less interactive organism should be capable of fewer permutations than would that of a more complex creature.

Psi in Inanimate Systems?

Carried to its logical conclusion, this line of thought suggests the ultimate in such depersonalization, the possibility of psi interaction between two inanimate systems. Possibly psi is a manifestation of life, and dependent on it. But one suspects that any principle that manifests through living systems should be detectable in some form in more simply organized matter. Galvani noted that his frog legs hanging by copper hooks on an iron bar kicked when they touched the iron, and went on to an extensive and insightful series of experiments on what he termed "animal electricity," believing it to be a manifestation of life. Nevertheless, Volta and others soon showed that the same phenomena could be developed in nonliving apparatus--i.e., batteries.

Whether psi offers the possibility of a parallel development appears to depend upon the relation of mind and matter. "Animal electricity" was clearly a physiological phenomenon; but psi is persistently identified with mind rather than body per se. Is "mind" a universal attribute of matter, manifesting in simple situations in ways that we do not detect or fail to identify? Or is mind a function of complexity? Would two large computers programmed for slightly different operations tend to interact? In any event, the difficulty of eliminating psi influence by the experimenter in any such situation is formidable.

5   SOME OBSERVATIONS ON REPEATABILITY

At this point, it is in order to consider what conditions information must satisfy to support scientific conclusions. First, it is not necessary that the data result from experiments; astronomy has managed very well on the basis of observations alone. What is necessary is that the observations be sufficiently numerous and accurate to afford an opportunity for the discovery of any consistent relations that may exist among the observed phenomena. It is not necessary that such relations conform to any known law, but only that they be orderly enough to justify a theoretical rationalization based on them.

The crux of the matter lies in the words orderly enough. Order necessarily means perceived order. It is an article of faith among scientists that all processes are orderly, that apparent chaos is a complex mixture of orderly events. Even processes involving isolated small particles conform to the probabilistic order specified by quantum mechanics. A common mistake is to demand that unfamiliar events such as psi phenomena should conform to a preconceived order, to an existing theoretical model. "Orderly enough," then, means relations among relevant variables sufficiently simple that a dedicated investigator can perceive them and formulate them intelligently.

Of course, such an extension of theory is not acceptable as an island. It must relate rationally to adjacent phenomenological areas. Usually the extension cannot be appended arbitrarily to the preexisting theoretical structure. Rather, the new rationalization supersedes the old, unifying both the new and the old areas of observation under a broader system of insight. Examples in physics of such a process are familiar. Attempts to assimilate electrical phenomena in terms of Newtonian mechanics were futile; but Maxwell's radical theoretical approach not only rationalized the diverse electromagnetic data--it revolutionized mechanics as well. Maxwell's theory in turn proved incapable of explaining the behavior of small particles. It was superseded by the radical assumptions of quantum mechanics, with their implications of a fundamentally statistical universe.

So much has been made of the issue of repeatability in parapsychology that it seems necessary to emphasize again that repeatability is desirable but not essential in scientific observations. To go back to the astronomical example, Kepler derived his revolutionary laws of planetary orbits from observations of apparent paths of planets that never are exactly repeated. Few if any events ever are exactly repeated. Scientific insight consists in discovering relationships among identifiable variables to which diverse events conform repeatedly.

Repeatability Is Abstraction

Repeatability thus implies the abstraction of certain elements of consistency from situations that differ in detail. A lightning stroke is never exactly repeated, but the qualitative characteristics that constitute the concept lightning are consistently repeated. No eclipse track on earth ever is repeated, but we understand eclipses to the point of boredom.

The demand for repeatability, then, is really a demand for insight. The factors upon which repeatable results depend cannot be prescribed a priori; they must be sought within the context of the phenomena. Eclipses are regarded as repeatable rather than capricious events only because they are consistent with gravitational theory. Individual positions and motions of sun, moon, and earth at eclipse never are exactly repeated, but the parameters of them are understandable and assignable as consequences of the inclusive theory, the applicability of which is repeatable. Without the unifying concept of gravitational theory or an empirical approximation derived from long experience, eclipses appear as capricious events.

Anyone who believes that physical experiments are inherently repeatable should examine the results of a freshman laboratory session! Even in sophisticated physical experiments, repeatability is a matter of degree. It depends upon the understanding by the experimenter of the variables involved in the experiment and of their relative significance, and his ability to control these variables. And control does not necessarily mean holding them constant. If someone measures the speed of sound in air and gets different results at different temperatures, he does not despair at the capriciousness of his experiment. He recognizes that temperature is a significant factor and uses the "capriciousness" itself to evaluate the effect.

Repeatability in Experiments with Humans

It is a long step, of course, from such a simple and well-understood example to a parapsychological experiment, or even one in psychology. Even if measurable physical factors could be found in psi phenomena, the data probably would be complicated seriously by inconstant personal factors. It is not surprising that the meager evidences of consistency between scoring levels and certain psychological variables are themselves inconstant. It is important, of course, to find means of improving the stability of such evidences of order; but we should understand that doing so does not in itself improve the scientific validity of the results. It only makes the results easier to rationalize.

In an experiment in which a human personality is a vital component, it is obviously impracticable and perhaps impossible in principle to control all variables, or even to evaluate them. For this reason, psi experiments with simple organisms as subjects are especially attractive. As noted earlier, it is plausible to expect that these creatures will exhibit less "capriciousness" (i.e., complexity) than will humans. If these simpler organisms actually are functioning as psi agents and not merely reflecting the experimenter's influence, we may hope that intensive work with them will lead to significant improvements in clarifying psi relationships.

The results of experiments involving human subjects probably will remain highly variable and therefore very difficult to interpret. The nuances of personality variables are so numerous and elusive that close control or evaluation of them probably will remain impossible. In that event, any conclusions from such work will necessarily continue to

depend heavily upon statistical evaluation, with a high degree
of unpredictability.

6   CONCLUSION

The intractability of psi with respect to physics is
frustrating, but it need not be cause for despair.   After all,
psi does interact with the physical world--in PK, in clairvoyance, in precognition.   But its close identification with
psychological rather than physical correlates lends support
to the idea that psi manifestations are in a fundamental sense
parallel to the more familiar manifestations of mind through
the body.   Such a distinction between mind and body need
not imply that one's mind is a preexisting or independently
existing entity, but it does suggest a level of function that
in both psi and sensorimotor aspects transcends the recognized capabilities of physical systems.   If this conjecture is
correct, we must regard psi manifestations not as an isolated anomaly to be investigated and clarified, but as an integral portion of the entity we call mind.   In that case, we
must expect that the elucidation of psi will come only as one
phase of the evolution of understanding of the broader phenomena of subjective mind and the mind-body complex.

REFERENCES

Birge, W. R.   "A New Method and an Experiment in Pure
     Telepathy. "   Journal of Parapsychology, 12 (1948), 273-
     88.
Brier, R. M.   "PK on a Bio-Electrical System. "   Journal
     of Parapsychology, 33 (1969), 187-205.
Chari, C. T. K.   "Precognition, Probability, and Quantum
     Mechanics. "   Journal of the American Society for Psy-
     chical Research, 66 (1972), 193-207.
Craig, J. G. , and Treurniet, W. C.   "Precognition in Rats
     as a Function of Shock and Death. "   In W. G. Roll,
     R. L. Morris, and J. D. Morris (eds.), Research in
     Parapsychology 1973 (Metuchen, N. J. :   Scarecrow Press,
     1974), p75-8.
Duval, P. , and Montredon, E.   "ESP Experiments with
     Mice. "   Journal of Parapsychology, 32 (1968), 153-66.
Eisenbud, J.   "Psi and the Problem of the Disconnections
     in Science. "   Journal of the American Society for Psy-
     chical Research, 50 (1956), 3-26.
_____ .   The World of Ted Serios.   New York: William

Morrow, 1967.

Fisk, G. W., and West, D. J. "Dice-Casting Experiments with a Single Subject." Journal of the Society for Psychical Research, 39 (1958), 277-87.

Forwald, H. Mind, Matter, and Gravitation: A Theoretical and Experimental Study. New York: Parapsychology Foundation, 1969 (Parapsychological Monographs, no. 11).

Grad, B. "The 'Laying On of Hands'": Implications for Psychotherapy, Gentling, and the Placebo Effect." Journal of the American Society for Psychical Research, 61 (1967), 286-305.

_____, Cadoret, R. J., and Paul, G. I. "The Influence of an Unorthodox Method of Treatment on Wound Healing in Mice." International Journal of Parapsychology, 3 (1961), 5-24.

Hoffman, B. "ESP and the Inverse-Square Law." Journal of Parapsychology, 4 (1940), 149-52.

Honorton, C. "Apparent Psychokinesis on Static Objects by a 'Gifted' Subject." In W. G. Roll, R. L. Morris, and J. D. Morris (eds.), Research in Parapsychology 1973 (Metuchen, N.J.: Scarecrow Press, 1974), p128-31.

Humphrey, B. M., and Rhine, J. B. "A Confirmatory Study of Salience in Precognition Tests." Journal of Parapsychology, 6 (1942), 190-219.

McMahan, E. A. "An Experiment in Pure Telepathy." Journal of Parapsychology, 10 (1946), 224-42.

Mitchell, E. D. "An ESP Test from Apollo 14." Journal of Parapsychology, 35 (1971), 89-107.

Osis, K. "ESP Over Distance: A Survey of Experiments Published in English." Journal of the American Society for Psychical Research, 59 (1965), 22-42.

_____. "What Can Be Done in Space Experiments That Cannot Be Done in Earth Experiments?" In W. G. Roll, R. L. Morris, and J. D. Morris (eds.), Research in Parapsychology 1972 (Metuchen, N.J.: Scarecrow Press, 1973), p54-5.

_____ and Fahler, J. "Space and Time Variables in ESP." Journal of the American Society for Psychical Research, 59 (1965), 130-45.

Pratt, J. G., and Keil, H. H. J. "Firsthand Observations of Nina S. Kulagina Suggestive of PK Upon Static Objects." Journal of the American Society for Psychical Research, 67 (1973), 381-90.

Rhine, J. B. "Evidence of Precognition in the Covariance of Salience Ratios." Journal of Parapsychology, 6 (1942), 111-43.

_____. "Telepathy and Other Untestable Hypotheses."

Journal of Parapsychology, 38 (1974), 137-53.

_____ and Humphrey, B. M. "The PK Effect: Special Evidence from Hit Patterns: I. Quarter Distributions of the Page." Journal of Parapsychology, 8 (1944), 18-60. (a)

_____ and _____. "The PK Effect: Special Evidence from Hit Patterns: II. Quarter Distributions of the Set." Journal of Parapsychology, 8 (1944), 254-71. (b)

_____, _____ and Pratt, J. G. "The PK Effect: Special Evidence from Hit Patterns: III. Quarter Distributions of the Half-Set." Journal of Parapsychology, 9 (1945), 150-68.

Rhine, L. E., and Rhine, J. B. "The Psychokinetic Effect: I. The First Experiment." Journal of Parapsychology, 7 (1943), 20-43.

Rush, J. H. "The Potential Significance of Psi Experimentation Involving Spacecraft." In W. G. Roll, R. L. Morris, and J. D. Morris (eds.) Research in Parapsychology 1972 (Metuchen, N.J.: Scarecrow Press, 1973), p58-9.

Schmeidler, G. R. "An Experiment on Precognitive Clairvoyance." Parts I, II, Journal of Parapsychology, 28 (1964), 1-27; Parts III, IV, V, Journal of Parapsychology, 28 (1964), 93-125.

_____. "PK Effects Upon Continuously Recorded Temperature." Journal of the American Society for Psychical Research, 67 (1973), 325-40.

Schmidt, H. "Quantum Processes Predicted?" New Scientist, Oct. 16, 1969, 114-5. (a)

_____. "Precognition of a Quantum Process." Journal of Parapsychology, 33 (1969), 99-108. (b)

_____. "A PK Test with Electronic Equipment." Journal of Parapsychology, 34 (1970), 175-81. (a)

_____. "PK Experiments with Animals as Subjects." Journal of Parapsychology, 34 (1970), 255-61. (b)

_____. "Some Psi Tests Related to Space Flight." In W. G. Roll, R. L. Morris, and J. D. Morris (eds.) Research in Parapsychology 1972 (Metuchen, N.J.: Scarecrow Press, 1973), p55-7.

Stevenson, I., and Pratt, J. G. "Exploratory Investigations of the Psychic Photography of Ted Serios." Journal of the American Society for Psychical Research, 62 (1968), 103-29.

_____ and _____. "Further Investigations of the Psychic Photography of Ted Serios." Journal of the American Society for Psychical Research, 63 (1969), 352-64.

Tanagras, A. "The Theory of Psychobolie." Journal of

the American Society for Psychical Research, 43 (1949), 151-4.

Ullman, M. "An Informal Session with Nina Kulagina." Proceedings of the Parapsychological Association, 8 (1971), 21-2.

Watkins, G. K., and Watkins, A. M. "Possible PK Influence on the Resuscitation of Anesthetized Mice." Journal of Parapsychology, 35 (1971), 257-72.

R. B. Roberts

A THEORY FOR PSI

My interest in the field of parapsychology dates from
a lecture in sophomore psychology in 1930. In the course
of the lecture Professor Langfeld stated that he had carried
out an experiment which proved that J. B. Rhine's work was
wrong. As it seemed quite illogical to claim that a failure
to repeat an experiment constituted disproof, I read Rhine's
papers and they roused an interest in the field that has remained with me to the present.

In 1930 nuclear physics was in its infancy. Artificial
disintegration of nuclei was still in the future. So were the
neutron, the positron, and the present long list of mesons.
Stanley had just succeeded in crystalizing tobacco mosaic
virus, but he had no idea of how it was synthesized. Goddard was starting his work with rockets.

Now nuclear physics is the basis of an industry. We
have all sorts of radioactive isotopes available at the local
distributor. A part of the power lighting of this room comes
from nuclear reactions. The synthesis and assembly of vi-
ruses have been described in great detail. And the de-
scendants of Goddard's rockets have taken men to the moon.

Other fields have made comparable strides. Plate
tectonics has revolutionized geology. Astronomy has turned
up pulsars, quasars, and black holes, all unheard of in
1930.

Compared to other fields of science, parapsychology
has been static and it is easy to see why some have no
confidence in the existence of the phenomena it studies. I
have had a few personal experiences that I cannot attribute
to errors, hoaxes, fraud, or chance, and so I remain con-

vinced that it is a legitimate but difficult field of research. Moreover, it is a field in which the concepts are far-reaching and intellectually intriguing. Why then has progress been so slow?

First and foremost is the difficulty of instrumentation. I doubt that the other fields would have moved very fast if the signals were always buried in the noise and experiments could not be routinely repeated. Ball lightning remains a mystery. We are all familiar with this problem.

A second difficulty is one that could be remedied: this is the lack of well-recognized theories. In physics the experimental work was guided by quantum theory and relativity. Theory led to the search for the neutrino and now is the basis for efforts to detect quarks. In biology the gene was a theoretical unit of heredity for years before it was recognized to be a sequence of DNA. Later the central dogma of DNA-RNA protein was formulated. These theories did not need to be correct; they simply had to be clearly stated and recognized. Then the experimentalists set out to support or disprove them.

It is my belief that the development of theory in parapsychology has been inhibited by intuitive feelings that unless a theory explains the basic mechanism of psi it will be useless. This is asking too much of a theory. Newton did not explain how or why one mass attracts another; he simply described the effect in general and quantitative terms. The same is true of relativity, quantum mechanics, and so forth. A theory simply substitutes one central mystery for numerous minor puzzles. To be useful a theory only needs to (a) arrange the facts in a pattern that is logical and therefore easy to remember, (b) explain numerous specific effects in terms of one unexplained phenomenon, and (c) make predictions subject to disproof and thereby to suggest experiments to support or disprove it.

To illustrate the value of the simplest kind of a theory, let us arrange the various phenomena of parapsychology as follows:

Organism to Organism	-	Telepathy
Object to Organism	-	Clairvoyance
Organism to Object	-	Psychokinesis
Object to Object	-	?

The listing of the first three classes suggests that the fourth class should be included for completeness. A moment's thought brought the realization that as opposed to "objects," the word "person" would be insufficient in this listing in that it omitted animals. When the thought was developed further, it was realized that "organism" should be used rather than "animal" so as to include plants and micro-organisms.

The development of a theory requires choices and precision. The effects listed imply as a minimum a transfer of information, but information can be transferred in different ways. As an analogy, a submarine can be detected by passive listening or by sonar. To make the theory as precise as possible, let us assume that the information transfer of psi is analogous to passive listening. This point might be subject to disproof.

Next, let us assume that there is no transfer of energy and, as a corollary, no transfer of momentum. This assumption places stringent limitations on the activities of poltergeists. It requires, for example, that if an object rises (as a result of PK) it might do so at the expense of its thermal energy; if so, its temperature would fall.

However, a body rising at the expense of its thermal energy would gain in free energy and thereby violate the Second Law of Thermodynamics. For the strictest conservatism let us assume that the Second Law holds. Then if a body rises as a result of PK it must do so at the expense of its internal free energy, as is the case when a rocket is launched.

With these three assumptions we are left with the theory that paranormal phenomena are due to interactions among organisms and objects that involve the transfer of information but no transfer of energy or momentum. Does this theory, which is strictly conservative, leave room for psi? To my knowledge it does. I am not aware of any hard evidence for energy transfer. Secondly, is it useful in any way?

First of all, it suggests a new class of interactions between objects. Ordinarily such interactions involve energy transfer, but there is one situation at least where information transfer might cause observable effects. Numerous solutions (for example, silica, urea, and magnesium sulfate) are not optically active but crystals formed from them are either right- or left-handed. Possibly the proximity of an existing left-handed crystal could influence the probability of forming another left-handed crystal from solution.

Second, the theory poses the question as to why interactions involving organisms are the only ones observed to date. Special properties of organisms are their complexity, the rapid rate of chemical reactions in them, their ample supplies of free energy, and their capacity to assume many different states of equal energy. These properties provide a situation where a trivial difference in information can be amplified into a detectable signal. A point mutation, for example, is caused by a very small change in the information, one nucleotide changed out of the billions present. Yet such a mutation can be lethal.

Next, the theory implies a division of the problem into three parts: the properties of the "emitter" (for lack of a better word), the properties of the recipient, and the dependence of the space-time relationship between the two. At present it hardly seems worthwhile postulating any details of the space-time relationship since we lack a quantitative receiver. The experimental difficulties are worse than those that would be faced in attempting to deduce the inverse square law of light propagation by observing the distance at which a man can read the headlines of a paper. Precognition, of course, shows clearly that the usual time relationships do not apply.

More has been learned about the properties of the recipient, but the main conclusion to be drawn is that recipients are highly variable. The sheep-goat experiments, for example, indicate that people are far too complex to act as reliable instruments. Possibly mice or fruit flies would be better.

Finally, the theory suggests that computers could be valuable in determining what constitutes an emitting object. The computer can be programmed to offer random targets for guessing. Beside the advantages of eliminating recording errors and the tedium of analyzing the results, the computer program can be arranged to provide a number of significantly different situations. The target can be chosen before or after the guess to determine whether precognition gives the same result as postcognition. More importantly, the program can be chosen to determine what constitutes a target. The target number can be printed out before the guess, after the guess, or not at all. These different modes of operation can be switched in a known or random fashion during the runs. If these three modes all give the same positive result, one might postulate that the subject can read the number stored in the computer's memory. Such a reading could then be made considerably more difficult by choosing three random numbers. The first would serve to encode the target while the second would designate the storage location. The third random number would be the target, but it would be transformed within a microsecond to its coded representation and stored at an address known only to the computer. Alternatively, the true target might never occur, only its code number. This storage of a message encoded in an unknown way and stored at an unknown location is quite similar to pure telepathy.

The possibility of PK effects on the computer's choice of targets can be eliminated by the use of pseudo-random numbers. Such experiments could rule out any theory based on the requirement of a real object as the emitter.

My purpose in running through this exercise is not to present a theory which I believe to be good or even new. It is simply to illustrate the usefulness of even the simplest sort of theory as a guide to what experiments are most significant. I venture to say that if even this crude attempt at a theory had been widely recognized in 1930 it would have been disproved many times over by now and it would have been superseded by a series of better theories.

A second purpose is to offer a poor theory in the hope that it will stimulate someone to devise a better one.

Part II

PARAPSYCHOLOGY AND BIOLOGY

For every ability of human beings, from learning to selective attention to ESP, we ask biological questions. Is this an ability of other kinds of advanced animals? Of simple animals? Of all living things? Does the ability differ in distinctive ways from one species to another? What differences are there within a species and how strong is their genetic component? What biological structures or functions are necessary for any given ability? What special physiological conditions facilitate it or inhibit it? What concomitant physiological changes occur when it is exercised? After it is exercised, what are the effects upon other ongoing processes?

Questions like these are numerous and probably are similar for almost any function. The answers vary and are sparse even in comparative psychology where there has been so much research on the learning process. They are especially sparse in parapsychology.

The reason for this sparsity is simple enough. Few scientists do any parapsychological research; even of these few, most have full-time work of a different sort, such as teaching, so that they can spend little time on experimentation. Not long ago it was estimated that only about 20 or 25 papers on parapsychological research were published in the average year and even now the number is not much greater. Of these reports, few dealt with biological questions. This in turn meant that any single question was likely to be handled in only a few reports, each dealing with a particular method or drug or narrow population and thus giving an overspecific answer to the broad general issue to which it can be seen to be addressed.

Some of these reports yielded such provocative findings that they well deserve follow-up. An example is B. R. Bhadra's research on the tie-in between ESP success and somatotype or body build ("Physique in Relation to ESP Performance," Journal of Parapsychology, 32 (1968), 131). Bhadra tested a large sample of college students in India, using a standard laboratory ESP procedure. He found a clear indication that most ectomorphic subjects (i.e., those most markedly "all skin and bone," who were slender and had linear, fragile bodies) had a lower rate of ESP success than the others. Would this hold true of other populations as well? Would it be true also for scores on tests that were conducted under pleasantly sociable, personalized conditions as opposed to the tension-producing conditions of the classroom or laboratory? If so, what would be found for other abilities in young persons of this body type? Would they show compensating strengths in some disparate areas? Suppose, for example, that subsequent research finds that when ESP scores are low, social ease, empathy, divergent thinking, and creativity scores tend also to be low, but that at the same time, in contrast, alertness, concentration, decent social reserve, and convergent reasoning scores are high. Such findings, or any other pattern of positive findings, could put us on the road toward developing better concepts of the relation of body build to physiological functioning, and thence to its relation to behavior and to success in ESP or other tasks. Isolated studies like Bhadra's need to be replicated and extended and this has not been done.

But some things have been done and they are well set forth in Dr. Robert L. Morris' article, which begins this section. Some ESP and PK research with animals suggests that they too have these abilities; some research on physiological processes in relation to ESP success gives clues about the complex pattern of body changes that needs to be examined further. The work that has been done is interesting. The gaps are glaring. You will find here both an overview of what findings have so far been obtained and a challenge to fill out the picture by obtaining more.

Dr. Morris's article organizes the research systematically, using three categories: the input of information (ESP), the processing of information (the relation of ESP to brain or perhaps to other body changes) and the output of information (PK). His emphasis is on the first of these categories, with minor emphasis on the second.

The other article in this section, by Dr. Bernard R. Grad, overlaps only slightly. Its emphasis is on the output side, and specifically on a possible application of that output. This possible application is the use of PK to influence body processes in other organisms.

When put in such coldly abstract language, Dr. Grad's topic may seem merely a reasonable extension of earlier concepts. It may strike you as only one more topic to investigate, not distinctively different from any of the others here. And so it is, in one sense. But in another sense it is radically different, with implications verging on the mystical, the superstitious, or the absurd. "The use of PK to influence body processes in other organisms" is a polysyllabic way of describing faith healing, or psychic healing, or even (when malignant instead of beneficent) the causing of death or bodily injury to others through a curse or evil wish without overt physical action. It overlaps with witchcraft. It is a laboratory examination of "black" or "white" magic.

This then is an area of investigation with exciting and perhaps bizarre, even frightening possibilities. You may find, as you read Dr. Grad's report, that you are dismayed at seeing the strength of evidence that such processes occur. Surely, when you have read it, you will hope that replication in other laboratories will be undertaken and--if positive results are obtained there too--that the implications and applications of this process be further explored. If such things happen, we need to know more about them.

Robert L. Morris

BIOLOGY AND PSYCHICAL RESEARCH

THE GENERAL QUESTION OF PSYCHE AND BIOLOGY

Given that human beings are biological organisms, one can still debate how much of our psyche, our mental life, is biological in nature. Although the interdependence of mind and body has been a philosopher's debate since the days of Aristotle, it has in recent years come into its own within the mental health science, particularly in psychiatry and psychosomatic medicine. Science has come to realize that our mental life is so tightly bound in with central nervous system activity that we cannot hope to achieve a thorough understanding of behavior and experience unless we understand its biological concomitants. The study of the biological aspects of mental events (or behavioral events, if you prefer) is often called psychobiology. It embraces a wide range of disciplines ranging from biochemistry and biophysics to social and clinical psychology. As we shall see shortly, psychical research also belongs on the list.

Psychobiological studies have established undeniable links between overt behavior and experience, and events in our central nervous system. These links are found in three major areas: the input of information, the storage of information, and the output of information. A fair amount is known about how information gets into and out of the body. But how it is processed, how it relates to actual experience, thoughts, etc., is still very much a matter of speculation.

It seems evident that memory and thought are related to activation or reactivation of some complex biochemical sub-system within the higher structures of the brain. Three kinds of relationships can be suggested: (a) thought is activation, (b) thought has a one-to-one correspondence with

48

specific activation, and (c) thought is interfaced with the physical body through activation of components of the central nervous system, but not necessarily on a one-to-one basis and not necessarily involving reactivation of specific structures. Our general problem is as follows: behavior and experience appear to interact heavily with the physiology of our bodies. However, we cannot specify at present what the extent of that interaction is. Psi is manifested through behavior and experience, so it must also interact heavily with our physiology. Thus to the extent that we want to understand and use psi, we must understand how it relates to biological factors and is influenced by them. And since we do not know how extensive the interaction between psyche and biology is, perhaps as we learn more about psi and its biological relationships we will learn more about whether there is some aspect of self, some mind-stuff above and beyond nervous system biochemical activity that is necessary for mental activity to take place. Many have argued that psi itself, as apparent communication without dependence on known physical principles, directly implies the existence of such an aspect to mind.

We are obviously a very long way from acquiring the extensive bodies of data needed to provide scientific answers to the problems posed above. However, there are some preliminary questions that can be intellectually explored and perhaps tied in with present research findings.

A Set of Terms for Psi

Before we pursue specific questions and their related research, we should agree upon a useful set of terms. Psi means communication between organism and environment without the use of known channels of information exchange. A regular communication system has a source, a receiver, a message (information), and a channel. Any message is sent from the source to the receiver via a particular means, or channel. If I speak to you, I am the source, you are the receiver, what I say is the message, and sound waves are the channel.

Studies of psi are of two sorts: those that explore designated organisms as receivers of information through unknown means (telepathy, clairvoyance, and precognition) and those that explore designated organisms as sources of information sent to receivers through unknown means (psycho-

kinesis and telepathy). In discussing studies on the psychobiology of psi, this general terminology will be used rather
than those terms which were traditionally associated with
parapsychology.

CENTRAL NERVOUS SYSTEM COMPLEXITY AND PSI

The central nervous system (CNS) varies greatly from
species to species in its anatomical and physiological characteristics. By examining psi throughout the animal kingdom, we may therefore learn what CNS characteristics seem
most related to psi functioning, and in what ways.

The Distribution of Psi Throughout the Animal Kingdom

Does psi in some form or another occur throughout
the animal kingdom, including simple organisms? There are
two forms of evidence bearing on this question, anecdotal
and experimental.

Anecdotal evidence. In considering the material in
this section the reader should bear in mind the following
problems with anecdotal evidence: deliberate fraud; distortion in perception of the original events; distortion in reten-
tion of the original events; distortion in reporting the original events; impossibility of exactly recreating the original
events to look for additional factors not known to the re-
porters; distortion and/or selective reporting by the investigator; and difficulty in assessing how unusual the event is,
i.e., how often, if at all, it would occur by chance.

There have been several surveys of anecdotes suggesting psi in animals. Perhaps the most rigorous is that
by Rhine and Feather (1962). They summarized the case
material collected at the (then) Duke Parapsychology Laboratory and described five categories of behavior suggesting psi:
Homing; psi-trailing; reaction to impending danger; reaction
to a distant death; and anticipation of a positive or rewarding
event.

Homing, the ability of an animal to return to its
home when removed a considerable distance in any given direction and released, has been documented in many species
of birds, as well as some mammals and reptiles and even
a few organisms as low as mollusks (see Thorpe, 1963).

However, there is increasing evidence that such abilities are mediated by a variety of subtle environmental cues that we humans normally do not think about, such as celestial patterns (see Matthews, 1968), terrestrial magnetism gradients (see Reich, cited in Dröscher, 1969), and so on. Thus it is presently uncertain whether or not homing can truly be considered as evidence for psi in any particular species of animal.

Psi-trailing presents a different story. In a typical psi-trailing case, an owner moves to a distant location and leaves a pet behind. The pet then disappears, only to turn up later at the new home of the owner, where it has never been before. How did the pet know where to go? Heightened sensory capacity or "blind luck" seem very unlikely with great distances. Rhine and Feather (1962) found 25 cases involving distances traveled of over 30 miles, cases in which the witnesses seemed reliable, supportive data were available, the pet involved had a readily distinguishable characteristic, such as a scar, or nametag, and so on. Involved were 10 dogs, 12 cats and three birds, all typical pet species.

Many of the cases involving reactions to impending danger to the animal or an owner may involve cues of which we humans are generally unaware. For instance, grazing animals reportedly may leave the slopes of a volcano days before there are signs of an eruption. Perhaps they are responding to minute ground tremors of the sort that we now know do occasionally signal volcanic activity. Other cases are harder to explain; e.g., dogs' refusing to enter vehicles that later crash and horses shying from faulty bridges before setting foot on them.

Cases involving responses to distant death or discomfort of an owner are occasionally very impressive. In one case, a dog was boarded at a veterinarian's while the owners visited Florida. One morning the animal started howling and showing other signs of great distress, which lasted for a full hour. The veterinarian noted this odd behavior and reported it to the family upon their return. They were astonished, for at the start of the hour in question they had been marooned on the roof of their car in a flash flood and had been rescued an hour later. In other cases, dogs have suddenly started to howl at the time of their distant owners' deaths.

Likewise, cases involving anticipation of positive events are sometimes quite impressive. Typically, a dog whose master is away at school or in the service may suddenly show signs of excitement, running repeatedly to the front door or gate, only to find that a short time later the missing master arrives at home unexpectedly, unanticipated by the humans in the household.

No exact tabulation of species exists for these last three kinds of cases, although far and away the most frequent stories involve mammals who have had apparent close relationships with humans.

Two other surveys of interest are those by Bayless (1970) and Gaddis and Gaddis (1970). The former emphasizes case material relating to the survival question, such as unusual responses of animals in apparent haunted houses, when accompanying humans who see apparitions, when present during mediumistic phenomena, and so on. Given that the animals seem responsive to such circumstances, it is difficult to separate out sensory information, including odors, that is provided by the humans involved. Gaddis and Gaddis cite many cases of ususual animal performances, including examples of apparently very intelligent animals, cases of animals' displaying extraordinary devotion to masters, and anecdotes such as psi-trailing cases, suggesting that animals can respond to distant information to which they have no apparent sensory access. The material related to psi presented in these two works also deals almost exclusively with mammals that come into frequent contact with humans, plus a few cases involving birds.

Two other kinds of cases have often been offered as possible evidence for psi: "clever" animals and "hive" behavior, both of which the present author discusses in more detail elsewhere (Morris, 1970). Clever animals are animals that seem able to respond appropriately to questions by barking, pawing, or pecking the correct number of times, spelling out appropriate words by indicating in sequence lettered blocks from a tray, and so on, in such a way as to appear able to converse intelligently. Although many animals have certain forms of counting ability and some, such as chimpanzees and porpoises, seem able to make use of language systems, we now think that most if not all such "clever" animals are in fact responding to subtle and often unconscious body movement cues provided by people who know the correct answer. Rosenthal (in an introduction to

Pfungst, 1965) provides a good summary of how this would work. Some cases remain difficult to explain, however, in that results were still obtained when the animal was screened from all humans who knew the correct answer (e.g., White, 1964b, and Wood and Cadoret, 1958, both with dogs). Some of the work done by the famous Russian animal trainer Durov may also fit in here (see Bechterev, 1949).

Several early naturalists were impressed by the un-usual group precision in the social behavior of hive insects, bird flocks, and schools of fish, behavior which seemed so simultaneous that it could not have been communicated through normal means. We now have a better understanding of how animals communicate through subtle postural changes, release of chemicals (pheromones) into the air or water, and so on, and we no longer see the need to label such group behavior as "due to psi."

In summary, there is very little good anecdotal evi-dence suggesting the presence of psi in animals having simple central nervous systems. Most of the cases come from domesticated mammals, especially pets, and the re-mainder from birds. Humans collect more anecdotes in general about animals with which they are in daily contact and with which they are emotionally involved, so the empha-sis on dogs, cats, birds, and horses in such anecdotes does not in itself rule out the presence of undetected forms of psi in lower organisms. Likewise, it should be remembered that anecdotes cannot be construed as proof of the presence of psi in and of themselves since there are obviously selec-tive and biasing factors in their reporting, but they can pro-vide strong supporting evidence.

Experimental evidence based on choice behavior.   In doing controlled studies with animals, the first question that arises is: how do we get the animal to let us know that it has indeed become aware of information about its environ-ment through unknown means? The main research strategy has been to present the animal with the opportunity to make a series of specific choices such that a correct choice leads to an event more advantageous to the animal than an incor-rect choice. The animal must not have access, of course, to any information through normal channels about which choice is the correct one.

Osis and Foster (1953) did several experiments with kittens run in a two-choice T-maze. The kittens were re-

quired to choose which of the two arms of the maze led to
concealed food. A choice consisted of actually entering one
of the two arms of the maze. Olfactory cues were mini-
mized by a fan blowing air toward the food cup positions,
and because of the shape of the maze the cups themselves
were not visible to the kittens at the time they actually made
their choices. The kittens scored positively under "good"
conditions such as affectionate handling and negatively under
"poor" conditions in which distractions were deliberately introduced. The evidence for psi was weakest when the animals were showing rigid or stereotyped choices, such as always going to the right arm, and so on.

Bestall (1962) used male mice run in a two-choice
maze. Each mouse made one choice. Some time after all
the mice had made their choice, a randomization procedure
determined for each mouse which side was correct and
which side incorrect. Correct choosers were given access
to a female six hours later; incorrect choosers were put to
death. Bestall obtained positive results with this procedure,
and even found suggestive evidence for cyclic variations in
scoring from day to day.

Craig and Treurniet (1974) used a similar procedure
with rats in a two-choice maze. The rats showed no tendency to choose the correct side, but those which did so
tended to take longer to run the maze. This was found in
two successive studies. In a later study, Treurniet and
Craig (1975) found a suggestive relationship between success
and phase of the moon.

Duval and Montredon (1968) used mice in a slightly
different two-choice procedure. The basic procedure was
as follows: the animal was placed in a small cage divided
in two by a low partition which the animal could easily
cross. At periodic intervals a mild shock was administered
to the floor on one side or the other. A logic circuit recorded the animal's position. At regular intervals a random
number generator designated one side or the other as the
side to be shocked. Shock was administered for five seconds if the animal was on that side at the time the shock
was selected. A printout of the animal's position plus the
side designated as shock each time provided automated recording of the data. The overall results were positive but
weak, e.g., the mice avoided the shock somewhat more
often than not. On many occasions the mice showed non-
choice behavior; e.g., they either did not move from trial

to trial or else moved only in immediate response to shock. When such trials were eliminated, the results became quite strong. This finding was obtained also in followup work by the same team.

This line of research was in recent years followed up extensively by Walter J. Levy and several coworkers in a set of well-designed and well-instrumented studies (e.g., Levy, 1972). Unfortunately, Levy has admitted that in a recent study he manipulated his equipment to inflate the scoring rate artificially. Thus all past research results with which he was personally involved one way or another must be held in abeyance, pending the outcome of independent attempts to replicate his findings. Levy's work therefore will not be treated as part of the evidence we are considering in this paper.

Schouten (1972) used drops of water as a reward for thirsty rats rather than shock as a punishment. The rats were given two levers to depress, only one of which would give them access to water at a given moment. Which lever led to water was determined by a randomizing device that designated the target lever before the rat was allowed to select. Schouten found that his animals also scored best (e.g., pressed the lever that led to the water) when they were not showing rigid or stereotyped behavior, such as always choosing the same lever. He also found suggestive evidence that having another animal aware of the correct choice helped the subject animal to make that choice. These results were not confirmed in three follow-up studies using similar but not identical procedures (Schouten, 1973).

Parker (1974) used hungry gerbils given two levers to depress, one of which when pressed at a given moment would allow the animal access to a sunflower seed. A pre-programmed punch-tape determined which lever led to food. The results were positive overall, and were still better when the animals were not showing rigid or stereotyped behavior. Broughton and Millar (1975) attempted to repeat this study, using the same equipment in the same laboratory and even some of the same animals, but obtained chance results.

Terry and Harris (1975) used thirsty rats in a procedure similar to that of Schouten. They found slightly below-chance results overall, but strong positive results when the animals were not showing rigid or stereotyped behavior. Only one study was done.

Rhine (1971) investigated a trainer-and-dog interaction in the location of dummy underwater mines buried four inches in the sand in one of five randomly selected shallow water sites. The dog, guided by the trainer (who did not know where the dummy was buried), would register its guess by sitting down in the water at one of the five possible locations, as it had earlier been trained to do. Results were very strong, but interpretation is difficult since (a) the dog may have been able to tell where the dummy was buried by the compactness of the sand as it walked from place to place, and (b) the trainer may have located the targets in the same way, or perhaps through his own psi, and communicated non-verbally to the dog that it was time to sit down.

The final study (Wood and Cadoret, 1958) in this section involves an interesting procedure applied to a "clever" dog, Chris. He was taught by his owner, George Wood, to "guess" down through a stack of standard ESP cards enclosed in opaque envelopes by pawing on Wood's extended forearm once for circle, twice for square, and so on. Wood, who did not know the identity of any of the enclosed cards, presented them one by one to Chris and recorded his responses. This procedure produced very strong positive results when Wood and Chris worked together alone, with Mrs. Wood preparing the target order on a blind basis. When an outside investigator, Cadoret, was called in to witness the results, Chris's scores became negative to a statistically meaningful degree. Unfortunately, further studies were not done to find out if this shift was similar to the often-reported negative scoring of humans in the face of stress.

Experimental evidence based on general behavior patterns. Several preliminary studies have used general activity level to assess an animal's responsiveness to impending and/or distant events of emotional importance for the animal. The present author (Morris, 1967) placed rats one at a time in an open field maze and counted the number of 12" x 12" floor squares traversed by the rat during two minutes. A second experimenter then either killed the rat or spared it, according to a random plan. Overall, no significant difference was found in the animals' activity. However, when those animals that had never run in the apparatus before were considered separately, the ones about to die showed no activity whereas those who were to continue living showed activity. Schmidt (1970b) was unable to obtain results using this procedure, however, and Craig and Treurniet (1974) found that rats who were about to die within 24 hours were more active than those that would live on for several weeks.

Morris (1967) also found in one study that goldfish activity level was related to whether or not the fish was about to be held aloft briefly. In later work, however (Morris, 1972), this finding was not repeated when an improved procedure was used.

Experimental evidence based on human-animal interactions. Several studies involve examination of human-animal interactions, in which a human attempts to influence the behavior of an animal.

Reitler (1962) noted that a colony of sea worms, Tubifex, gave regular responses to the presence of a human observer without the apparent use of sensory cues. However, there may well have been biophysical cues produced by the observer's proximity that could be processed by Tubifex in ways not considered at the time. Watkins and Watkins (1971) reported successful studies in which humans, especially "healers," attempted to revive target anesthetized mice earlier than control mice anesthetized at the same time. Their results were repeated in the same laboratory by Wells and Klein (1972). Metta (1972) found some evidence that a human could influence butterfly larvae to crawl into specified sectors of a petri dish. Extra (1972) did two studies which found some evidence that a human could influence rat running behavior in a shuttle box.

Richmond (1952) found evidence that he could influence the direction of locomotion of paramecia viewed through a microscope. Randall (1970) used a better experimental design and was unable to repeat Richmond's results (nor was Knowles, cited in Randall, 1972b). Later, Randall (1971) found some evidence that wood lice could be influenced to enter one of five sectors of a circular board, as well as evidence (Randall, 1972a) that gerbils could be influenced to jump on certain blocks of wood as opposed to others. He does not regard his results as conclusive, however. Osis (1952) attempted to influence kittens in a two-choice maze. As in his kitten ESP work with Foster mentioned above, there were predicted high runs and predicted low runs, depending upon running conditions and treatment of the kittens. Predicted low runs produced statistically significant psi-missing, whereas the predicted high runs produced only slightly positive results.

The present author (Morris, 1974) found significant evidence that a kitten in an open field apparatus tended to become very peaceful during times when its distant owner had self-induced a very vivid experience of visiting the kitten in the open field and playing with it.

The present set of studies raises an interesting issue, in that we are dealing with an organism designated as source attempting to communicate with another organism designated as receiver. If communication occurs, we are not necessarily bound to assert that both organisms "have psi," since the organism designated as source may not have been the only available source of information (e.g., a target record is usually present), and the receiver may have been induced to behave as it did indirectly (e.g., the human source may have had its psi influence over some purely physical aspect of the environment, such as a slight modification of the temperature or wind currents or chemical gradients in the milieu, which itself biased the animal's behavior). From the standpoint of logic, therefore, we cannot yet assume that the success of the studies in this section demonstrates the presence of psi in the non-human species involved.

Experimental evidence using the animal as source. An additional set of studies has involved experiments in which the psi abilities of animals have been tested through psychokinesis procedures (Schmidt, 1970a; Watkins, 1971). Cockroaches, lizards, chickens, and cats are placed in mildly unpleasant environments. Factors affecting the pleasantness of the environment, such as periodic shock or stimulation from a heat lamp (in a cold environment), are controlled by a random number generator. The hypothesis is that the animals will influence the generator in such a way as to make the environment less unpleasant. The results are mixed. Schmidt's cockroaches were shocked more often than one would expect by chance rather than less often; Watkins' lizards in cool environments showed different tendencies to receive heat from a heat lamp depending on barometric pressure and humidity of the surrounding environment. For Schmidt's study there exists the possibility that Schmidt himself, who doesn't like cockroaches, might have been the real PK agent. The mixed results of the Watkins study are interpretable as consistent with the differing heat needs of the lizards as they found themselves in different environments. Schmidt (1974a) has recently found a similar effect when brine shrimp were exposed to brief electric shock controlled by a random generator. However, this effect is not in his opinion (Schmidt, 1974b) construable as a stable phenomenon.

Unfortunately, all of the studies of this sort may be interpreted as human psi in that the human experimenter (who wants the study to succeed) rather than the animal may be influencing the outcome of the randomizing device. Thus these studies can be taken only as raising the possibility that the non-human species involved are capable of serving as psi sources, but they do not in themselves demonstrate it.

Summary of the experimental evidence bearing on the distribution of psi in animals. As mentioned above, the last two categories of experimental evidence are ambiguous as to interpretation in that the animals involved need not necessarily have been functioning directly in a psi communication system. This is unfortunate because the species involved cover a wide range of central nervous system complexity, from kittens to insects, crustacea and sea worms. Metta's work with butterfly larvae raises interesting possibilities for looking at CNS complexity from a developmental standpoint. It should be added at this time that if in fact the animals themselves are really showing psi--i. e. , are participating directly as source or receiver in a true psi communication system--this should gradually become evident with more and more programmatic research designed to tease out correlational variables.

Of the first two kinds of experimental studies, in which the animals do seem more directly involved, 12 studies involved small rodents. Of these, five give straightforward positive results, two give secondary results only, three give chance results, and two (Craig, 1973; Morris, 1967) give conflicting but significant results with slightly different conditions. Two of these five studies involved precognition procedures, which raise the possibility that a human may have been producing the psi effect rather than the animal (e.g. , Morris, 1973). Three studies involved house pets, each of which produced fairly strong results, but two of which (Osis and Foster, 1953; Rhine, 1971) may possibly have been due to some form of subtle environmental cues. The third (Wood and Cadoret, 1958) may conceivably have been due to Wood being the actual psi receiver, who then unconsciously tensed or relaxed the muscles in his outstretched arm in such a way as to cue Chris. The final two studies involved goldfish. The first study, which worked, allowed a human to determine the target by throwing dice, thus allowing the human to be the psi communicator rather than the fish. When the procedure was modified to eliminate this possibility (Morris, 1972), the results disappeared.

Thus the evidence for psi in animal species is very complex and full of possible interpretational pitfalls. The bulk of the evidence suggests that mammals have psi ability, especially house pets and rodents, the two kinds of animals most commonly tested. Collectively, the evidence is rather strong, although perhaps not as definitive as we might like. With non-mammalian species, there is some suggestive evidence, but far more work must be done to clear up interpretational difficulties.

Although it is true that we do not know what research has been done but not reported, it seems clear that those few species that have been put to a fair amount of testing have shown some evidence of psi. Perhaps in the future more species will be tested, in ways that make sense in terms of their perceptual and behavioral peculiarities, to provide a more comprehensive answer to the question of distribution of psi within the animal kingdom.

Qualitative Aspects of the Distribution of Psi Throughout the Animal Kingdom

Since psi may be present at several levels of central nervous system complexity, additional questions come up about the ways in which it may be manifest between and within species.

Differences in strength within and between species. Although we obviously do not have enough data on hand to assess which species show more or less psi, the question itself deserves thought. It is an interesting one because if we can reliably show differences in strength, once again we may be able to learn something by seeing what anatomical and physiological factors are involved. Also, by relating psi strength to the natural ecology of the animal involved, we may be able to do further studies to learn how psi actually can function for the good of a species (including our own) in its natural environment.

For instance, do animals involved in strong prey-predator relationships show more psi than those that are not? Does the prey show more than the predator or vice versa? Does psi function as a mechanism for regulating and stabilizing population size? For example, if a population of grazing animals becomes so large that it threatens to consume its food supply too quickly, does their psi then dampen somewhat so that they become easier prey for predators? Likewise, if a predator population has eaten too much of its prey, perhaps the predator's psi will diminish and the prey will have an easier time escaping. This may appear to be asking for a supra-intelligent regulatory aspect in psi functioning within any given population. Although this can not be ruled out at present, there are cetainly several simpler mechanisms by which the regulatory function could operate. Psi may be stress-dependent so that animals in great general biological stress show very little psi, or perhaps even psi-missing. Or psi strength may be tied in to other aspects of biochemical fitness, in turn related to diet, thus becoming one more homeostatic regulatory device.

A related question is the functioning of psi in very crowded versus very sparse species. In crowded species, is there perhaps an excess of psi noise, too many competing sources? If so, do we come equipped with psi filtering devices, much as we do for other forms of information input? What about psi as a coordinating device within dense populations, à la the early naturalists? Is this completely unreasonable? What about psi in sparse populations in which social interactions must be timed well and occasionally maintained over some distance?

Various other ecological needs may affect psi strength: availability of food and water in general; the necessity of seasonal migration, maintenance and constant location of the young in a harsh environment, anticipation of natural catastrophe, and general efficiency of social interaction within and between neighboring species.

Certainly one theme that emerges from the anecdotal literature is that bonds of affection seem important in the display of psi. Perhaps we will come to find that affection, affiliation, love, go considerably beyond the complex stimulus-response associative learning theories used by most animal behavior scientists at present to account for these aspects of animal and human behavior. Perhaps psi provides an additional element to such interactions which in itself is affected by all these other variables of which we have been speaking.

Doing research along these lines will not be easy, however. Researchers in the area of animal intelligence have for some time been plagued with the problems of how to compare one species' intelligence with another's. For instance, we would expect the great whales to be extremely intelligent from what we know of their brain anatomy and physiology, especially when it comes to processing auditory (but not visual) information. Yet we know very little of their true capabilities because it is so difficult to find ways of posing behavioral problems for them to which they can respond in measurable ways. When we design studies for animals we tend to anthropomorphize extensively, even when we are aware of the problem. For instance, in a very well-planned study of human-dolphin interactions, Lilly (1967) used a three-environment living space for a young woman and a dolphin to explore together for a month's time while she tried to learn about his language structure and teach him ours. A great many very valuable things were learned from this study; however, much time was wasted while she tried in vain to teach the dolphin to pronounce her three-syllable first name. He finally learned how to roll on his side, letting water rush into one blow hole, meanwhile blowing out through the other and producing a good "mmm" sound, the first sound in her name. The full name was never learned. Had the known behavior and likely Umwelt of dolphins figured more strongly in the planning of this study rather than a task of more specific interest to the cultural world of humans, the time might have been more productively spent.

Likewise with tests of psi in animals, a fair test will require extensive thought about the natural ecology, perceptual world, and behavioral capacities of the species involved. Different procedures may have different motivational salience for the animal, thus producing results in different strengths. If human experimenters can indeed interact with their studies in the ways discussed earlier, their influence may be impossible to eliminate completely and must therefore in some way be controlled or allowed for in the experimental design. Also, the extent to which the testing environment really resembles the natural environment of the animal is undoubtedly a major factor. An environment (including the motivationally relevant target aspect) that resembles the natural environment will probably be responded to psychically in a natural way, thereby producing results more generalizable to the animal's world. If the environment is battleship gray or plexiglass and the target includes only electronic circuitry, the animal may show psi in ways quite unlike its usual ways in that it will be stressed trying to acquire information in general, making few perceptual assumptions, and so on.

And after all is said and done about the factors already mentioned, there is also the problem of the potential cancellation of two factors having equal but opposite effects. Such cancellation becomes a problem only when two factors are always co-present, which can often happen if one of the factors is basically a hidden one that is not included in the experiment intentionally or is a factor that has previously been ignored or judged as irrelevant.

Thus the research that is needed must be comprehensive and programmatic in nature, carefully thought out each step of the way, if we are to obtain answers to the questions we have been posing.

Similarities between human and animal work. Since we have not considered any work on psi in primates, one question that pops up is whether or not what we learn of psi in animals and how it is expressed has anything at all to do with the human condition. Perhaps psi occurs in quite different ways in central nervous systems that process information in the ways humans do. Although this question also is beyond the range of what we can talk about as a result of our currently gathered data, we can map out a plan of attack and look at some preliminary indications.

One approach is to fill in the missing links by working with primates, dolphins, and the like. At the time of his tragic death in an accident in Mexico City, the great neuroanatomist Raul Hernández-Peón had arranged to do a study of psi in dreaming spider monkeys implanted at several midbrain levels. The study was never carried out, nor has any other with primates that has been made public. Although one hears occasional rumors to the contrary, there are no studies on public record of psi research in dolphins.

Another strategy is to look for consistencies in the internal findings between animal and human results. Some similarities do emerge. Osis (1952) and Osis and Foster (1953) found that kittens treated poorly scored below chance, whereas kittens treated well scored positively. This is very similar to the findings of Honorton, Ramsey and Cabibbo (1975), who showed that when humans being tested on a

Schmidt binary random generator were treated abruptly and coldly by the experimenter they scored below chance, whereas those who were treated warmly scored well above. Along similar lines, Chris, the "clever" dog, scored positively when he was being tested by his owners. When Cadoret, the outside professional, participated, thereby (one assumes) increasing the stressfulness of the occasion for all concerned, the results were below chance. Negative human results in the presence of stressful conditions have often been reported. Thus there seems to be some evidence that animals, like humans, may show psi-missing under negative conditions.

Another common feature is exemplified in the findings by Osis and Foster (1953) that their kittens did best when they were going against a bias or patterned response which they had been showing in the immediately preceding trials. This finding is very similar to the response bias findings of Stanford (1967), in which humans who rarely call a specific ESP symbol (i.e., have a bias against it) tend to score quite well on that symbol when they finally do break their bias and call it. Interpretation of this similarity is unclear, but one possibility is that a bias is broken whenever an especially strong message comes through, implying that perhaps both humans and animals may process and filter psi information irregularly so that some messages are stronger than others even though motivational salience is constant.

The finding by Duval and Montredon (1968), Schouten (1972), Parker (1974), and Terry and Harris (1974) that animals score better on trials when they are not showing rigid behavior is also occasionally adduced as a specific finding to be compared with similar human results. In my opinion this finding shows only that when one tests for the presence of psi through giving the animal a choice one mainly finds psi when in fact the animal chooses. This is no more surprising than the discovery that a human will show psi when guessing ESP cards only when he varies his guesses and not when he calls the same card on each of the 25 trials. In other words, I do not see that this finding indicates in any way that the underlying processes of psi are similar in the various species involved. It only shows that psi is in fact occurring during those times at which it has an opportunity to occur.

Thus there is overall at least some indication that psi in animals may occur in roughly the same ways as it does in humans. Of course, much more work along these lines needs to be done.

THE PSYCHOBIOLOGY OF PSI INFORMATION PROCESSING IN HUMANS

Considering the uncertainties of interpretation regarding the distribution of psi in less complex central nervous systems, we should certainly devote space to questions about the biological aspects of positive psi performance in humans per se. Unfortunately, the relevant studies in humans are almost exclusively confined to psychophysiological studies, and we are still very uncertain about many aspects of interpretation of psychophysiological results themselves.

Psychophysiology is the study of relationships between measurable physiological signals and the reported cognitive activity within the organism being measured. The best-known studies within this field of inquiry have been those relating autonomic nervous system activity and emotional states. General arousal or excitement makes the heart beat faster. Fear or sudden shock is accompanied by a pale face due to constriction of the peripheral blood vessels; embarrassment or anger is accompanied by a red face due to expansion of these vessels. When we see something we like, the pupils of our eyes expand; when we see something we don't like, they contract. All of these reactions are controlled by the sympathetic and parasympathetic branches of the autonomic nervous system. Such reactions are generally considered to be adaptive responses of the body to strong stimulation from the environment.

Of specific interest are the relationships between the electrical activity of the cerebral cortex and cognitive processes, especially the alpha rhythms (8-13 Hz) as obtained from EEG recordings from the scalp surface. The power source and pacing mechanism for these rhythms are generally believed to be due to bioelectric activity in cortical cell dendrites, paced or regulated by centers in the thalamus which communicate with various areas of the cortex by a network of neural fibers (the thalamocortical projection system). Most of the evidence comes from animal research. For a more thorough discussion, see Anderson and Anderson (1968). A dissenting view is that offered by Lippold (1973), who builds an interesting case for the possibility that alpha rhythms are produced by modulated corneoretinal potentials and that relationships between alpha abundance and deployment of attention are produced by differences in the motor activity of the eyes.

Presence of an occipital alpha rhythm is, for most people, associated with a feeling of "relaxed awareness" which does not involve visual imaging or the processing of visual information (Lindsley, 1960). Some people, however, do not appear to have a recordable alpha rhythm. Mulholland and Peper (1971) have noted that the absence of an alpha rhythm during the process of paying specific attention to aspects of the visual environment may be due to the kinds of eye movements we make at those times and which we do not make during "relaxed awareness." Also, the alpha rhythm can be produced by extreme elevation of the eyeballs (e.g., Fenwick and Walker, 1969) and increased by behavior leading to cerebral vasoconstriction, such as hyperventilation (Darrow and Pathman, 1943).

Several writers, especially White (1964a), have noted that a general state of relaxed awareness free of extraneous thoughts has been reported by many to lead to strong psi experiences. Several workers have attempted to relate aspects of the occipital alpha rhythm to ESP scoring success in choice behavior tests. Some of these have found no meaningful relationship (Morris and Cohen, 1969; Wallwork, 1952). Some have found a negative relationship between amount of alpha and ESP score, for unselected subjects (Honorton and Carbone, 1971; Stanford and Lovin, 1970). Others have found a positive relationship (Cadoret, 1964; Honorton, 1969; Morris, Roll, Klein and Wheeler, 1972; Honorton, Davidson and Bindler, 1971). Of these, the first three studied people preselected for ESP ability. The fourth used people preselected for alpha abundance. Lewis and Schmeidler (1971), using unselected subjects, found a positive relationship between psi scoring and alpha abundance when their subjects were unaware that they were performing an ESP task and a negative relationship when they were aware. Stanford (Stanford, 1971; Stanford and Stanford, 1969) found no relationship between ESP scoring success and amount of alpha, but did find a positive relationship between ESP scoring success and an increase in the dominant frequency of the alpha rhythm from just prior to the ESP test to the test itself. Other studies have not looked at alpha frequency shifts. Stanford interprets this increase in alpha frequency as a possible "coping" effect in which the subject continues to be in a state of relaxed awareness, but is at some level becoming mobilized for what he may view as a difficult ESP task ahead.

Two EEG studies involving free response ESP tests
have been done. Stanford and Stevenson (1973) asked the
subject to clear his mind, then allow an image to form of
the line drawing serving as target. During the mind-clearing
period, alpha frequency was negatively related to ESP success. An increase in alpha frequency from mind clearing to
image formation was positively related to ESP success.
Amount of alpha was not related to ESP success. Rao and
Feola (1973) used a subject who was very familiar with
biofeedback and meditation techniques. He was asked to
produce either high or low alpha during periods of concentration upon target pictures from magazines. His success
was higher during the times he was asked to produce high
alpha than during the times of low alpha.

The EEG results considered as a whole are confusing;
this is doubtless due in part to differences in procedure, the
nature of the test, experimenter hypotheses, subject characteristics, and so on. The EEG measures taken may serve
primarily as indicators of what kind of internal state is
most conducive to the kind of psi called for under the given
circumstances. Perhaps a positive relationship between
amount of alpha and psi success is only to be expected in
situations highly conducive to the production of both.

Other psychophysiological variables have not been extensively assessed. Otani (1955) found that psi performance
was higher when the galvanic skin response measure indicated the person was relatively relaxed. Other preliminary
findings have suggested that a general state of relaxation is
conducive to psi. Braud and Braud (1973, 1974) found this
to be the case, employing a standard relaxation technique
to facilitate psi. In later work they have used psychophysiological instrumentation to generate potentially an entire
syndrome of psi-conducive physiological variables. Included
are: reduced EMG activity; low frequency, high amplitude
EEG; reduced heart rate and blood pressure; reduced GSR;
reduced oxygen consumption; and reduced blood lactate level
(Braud and Braud, 1975).

One additional point of interest concerns the use of
psychophysiological measurements as the ESP response itself. Dean (1962) used peripheral vasoconstriction and vaso-
dilation as an indicator of emotional response to names of
emotional importance to agent and/or receiver being "sent"
at various times by an agent. The procedure has produced
some success and deserves to be followed up. Duane and

Behrendt (1965) found some evidence that inducing alpha in one identical twin led to alpha in the other twin, who was located at a distance from the first. This was found for only one pair of twins particularly, out of a total of 13 tested.

The last two studies are of potentially great interest since they bypass whatever processing is involved in converting an internal impression into an overt, willed verbal or motor response, thereby perhaps allowing a clearer look in some respects at certain aspects of the internal processing of the psi message. Further work along these lines would need to involve several measures in order to examine the relevance of the Brauds' syndrome for such a nonverbal task.

Taken collectively, these psychophysiological studies do not yet tell us much about the biological aspects of processing psi in the human organism, but they represent a good start along several lines to be followed up by more programmatic research and more sophisticated instrumentation. A general picture is emerging which indicates that for certain kinds of psi tasks, perhaps especially free-response tasks, a state of relaxed awareness in which one is not actively processing sensory information is conducive to psi success. Whether or not this is the only conducive receiver state, and whether or not it pertains to all testing circumstances, remains to be seen. Obviously there are many spontaneous cases and experimental data to indicate that psi can transpire during very activated receiver states (e.g., Rhine, 1964).

It should also be noted that at present we have no real information about optimum internal states for organisms serving as psi sources (designated agents in telepathy studies or in psychokinesis studies).

SUMMARY AND POSSIBLE IMPLICATIONS

It seems likely that psi is present throughout a range of biologically complex organisms. Within humans, psi appears to be relatable to several aspects of human psychophysiology that may tell us a great deal eventually about biological aspects of psi processing. Psi ability may be related to several biologically-dependent aspects of the central nervous system such as attention deployment, peripheral and central sensory input filters, retrieval systems (memory), total information storage capacities, response capacities of the organism, and other aspects present in the species involved.

Because of this involvement, psi should be amenable to evolutionary change. As it changes, it should produce variation within and between species as the species interact with environmental pressures

We know nothing at present of the specifics of these interactions and their potential for interfacing psi with the ongoing life adjustment of the species involved. Some possibilities are the following:

Psi may not be a very efficient way to acquire information; thus for species whose individual organisms have very effective means of information processing through the senses, increased reliance upon the use of psi may be selectively disadvantageous.

Psi-missing during times of great stress may be an effective regulator of population size and may provide an effective negative reinforcer for potentially bad habits.

Psi may facilitate temporary expansion into new ecological environments, until the organism or its species develops completely effective adaptive mechanisms.

Psi may facilitate general affective communication and guide the development of behavior patterns that serve as social communicators.

Psi may help to maintain the bonds among adults and between parents and young.

Psi may allow, for organisms capable of serving as psi sources, the partial regulation of salient aspects of its environment.

Psi may provide for the development of important individual differences at an early age, as an organism interacts emotionally with others in the environment and as it learns to make choices (or avoid making choices) when it has access to only limited information.

These are still only speculations, but it is evident that psi does interact with organisms as biological entities, and that our understanding of psi and our understanding of these organisms themselves will be woefully incomplete until we understand the real nature of such interactions.

REFERENCES

Anderson, P., and Anderson, S. A. Physiological Basis of the Alpha Rhythm. New York: Appleton, 1968.

Bayless, R. Animal Ghosts. Secaucus, N.J.: University Books, 1970.

Bechterev, W. " 'Direct Influence' of a Person Upon the Behavior of Animals. " Journal of Parapsychology, 13 (1949), 166-76.

Bestall, C. M. "An Experiment in Precognition in the Laboratory Mouse. " Journal of Parapsychology, 26 (1962), 269 (abstract).

Braud, L. W., and Braud, W. G. "Further Studies of Relaxation as a Psi-Conducive State. " Journal of the American Society for Psychical Research, 68 (1974), 229-45.

Braud, W. G. and Braud, L. W. "Preliminary Explorations of Psi-Conducive States: Progressive Muscular Relaxation. " Journal of the American Society for Psychical Research, 67 (1973), 26-46.

_____ and _____. "The Psi-Conducive Syndrome: Free-Response GESP Performance Following Evocation of 'Left-Hemispheric' vs. 'Right-Hemispheric' Functioning. " In J. D. Morris, W. G. Roll, and R. L. Morris (eds.), Research in Parapsychology 1974 (Metuchen, N.J.: Scarecrow Press, 1975), p17-23.

Broughton, R., and Millar, B. "An Attempted Confirmation of the Rodent ESP Findings with Positive Reinforcement. " In J. D. Morris, W. G. Roll, and R. L. Morris (eds.), Research in Parapsychology 1974 (Metuchen, N.J.: Scarecrow Press, 1975), p73-5.

Cadoret, R. J. "An Exploratory Experiment: Continuous EEG Recording During Clairvoyant Card Tests. " Journal of Parapsychology, 28 (1964), 226 (abstract).

Craig, J. G. "The Effect of Contingency on Precognition in the Rat. " In W. G. Roll, R. L. Morris, and J. D. Morris (eds.), Research in Parapsychology 1972 (Metuchen, N.J.: Scarecrow Press, 1973), p154-6.

_____ and Treurniet, W. C. "Precognition in Rats as a Function of Shock and Death. " In W. G. Roll, R. L.

Morris, and J. D. Morris (eds.), Research in Parapsychology 1973 (Metuchen, N.J.: Scarecrow Press,
1974), p75-8.

Darrow, C. W., and Pathman, J. H. "The Role of Blood
Pressure in Electroencephalographic Changes During
Hyperventilation." Federation Proceedings, 2 (1943), 9
(abstract).

Dean, E. D. "The Plethysmograph as an Indicator of ESP."
Journal of the Society for Psychical Research, 41 (1962),
351-3.

Dröscher, V. The Magic of the Senses. New York: Dutton,
1969.

Duane, T. D., and Behrendt, R. "Extrasensory Electroencephalographic Induction Between Identical Twins."
Science, 1,950 no. 3694 (1965), 367.

Duval, P., and Montredon, E. "ESP Experiments with
Mice." Journal of Parapsychology, 32 (1968), 153-66.

Extra, J. F. M. W. "GESP in the Rat." Journal of Parapsychology, 36 (1972), 294-302.

Fenwick, P. B. C., and Walker, S. "The Effect of Eye
Position on the Alpha Rhythm." In C. R. Evans and
T. B. Mulholland (eds.), Attention in Neurophysiology
(New York: Appleton, 1969), p128-41.

Gaddis, V., and Gaddis, M. The Strange World of Animals
and Pets. New York: Cowles, 1970.

Honorton, C. "Relationship Between EEG Alpha Activity
and ESP Card-Guessing Performance. Journal of the
American Society for Psychical Research, 63 (1969),
365-74.

_____ and Carbone, M. "A Preliminary Study of Feed-
back-Augmented EEG Alpha Activity and ESP Card-
Guessing Performance." Journal of the American Society for Psychical Research, 65 (1971), 66-74.

_____, Davidson, R., and Bindler, P. "Feedback-
Augmented EEG Alpha, Shifts in Subjective State, and
ESP Card-Guessing Performance." Journal of the
American Society for Psychical Research, 65 (1971),
308-23.

_____, Ramsey, M., and Cabibbo, C. "Experimenter
Effects in Extrasensory Perception." Journal of the
American Society for Psychical Research, 69 (1975),
135-9.

Levy, W. J. "The Effect of the Test Situation on Precognition in Mice and Birds: A Confirmation Study."
Journal of Parapsychology, 36 (1972), 46-55.

Lewis, L., and Schmeidler, G. R. "Alpha Relations with
Non-Intentional and Purposeful ESP After Feedback."

Journal of the American Society for Psychical Research, 65 (1971), 455-67.

Lilly, J. C. The Mind of the Dolphin. Garden City, N.Y.: Doubleday, 1967.

Lindsley, D. B. "Attention, Consciousness, Sleep and Wakefulness." In J. Field, H. W. Magoun, and V. E. Hall (eds.), Handbook of Physiology, Section II: Neurophysiology III (Washington: American Physiological Society, 1960), p1153-593.

Lippold, O. The Origin of the Alpha Rhythm. London: Longmans, Green, 1973.

Matthews, G. V. T. Bird Navigation, 2d ed. Cambridge, England: Cambridge University Press, 1968.

Metta, L. "Psychokinesis on Lepidopterous Larvae." Journal of Parapsychology, 36 (1972), 213-21.

Morris, R. L. "Some New Techniques in Animal Psi Research." Journal of Parapsychology, 31 (1967), 316-7 (abstract).

_____. "Psi and Animal Behavior: A Survey." Journal of the American Society for Psychical Research, 64 (1970), 242-60.

_____. Unpublished manuscript, 1972.

_____. "Complex Psi and the Concept of Precognition." In W. G. Roll, R. L. Morris, and J. D. Morris (eds.), Research in Parapsychology 1972 (Metuchen, N.J.: Scarecrow Press, 1973), p95-7.

_____. "The Use of Detectors for Out-of-Body Experiences." In W. G. Roll, R. L. Morris, and J. D. Morris (eds.), Research in Parapsychology 1973 (Metuchen, N.J.: Scarecrow Press, 1974), p114-6.

_____ and Cohen, D. "A Preliminary Experiment on the Relationship Among ESP, Alpha Rhythm and Calling Patterns." Proceedings of Parapsychological Association, 6 (1969), 22-3.

_____, Roll, W. G., Klein, J., and Wheeler, G. "EEG Patterns and ESP Results in Forced-Choice Experiments with Lalsingh Harribance." Journal of the American Society for Psychical Research, 66 (1972), 253-68.

Mulholland, T. B., and Peper, E. "Occipital Alpha and Accommodative Vergence, Pursuit Tracking, and Fast Eye Movements." Psychophysiology, 8 (1971), 556-75.

Osis, K. "A Test of the Occurrence of a Psi Effect Between Man and the Cat." Journal of Parapsychology, 16 (1952), 233-56.

_____ and Foster, E. B. "A Test of ESP in Cats." Journal of Parapsychology, 17 (1953), 168-86.

Otani, S. "Relations of Mental Set and Change of Skin Resistance to ESP Score. " Journal of Parapsychology, 19 (1955), 164-70.

Parker, A. "ESP in Gerbils Using Positive Reinforcement. " Journal of Parapsychology, 38 (1974), 301-11.

Pfungst, O. Clever Hans. Introduction by R. Rosenthal. New York: Holt, Rinehart and Winston, 1965.

Randall, J. L. "An Attempt to Detect Psi Effects with Protozoa. " Journal of the Society for Psychical Research, 45 (1970), 294-6.

————. "Experiments to Detect a Psi Effect with Small Animals. " Journal of the Society for Psychical Research, 46 (1971), 31-9.

————. "Two Psi Experiments with Gerbils. " Journal of the Society for Psychical Research, 46 (1972), 22-9. (a)

————. "Recent Experiments in Animal Parapsychology. " Journal of the Society for Psychical Research, 46 (1972), 124-35. (b)

Rao, K. R. , and Feola, J. "Alpha Rhythm and ESP in a Free Response Situation. " In W. G. Roll, R. L. Morris, and J. D. Morris (eds.), Research in Parapsychology 1972 (Metuchen, N. J. : Scarecrow Press, 1973), p141-4.

Reitler, R. "ESP in a Primitive Animal. " Indian Journal of Parapsychology, 3 (1962), 1-11.

Rhine, J. B. "Special Motivation in Some Exceptional ESP Performances. " Journal of Parapsychology, 18 (1964), 42-50.

————. "Location of Hidden Objects by a Man-Dog Team. " Journal of Parapsychology, 35 (1971), 18-33.

———— and Feather, S. R. "The Study of Cases of 'Psi-Trailing' in Animals. " Journal of Parapsychology, 26 (1962), 1-22.

Richmond, N. "Two Series of PK Tests on Paramecia. " Journal of the Society for Psychical Research, 36 (1952), 577-88.

Schmidt, H. "PK Experiments with Animals as Subjects. " Journal of Parapsychology, 34 (1970), 255-61. (a)

————. Personal communication, 1970. (b)

————. "Animal PK Tests with and without Time Displacement. " Unpublished manuscript, 1974. (a)

————. Personal communication, 1974. (b)

Schouten, S. "Psi in Mice: Positive Reinforcement. " Journal of Parapsychology, 36 (1972), 261-82.

————. "Psi in Mice: Role of Target, Spatial Position of Target and Response Preferences. " Unpublished manuscript, 1973.

Stanford, R. G. "Response Bias and the Correctness of ESP Test Responses." Journal of Parapsychology, 31 (1967), 280-9.

_____. "EEG Alpha Activity and ESP Performance: A Replicative Study." Journal of the American Society for Psychical Research, 65 (1971), 144-54.

_____ and Lovin, C. "EEG Alpha Activity and ESP Performance." Journal of the American Society for Psychical Research, 64 (1970), 375-84.

_____ and Stanford, B. E. "Shifts in EEG Alpha Rhythm as Related to Calling Patterns and ESP Run-Score Variance." Journal of Parapsychology, 33 (1969), 39-47.

_____ and Stevenson, I. "EEG Correlates of Free-Response GESP in an Individual Subject." Journal of the American Society for Psychical Research, 66 (1973), 357-68.

Terry, J., and Harris, S. "Precognition in Water-Deprived Rats." In J. D. Morris, W. G. Roll, and R. L. Morris (eds.), Research in Parapsychology 1974 (Metuchen, N.J.: Scarecrow Press, 1975), p81.

Thorpe, W. H. Learning and Instinct in Animals. Cambridge: Cambridge University Press, 1963.

Treurniet, W. C., and Craig, J. G. "Precognition as a Function of Environmental Enrichment and Time of the Lunar Month." In J. D. Morris, W. G. Roll, and R. L. Morris (eds.), Research in Parapsychology 1974 (Metuchen, N.J.: Scarecrow Press, 1975), p100-2.

Wallwork, S. C. "ESP Experiments with Simultaneous Electroencephalographic Recordings." Journal of the Society for Psychical Research, 36 (1952), 697-701.

Watkins, G. K. "Possible PK in the Lizard Anolis sagrei." Proceedings of the Parapsychological Association, 8 (1971), 23-5.

_____ and Watkins, A. M. "Possible PK Influence on the Resuscitation of Anesthetized Mice." Journal of Parapsychology, 35 (1971), 257-72.

Wells, R., and Klein, J. "A Replication of a 'Psychic Healing' Paradigm." Journal of Parapsychology, 36 (1972), 144-9.

White, R. A. "A Comparison of Old and New Methods of Response to Targets in ESP Experiments." Journal of the American Society for Psychical Research, 58 (1964), 21-56. (a)

_____. "The Investigation of Behavior Suggestive of ESP in Dogs." Journal of the American Society for Psychical Research, 58 (1964), 250-79.

Wood, G. H., and Cadoret, R. J. "Tests of Clairvoyance in a Man-Dog Relationship." Journal of Parapsychology, 22 (1958), 29-39.

Bernard R. Grad

THE BIOLOGICAL EFFECTS OF THE "LAYING ON OF HANDS" ON ANIMALS AND PLANTS: IMPLICATIONS FOR BIOLOGY

Introduction

The prescientific healing practices of primitive communities were for a long time of interest only to the mis-
sionary, the venturing traveler, and the anthropologist.
However, medical scientists gradually came to realize that
not all folk remedies are worthless. Medically useful substances such as digitalis, curare, reserpine, and quinine
were first used as therapeutic agents by scientifically naive
people. More recently, other practices of primitive medicine have become the object of study (Kiev, 1966, 1972;
Prince, Leighton and May, 1968), but interestingly enough,
healing by the laying on of hands, which was long used by
the ancient Chinese, Indians, Egyptians, and Greeks and
which figured large in the origin of the Christian Church,
has been completely ignored by the scientific community.
Whatever the reasons, no serious scientific study of this
method of healing was undertaken prior to 1957, when a
series of experiments was begun by the author, a biomedi-
cal researcher, with a man (O. E.) who, on the basis of a
decade's experience, claimed to be able to heal some dis-
eases in humans and common domestic animals by the laying on of hands.

Methods and Results

For the animal studies, mice were selected because
the expense of purchase, housing, and maintaining the number required to establish statistical significance of the findings would not exceed the modest budget and space available.

76

To administer the treatment, a cage made of galvanized iron was divided into compartments, each large enough to allow the mice to turn around and to make themselves comfortable, but not large enough to permit the animals to move from one place to another. Eight to 10 mice were placed in the treatment cage at one time. The size of the cage was adjusted to the size of O. E. 's hand so that when he held one hand on top of the cage and the other on the bottom, all the mice were covered. The compartments were covered with a fine wire mesh, also made of galvanized iron, to prevent the animals from escaping. The bottom of the cage was solid.

Before beginning the hand-treatment, and before the animals were divided into control and treatment groups, it was found necessary to train them to become accustomed to frequent removal from the housing cage to the treatment cage and to being in the treatment cage for at least 15 minutes. This was done by placing the mice in the treatment cage twice daily, five days a week, for two weeks before beginning the experiment. Also, all mice were gently stroked for a minute or two during this period to make them calm. Mice that remained restless and showed excessive efforts to escape from the treatment cage at the end of the training period were eliminated from the experiment. The stroking of the mice was stopped when the mice were divided into treatment and control groups. When hand-treatment was begun, control mice were also placed in the treatment cages; in some experiments these controls were given no treatment at all, while in other experiments they were exposed to heat delivered by insulated electrothermal heating tapes, the heat delivered to the mice being adjusted so as to be the same as that produced by the warmth of the healer's hands. This was done by measuring the temperature in the containers under the two different conditions.

During the treatment, O. E. 's hands did not touch the mice underneath the wire mesh nor did he move his hands about. Hand treatment, in all the animal experiments, was given for 15 minutes at a time, morning and evening, five times a week. When treatment was given on Saturday, it was given only once. No treatment was given on Sundays.

The Effect on Goiter

Because O. E. had claimed success in the treatment

of thyroid disease in man, it was decided, first of all, to test whether he could influence by laying on of hands the rate of development of goiters artificially produced in mice. Goiters can be readily produced in animals by feeding them a diet deficient in iodine, and also by feeding them goitrogens, chemicals which interfere with the uptake of iodine by the thyroid gland. Therefore, in our first experiments, an iodine-deficient diet and a goitrogen, thiouracil, were fed to mice, and the rate of increase in the size of the thyroid gland, in both control and treated mice, was determined by weighing the thyroids of mice sacrificed at suitable time intervals.

The first experiment used 70 mice, separated into three groups: two control and one treated. Both control groups were placed in metal cages at the same time as the mice receiving hand-treatment: one control group received no treatment at all, while the other received the heat treatment mentioned above; the third group received hand-treatment by O. E. The experiment lasted 40 days, with O. E. hand-treating the mice for the first 20 days and J. B. treating them the same way for the remaining time. (J. B. was working in the laboratory at the time these experiments were undertaken, and it was subsequently shown that he could also produce significant telekinetic effects in animals and plants by the laying on of hands.)

The results show that the thyroids of the two control groups increased in size significantly faster, when consuming an iodine-deficient diet and thiouracil, than did the thyroids of the mice receiving the hand-treatment (Table 1, $P < .001$). Inasmuch as the thyroids of the control mice receiving the heat treatment did not grow significantly slower than did those of the nonheated controls (Table 1, $0.30 > P > 0.20$), the heat produced by the warmth of the hands during O. E.'s treatment could not have been responsible for the significant inhibition, which the hand-treatment produced, in the rate of goiter development in the mice.

That heat could not have been responsible for the significant inhibition of goiter development was further shown by a second experiment involving 37 mice separated into two groups; a control group, and a group which was treated, not by O. E. directly, but by placing the mice in direct contact with wool and cotton cuttings which had been held in O. E.'s hands for 15 minutes, once on the first day of the experiment and twice during the next 24 days, the entire

Table 1. The Effect of Hand-Treatment by O. E. and J.B. on the Increase in Thyroid Weight (Mgm.) of Caworth Farm Female Mice on Remington's Iodine-Deficient Diet (RIDD) and 1 Per Cent Thiouracil.

Treatment	On purina fox chow and H_2O	On RIDD and H_2O for 11 days	On RIDD and 1% thiouracil for: 2 wks	3 wks	4 wks
None		3.01 ± 0.31 (5)	6.25 ± 0.77 (6)	9.78 ± 0.91 (7)	9.47 ± 0.48 (7)
Heat	2.48 ± 0.24 (6)		7.72 ± 0.71 (7)	8.24 ± 0.39 (7)	11.86 ± 0.53 (6)
O.E./J.B.			4.83 ± 0.50 (7)	6.66 ± 0.34 (7)	8.46 ± 0.74 (5)

Table 2. The Effect of O.E.-Handled Cuttings on the Increase in Thyroid Weight (Mgm.) of Caworth Farm Female Mice on Remington's Iodine-Deficient Diet (RIDD) and 1 Per Cent Thiouracil

Treatment	On purina fox chow and H_2O	On RIDD and H_2O for 10 days	On RIDD and 1% thiouracil for: 2 wks	3 wks	4 wks
Control	1.92 ± 0.21 (6)	2.03 ± 0.14 (2)	5.59 ± 1.02 (4)	7.07 ± 1.04 (5)	9.59 ± 1.38 (6)
O.E.		2.19 ± 0.31 (3)	3.75 ± 1.17 (4)	5.51 ± 0.97 (4)	7.14 ± 1.70 (3)

Note: The numbers in parentheses in both tables are numbers of animals for which the adjacent mean and standard error were calculated.

experiment lasting 42 days. Ten grams of cuttings were placed in each cage, containing four or five mice, for one hour, morning and evening, six days a week. The control mice also received cuttings, but these were not held in the hands of the healer or any other person. The cuttings were dropped into the cage, and an hour later the mice were always found sitting on the cuttings spread out beneath them. All mice were fed the goitrogenic diet.

The results were the same as in the first experiment, i. e., the thyroid glands of the mice treated with the cuttings held in O. E. 's hands developed significantly more slowly than did the control mice on the goitrogenic diet (Table 2, $P < .001$).

Further experiments in this series were conducted on the rate of return of goiters to normal size after the mice were placed on a normal iodine diet. Here also, the influence of the hand-treatment on the mice, directly as well as indirectly via the influence of cloth cuttings, was tested and, in both situations, the rate of return of the goitrous thyroid to normal size was more rapid in animals receiving the hand-treatment by O. E., whether directly or indirectly.

The Effect on Wound Healing

A series of experiments was then undertaken to assess the effect of the laying on of hands on the rate of wound healing in mice. Mice were anesthetized and wounded by removing equivalent-sized patches of full skin from their backs. The removed skin was immediately weighed and the area of the wound measured by placing transparent plastic over it and tracing its outline with a grease pencil. These outlines were then transferred to paper, cut out, and weighed on a balance sensitive to .005 milligrams. Measurements were made again at the end of the first, eleventh and fourteenth days after wounding. Statistical analyses of the weights of the paper projections of the wounds revealed that the wounds of the two control groups were healing at the same rate, while those in the groups that had been treated by O. E. were healing at a significantly faster rate. A second experiment, repeated in the same way, yielded the same results. The results of these experiments are described in greater detail in an earlier publication (Grad, 1965).

Following this, a more elaborate double-blind experiment, involving 300 mice, was conducted in collaboration with doctors R. J. Cadoret and G. I. Paul of the University of Manitoba (Grad, Cadoret, and Paul, 1961). There were three groups in this experiment also: untreated control mice, mice treated by O. E., and mice treated by skeptical medical students. The metal cages in which the mice were housed were placed in heavy paper bags. In half of each group, the bags were stapled shut during the treatment, in the other half they were left open. In the open-bag series, O. E. and the students placed their hands inside the bags, one hand on top of the cage, the other supporting the cage from below. In the closed-bag series, they held the cage in the same way but outside the paper bags.

Again, statistical analyses conducted on the mean surface areas of the wounds on the fifteenth and sixteenth day after wounding showed that the wounds of the animals treated by O. E. were healing significantly faster than those of the other two groups in the open-bag series. The mice treated by the skeptical medical students healed more slowly than the mice that received no treatment at all. No statistically significant effect could be observed in the closed-bag series. However, even in this series O. E. 's mice healed faster than those in the other two closed-bag groups. Mice in the closed-bag series became overheated and hence agitated during hand-treatment. This was probably the reason why there were no significant differences in the closed-bag series, as there were in the open-bag one.

The Effect on Plant Growth

Having observed the biological effects of the laying on of hands on mice in the goiter and wound-healing experiments, it was decided to test the effect of such treatment on the growth of plants to see how widely in the biological realm this effect could be observed. Also, the plant experiments seemed to offer a less time-consuming method of observing the effect of hand-treatment than the animal experiments conducted hitherto.

The plant experiments went through several states of development. Among the findings which emerged from the pilot studies were the following: (1) the seeds should be studied while implanted in the soil (our preliminary experiments with the germination of seeds failed to yield signifi-

cant results). (2) The experiments should be conducted under some degree of inhibition of the normal growth of the
seeds. This was achieved by watering the seeds initially
with a 1 per cent sodium chloride solution. This, by itself,
has an inhibitory effect on the growth of plants, salt being
injurious to plant growth. Following watering with saline
were several days of drying, and subsequent watering with
tap water in suitable amounts and intervals so that plant
growth was just maintained but not allowed to flourish.
(3) Most interesting, at this stage, was the finding that significant differences could be obtained without the need for
O. E. to treat the plants directly with his hands; it was
enough to water the seeds with saline solutions which he
had previously held in his hands. Moreover, it was unnecessary for O. E. to treat the tap water added later to the
plants. Further details of these preliminary experiments
have been published (Grad, 1963). The thinking behind these
plant growth experiments was to create a state of need in
the plants, just as had been done in the animals in the goiter experiments when they lacked iodine and in the wound-
healing experiments when they lacked a piece of skin.

In the first experiments, O. E. held the saline solution in an open beaker between his hands for 15 minutes,
and the seeds watered by this solution produced a significantly greater yield of plants than did those watered with an
identical non-hand-treated saline solution.

A second experiment, identical in every way with the
first except that the hand-treatment of the saline was omitted,
showed no significant differences between the two groups.
This proved that the probability was extremely remote that
a difference of the magnitude observed in the first experiment would occur spontaneously.

Subsequently, four double-blind experiments were conducted in which the hand-treatment of the saline took place
in glass-stoppered reagent bottles rather than in open beak-
ers, as in the first experiment. In three of the four experiments, the stimulating effect of the treated saline was statistically significant. In the first and third experiments,
the significant differences were apparent in the height of the
plants, while in the second experiment, it was apparent in
the mean number of seedlings appearing above the surface
of the soil and in the mean yield of plant material. The
significant differences observed in growth between the control and treated plants are not explicable on the basis of dif-

ferences in the sodium concentration or pH between the control and saline solutions used to water them (Grad, 1964).

While these studies were being conducted, the question naturally arose as to what results would be obtained with subjects other than O. E. Consequently, a study (Grad, 1967) was set up to test the effect on plant growth of the laying on of hands conducted by three individuals (not including O. E.) as compared with an untreated control. The three subjects included J. B. , who had previously been used in the goiter experiment and who had a "green thumb"; a woman with a depressive neurotic reaction (R. H.); and a man with a psychotic depression (H. R.). The latter two subjects were patients in a psychiatric hospital.

The hypothesis was that there is a direct relationship between the mood of the persons doing the treatment and the subsequent growth of plants watered by these treated solutions. Thus, it was hypothesized that a solution held for 30 minutes in the hands of an individual in a confident mood would permit plants watered by this solution to grow at a faster rate than plants watered by identical solutions, but held for the same length of time by persons with a depressive illness or not held by anyone (the control group). The experiment also tested whether solutions held by depressed persons would inhibit plant growth relative to the control group.

In essence the procedure consisted of having each person hold a sealed bottle of normal saline between his hands for 30 minutes. The solution was then poured on barley seeds embedded in soil which was then dried in an oven for 48 hours. Following this, the pots containing the seeds were removed from the oven and watered at suitable intervals with tap water not treated by anyone. When the seedlings appeared above the soil their number was counted and their height measured. The determinations were continued until seedling growth reached a plateau, which occurred seven to nine days after they first appeared above the soil surface. The results obtained with the hand-treated and untreated saline solutions were then compared. The watering with saline, the subsequent drying, and the restricted watering with tap water were used as forms of experimental stress to the plants. This experiment was carried out under multi-blind conditions, the information necessary to identify the treatment of each potted plant being divided among five individuals.

The results showed that the seeds watered by the saline held by J. B. (who was in a confident mood at the time of hand-treatment on the saline) grew significantly faster than those in the remaining three groups, while the plants treated by the person with the psychotic depression (H. R.) showed the slowest rate of growth. Thus, this part of the hypothesis was supported by the experimental data. However, the plants treated by R. H., who had a neurotic depression, had a slightly higher growth rate than that of the controls, and this was contrary to expectations (Grad, 1967).

This difference in the growth of the plants treated by the two depressed persons relative to the control group might be explicable as follows: the growth rate of H. R. 's plants was slower than that of the controls because he was agitated and depressed at the time he was holding the saline solution in his hands; in so doing, something associated with his depression might have been transferred to the solution, which then inhibited the growth of the barley seeds. He never inquired as to why he was given a bottle to hold, and therefore he was not told.

On the other hand, when R. H. was given a bottle of saline to hold for 30 minutes, she inquired as to the reason for the procedure, and when told, she responded with an expression of interest and a decided brightening of mood. Also, it was observed that she cradled the bottle in her lap as a mother would hold her child. Thus, the important fact for the purpose of the experiment was not what her psychiatric diagnosis was, but what her mood was at the time she was holding the bottle, and she did not appear to be depressed at that time. Therefore, the growth of the plants was not inhibited when watered with the solution she held at that time.

In short, it would appear that a positive mood while holding the bottles favors a change in the solution which leads to a stimulation of cell growth compared with other solutions not held by anybody, or held by persons in a depressed state. Also, it would seem that a negative mood such as depression, while holding the solution, results in an inhibition of cell growth when such cells are watered by these solutions. Further studies are indicated here.

Discussion

Practitioners of the laying on of hands speak in terms

of an energy which flows from them--often they say through
them--to the diseased organism. In this connection, numerous studies have shown that primitive theories of illness,
whether originating in Africa, Asia, or America, have a universal pattern which centers around the loss of a vital spirit
from the body, or the intrusion of a foreign and harmful
spirit into the body (Clements, 1932), spirits being a per-
sonification of energy. Moreover, even in Western society,
people speak of lacking "energy" when they become ill or
grow old. Also, in the arts the idea of a "living force"
has never been excluded, as has occurred in science.

The historical background of the idea of a life force
may be summarized as follows: there are numerous stories
in the Bible which indicate that some power is being con-
veyed by the practice of laying on of hands. The story of
the blessing of Jacob by Isaac is one such example, while
the healings of Jesus are others. In later centuries, the
idea that a life force existed had numerous proponents, the
best known of these being Paracelsus, Van Helmot, Galvani,
and, of course, Mesmer. Of the persons who experimented
with and propounded the idea of a life energy in the 19th
century, Reichenbach, a German industrialist and scientist,
deserves special mention. For further information on the
early history of life energy, refer to Mann (1973).

However, despite the antiquity of the idea of a life
force and its wide acceptance by nonscientists, and despite
the efforts of people like Mesmer and Reichenbach, the
vitalists were fighting a losing battle in the 19th century.
This was because knowledge in the physical sciences was
growing apace by this time, and scientists came, more and
more, to feel that far from there being a life force which
permeated and governed the cosmos, no such force existed
at all, and that all events in the cosmos, including those
involving biological phenomena, could be explained by the
laws of physics and chemistry. Moreover, just at the time
that Reichenbach died, in 1869, Pasteur was proving vic-
torious in the battle of the so-called spontaneous generation
of matter. His opponents on this question were vitalists,
and with Pasteur's victory an atmosphere was created in
which it became extremely difficult for scientists to continue
to propound ideas about a life force, a situation which continues to our own time. For example, when Bastian per-
sisted in reporting on his experiments, challenging Pasteur's
view on spontaneous generation in the 1870's, he was forced
to retreat after being warned that this could abort his medi-

cal career. However, he returned to his experiments upon retirement several decades later.

So strong is the stand against vitalism that only a few scientists in our century continued to broadcast such ideas, in one form or another. One of these was Hans Driesch (1929, 1941-42), who postulated a vitalistic factor, the entelechy, which he defined as a nonspatial element automatically regulating the living organism. However, according to him it was not energy or matter because it lacked the characteristics of quantity, and as such was not explicable in physicochemical terms. Gurwitsch (1932), a Russian biologist, claimed that there was a mitosis-inducing radiation, and even specified that it had a wavelength around 2000 A. Burr (1972) evolved the idea, after several decades of experimental study, that there was an electrodynamic force field around organisms, which themselves were electrodynamic systems, which responded to electrical fields both from within and without the organism. He talked of "electric tides" from the sun and moon and wrote of their influence on the steady state of the organism. Later, Ravitz (1962) extended these studies into medicine, especially psychiatry.

However, the most insistent and probably the most forceful proponent of the idea of the life energy in our own time was Wilhelm Reich (1948), who began his professional career as a psychoanalyst of the Freudian school. He soon gained fame in his own right with the publication of Character Analysis in 1933. Whereas science tended to ignore Driesch and Burr, these neovitalists still maintained contact with and worked within the scientific community. However, Reich, a highly creative and original man who did not believe in half measures, broke with the scientific community completely and went his own way. Unfortunately, the consequences, for him, were also more tragic than for Driesch and others, for he died in jail where he was impounded for allegedly disobeying a court injunction prohibiting distribution of his "orgone [life energy] accumulators."

Obviously, the question as to whether or not a life force exists can only be solved by further experimentation. Unfortunately, this is easier said than done, for persons with a materialistic-mechanistic viewpoint find the ideas of a life force unacceptable a priori and this creates difficulties for research even at the present time of greater freedom. Mechanists, along with some vitalists, have repeatedly

claimed that it is not possible to conduct experiments testing
the existence of a life force. Reich and others have shown
that this is not so. However, it is important for those
claiming that there is a life force to sharpen their experiments more and more and to work to close the gap between
them and the scientific community at large.

Interestingly enough, even when biologists have rejected the idea of a life force, time and again they are
forced to use terminology which hints at its existence. For
example, Minot (1891) spoke of the animal's being born with
a "certain impulse," which is strong at first and which, as
it fades out during life, was responsible for aging and death.
He also spoke of a "power of growth." Murray (1926) wrote
of an "aliveness" and Pearl (1928) of an "inherent vitality"
which, the more rapidly it was consumed, the shorter was
the duration of life. Lansing (1956) wrote of aging as being
a product of "reduced growth potential." Selye (1946) spoke
of a fixed inherited reserve of "adaptation energy" which is
irreplaceably reduced by each stressful experience in life.
Comfort (1956) speculated that the organism is born with a
"program" which is succeeded by senescence when it runs
out. In referring to their patients, psychiatrists often speak
in terms of energy, although when confronted with this they
deny that they refer to any specific "life force." Although
all these scientists would certainly deny that they are vitalists, close observation of the living organism has its own
insistent way of suggesting that there may in fact be a life
force at the bottom of living functioning.

In our own experiments with the laying on of hands,
the simplest explanation would seem to be that there is in
fact a life force emanating from the hands of people, probably more in some than in others. How else can the plant-
stimulating effect of hand-treated saline from sealed bottles
be explained? Also, emotional states may be a factor in
the kind of energy produced. This energy, which had effects both on animals and plants, was able to work, as in
the case of the goiter experiments, not only to prohibit goiter formation in animals whose thyroids lacked iodine, but
once iodine was made available to such animals, was able
to accelerate the rate of return of the goiter to a normal
size. Thus, in these experiments there was actually an ac-
celeration of cell growth in the hand-treated groups, as
compared with the controls. Thus, it would seem that if
there is such energy, it is somehow very intimately associated with homeostatic mechanisms; that is, it tends to
operate so as to maintain the organism at its optimal level.

These studies also have relevance for psychotherapy, the placebo effect, the handling of the newborn and the young, and the mythology which has grown around menstruation over the centuries. Their connection has been discussed earlier (Grad, 1967). Also, from the author's laboratory experience, it would seem that every aspect of biological functioning is open for investigation, in the same way as already reported for goiter, wound healing, plant growth, and enzyme studies (Smith, 1972). Whether such studies will in fact take place may well depend on a complexity of factors of which the interests of scientists may only be one.

REFERENCES

Burr, H. S. The Fields of Life. New York: Ballantine Books, 1972.

Clements, F. E. "Primitive Concepts of Disease." University of California Publications in American Archeology and Ethnology, 32 (1932), 185-252.

Comfort, A. The Biology of Senescence. London: Routledge & Kegan Paul, 1956.

Driesch, H. The Science and Philosophy of the Organism. London: A. & C. Black, 1929.

_____. "Zur Problematik des Alterns." Zeitschrift für Alternsforschung, 3 (1941-42), 26-43.

Grad, B. "A Telekinetic Effect on Plant Growth. [I]." International Journal of Parapsychology, 5 (1963), 117-33.

_____. "A Telekinetic Effect on Plant Growth. II. Experiments Involving Treatment of Saline in Stoppered Bottles." International Journal of Parapsychology, 6 (1964), 473-98.

_____. "Some Biological Effects of the 'Laying On of Hands': A Review of Experiments with Animals and Plants." Journal of the American Society for Psychical Research, 59 (1965), 95-127.

_____. "The 'Laying On of Hands': Implications for Psychotherapy, Gentling, and the Placebo Effect." Journal of the American Society for Psychical Research, 61 (1967), 286-305.

_____, Cadoret, R. J., and Paul, G. I. "The Influence of an Unorthodox Method of Treatment on Wound Healing in Mice." International Journal of Parapsychology, 3 (1961), 5-24.

Gurwitsch, A. Die mitogenetische Strahlung. Berlin: Springer Verlag, 1932.

Kiev, A. Magic, Faith and Healing: Studies in Primitive
    Psychiatry Today. New York: Free Press, 1966.
    _____ . Transcultural Psychiatry. New York: Free
    Press, 1972.
Lansing, A. I. "What Is Aging?" Bulletin of the New York
    Academy of Science, 32 (1956), 5-13.
Mann, W. E. Orgone, Reich and Eros. New York: Simon
    & Schuster, 1973.
Minot, C. S. "Senescence and Rejuvenation. " Journal of
    Physiology, 12 (1891), 97-153.
Murray, H. A. "Physiological Ontogeny. A. Chicken Em-
    bryoes. VIII. Accelerations of Integration and Differen-
    tiation During the Embryonic Period. " Journal of Gene-
    ral Physiology, 9 (1926), 603-20.
Pearl, R. The Rate of Living. New York: Knopf, 1928.
Prince, R. , Leighton, A. H. , and May, R. "Therapeutic
    Process in Crosscultural Perspective: A Symposium. "
    American Journal of Psychiatry, 124 (1968), 56-69.
Ravitz, L. J. "History, Measurements and Applicability of
    Periodic Changes in the Electromagnetic Field in Health
    and Disease. " Annals of the New York Academy of Sci-
    ence, 98 (1962), 1145-201.
Reich, W. The Cancer Biopathy. New York: Orgone Insti-
    tute Press, 1948.
Selye, H. "The General Adaptation Syndrome and the Dis-
    eases of Adaptation. " Journal of Clinical Endrocrinol-
    ogy, 6 (1946), 117-230.
Smith, M. J. "The Influence on Enzyme Growth by the
    'Laying-On-of-Hands'. " In The Dimensions of Healing:
    A Symposium (Los Altos, Cal. : Academy of Parapsy-
    chology and Medicine, 1972), p110-20.

Part III

PARAPSYCHOLOGY AND PSYCHOLOGY

If we try to see where parapsychology belongs within the body of systematized knowledge, or try to fit it into Comte's hierarchy of sciences, we will probably come up with two answers, one theoretical and the other practical. The theoretical answer is that all sciences are potentially interconnected, and that they form a pattern less tidy than a hierarchy. We can speak of biophysics as readily as of biochemistry, and we sometimes relate even unlikely pairs, such as astronomy and psychology for problems of space travel. Theoretically, then, parapsychology could relate to almost any other field.

But the answer is different when we turn to some practical problem, such as deciding which department of a university should offer a course in parapsychology. Here our answer is likely to be that the newer name for psychical research is appropriate and that psychology offers the widest umbrella for most "parapsychological" findings. Responses of living organisms have been the source of our research data so far (though R. B. Roberts suggested earlier in this book that this might be unduly restrictive). All current findings, though not all theory, can therefore be subsumed under the general heading of behavior, though of course the behavior is of a special kind.

Support for this practical decision comes from another fact: more parapsychologists have research training in psychology than in any other area. About a third of the full members of the Parapsychological Association are psychologists. It follows that within parapsychology, the problems most likely to be studied are psychological ones: response bias and stimulus preference, or individual differences, or the effect on response of altered moods and states of consciousness. Our information about psychological

processes within parapsychology is thus richer and fuller
than about physical or biological ones.

The four papers that follow both present such information and reflect psychologists' natural concerns with other
broad issues; but they vary in the way they mix the two.
Dr. Irvin L. Child in the opening article explains how it
was his interest in achieving a proper fusion of humanist
problems and experimental method that led him to examine
a variety of topics, of which parapsychology was one; he
tells us that the strength of the evidence and the meaningful
relations he saw there made him study it more intensively
than he had planned. He reports some of the evidence he
considers important, and then turns to one of parapsychologists' major concerns: the repeatability of data.

The problem of repeatability is a major one for psychologists in almost every area. At the simplest level, if
we try to put together a set of sure-fire demonstrations for
the introductory course, we find few that we can rely on.
Knee jerks sometimes fail to show the expected twitch; reinforcement does not always result in conditioning if the subject's set is hostile or his level of information is inappro-
priately high or low; even color vision and stereoscopic fusion and constancy can show anomalies. P. Mussen tells
us that "independent replication of findings is a rare and
happy event in personality research" ("Early Socialization:
Learning and Identification," in T. M. Newcomb (ed.), New
Directions in Psychology, III, New York: Holt, Rinehart & Winston, 1967, p99). In parapsychology as in other
areas where experimenter-subject relations can be important,
the problem of repeatability is acute. Descriptions of procedure seldom tell us about the experimenter's personality,
the social setting, or the subject's prior expectations; and
without knowing about these it is hard or impossible to replicate research. Dr. Child, after examining this important
problem, finds hints in current work as to the most promising ways of solving it, and suggests adopting a research
strategy that includes appropriate instrumentation, increased
use of animals as subjects, and tasks in which the subject
is unaware of how ESP or PK can help him reach his goal.

The latter parts of Dr. Child's paper are interesting
to read in conjunction with Dr. LeShan's, which ends this
section. Both consider, though from different perspectives,
the twin dangers of overacceptance and overrejection of psi,
and the need for a tolerance of uncertainty in keeping to the
middle ground between them.

My own paper, which follows Dr. Child's, opens with a short unit on methodology and closes with a short unit on theory, but is mainly directed toward an overview of research findings. It addresses itself primarily to the question of whether the results of ESP and PK research mesh with psychological data on other forms of behavior. Its major conclusion is that in most cases the two fit well together and that where they do not, ESP provides new information that psychologists could profitably use in developing theories of general relevance.

The third paper, by Dr. Robert L. Van de Castle, examines a problem that is almost neglected elsewhere in this book, although probably all the contributors would agree that it is an important one. It stems from a criticism that is often made of psychology and that makes almost all psychologists wince a little each time they hear it: our laws about human behavior come mainly from what we find by testing college sophomores.

This is an overstatement, of course, but it has some truth in it. Even when we extend the age range of our subjects, a variant of the same criticism applies. Experiments are necessarily performed with the subjects who are available; and these are usually Westerners, reared in a middle-class setting. We worry, therefore, about how many of our generalizations reflect this social background rather than describing basic human processes. Does our middle-class Western training distort or limit the way subjects (and experimenters) perceive, reason, create, respond?

Dr. Van de Castle raises these questions forcefully and shows that they apply to parapsychology too. Further, he begins to answer them on the basis both of his reading and of his own research in parts of the world that are remote from us. Though the article gives only a short report of his findings, it suggests a provocative conclusion, shows the broadened perspective we need, and of course calls, as each of the papers does, for a substantial amount of further research.

Dr. Lawrence LeShan's closing paper in this unit refers only in passing to experimental findings. It emphasizes the experimenter rather than the experiment, and discusses in depth the rewards and difficulties of working in parapsychology. It brings the insights of a clinical psychologist to bear on the cognitive and motivational problems that

beset the research worker here and that probably apply also
to research workers in every field with far-reaching implications.

Irvin L. Child

PARAPSYCHOLOGY AND THE REST OF PSYCHOLOGY:
A MUTUAL CHALLENGE*

Introduction

Psychical research and its successor, parapsychology, are now almost a century old and provide a history of perennial challenge to the rest of psychology. Over and over they have presented evidence of events that psychology, as part of the body of accepted scientific knowledge, leads us to consider impossible--events that seem to contradict not only specific scientific generalizations, but even the basic presuppositions or modes of thought that underlie science and have proved so successful in predicting and controlling natural phenomena. Telepathy, clairvoyance, and psychokinesis are threatening enough in suggesting that we can communicate with each other and with the rest of nature without mediation by the sense organs we know or any substitute we find believable, and that people influence the non-human world without using muscles or glands and by processes we have not identified and fear we may never understand. To these seeming impossibilities is added precognition, which seems to have time running backward whereas in psychology and in the rest of science, as in daily experience, it runs inexorably forward.

To all these challenging phenomena the terms "psi," "psychic," and "paranormal" are applied. Like specific

---
*This paper, considerably longer than the comments presented at the Symposium, is based partly on colloquia or lectures given earlier by the author at Wesleyan University, Kenyon College, and U. C. L. A. Preparation of the paper was facilitated by a grant from the John E. Fetzer Foundation.

95

terms such as telepathy and clairvoyance, these words explain nothing; they merely call attention to phenomena that
seem impossible, yet apparently do happen.

What is new in the challenge these psi phenomena offer today is that the same old challenge is being put with increasing insistence, with renewed and ever-accumulating
evidence. I began to be aware of this several years ago
when I was planning a book called Humanistic Psychology
and the Research Tradition: Their Several Virtues (Child,
1973). Defining the humanistic approach very broadly as an
effort to understand man in the image of man rather than
as machine, animal, or mathematical equation alone, I
planned to argue that the humanistic approach and the scientific research tradition in psychology need each other--that
the humanistic view of man is sharpened, corrected, and
made more persuasive when checked against the careful test
of systematic observation, and that research on man is
better when guided by the human view. In searching for
topics to illustrate this general thesis, I discovered that
parapsychology provides a very apt one. Through reading
the general psychological journals and the journals on hypnosis (for this was another topic I had found to illustrate
my thesis), I had encountered a few articles on extrasensory
perception. They led me to look for the first time at the
parapsychological journals, and there I found abundant material for the chapter that was beginning to take form.

In my chapter on ESP, then, I summarized four recent developments that illustrated my general thesis. One
was a line of research initiated at U.C.L.A. by Thelma
Moss (Moss and Gengerelli, 1967, 1968). Bringing back into the methods of ESP research something of the strong emo-
tion so often associated with spontaneous psi occurrences,
this work showed that ESP could in this way be more readily
evoked for study. The outcome included the finding, verified in later research, that ESP seems more evident in artists than in other people (Moss, 1969). This finding is harmonious with other studies that form a second line of research with a humanistic approach--research on the personality characteristics and attitudes of people exhibiting ESP
contrasted with those who do not exhibit it. Gertrude
Schmeidler (Schmeidler and McConnell, 1958/1973), B. K.
Kanthamani (Kanthamani and Rao, 1973), and others have
for some years been pursuing this line of inquiry, and they
have (as a humanistic approach might suggest) found ESP to
be related to general openness and a positive attitude toward

psi phenomena. A third line of humanistic research is the important work on ESP and dreaming initiated by Montague Ullman and Stanley Krippner at Maimonides Medical Center, of which they have given a nontechnical account in their recent book with Alan Vaughan, Dream Telepathy (1973). A fourth line is the less decisive but equally intriguing work on ESP in other altered states of consciousness such as those associated with hypnosis, meditation, relaxation, and sensory isolation; to this work Charles Honorton (1974) has provided the most recent introduction.

All four of these humanistic turns in parapsychology have served to increase the evidence that psi phenomena are genuine occurrences, no mere products of misperception and misinterpretation of more familiar realities. All of them, too, increase the challenge to established science by giving hints about lines of inquiry that might be useful in bringing psi within the range of theories not alien to scientific modes of thought--by suggesting, in short, that science, like it or not, is stretching out to think about the previously unthinkable.

Just after I had enlarged my personal perspective by reading all this research on topics I had long neglected or that had just come into view, I encountered for the first time a person who seemed to display psi phenomena--a student in the Yale Law School named Bill Delmore. This firsthand view of phenomena which had previously been for me only remote and academic so greatly increased my interest that I shifted plans for an upcoming sabbatical semester and was fortunate enough to be able to spend it at the Institute for Parapsychology, the private research institute in Durham, North Carolina, founded by J. B. Rhine upon his retirement as a Duke professor. During an exciting stay there, I learned of recent developments on the other side of parapsychology, where it meets biology and physics rather than humanistic studies. Some of these offer special challenge to the general views of psychologists and other scientists; since these developments are considered in other papers in this volume, I will give them only brief attention before turning to the reverse challenge--the challenge to rather than from parapsychology.

Electronic Machines and Psi Research

The first of these recent developments on the natural-

science side of parapsychology has to do with instrumentation, with devising physical instruments useful in objectifying the study of psi phenomena and facilitating inquiry into
their sources. The leader in this development is Helmut
Schmidt. He is a physicist from Germany who began this
work while he was at the Boeing Scientific Research Laboratories in Seattle (Schmidt, 1969a, 1969b, 1969c) and later
came to the Institute for Parapsychology to continue it. The
first apparatus he constructed (described in Schmidt, 1970,
and pictured in Schmidt, 1971) is rather like some kind of
gambling machine; but money is not at stake, only the
pleasure of being right or the disappointment of being wrong.

The subject in Schmidt's first experiments had on a
table in front of him an apparatus with four buttons, each
with a small light bulb behind it. When the subject pressed
any one of the buttons, one of the bulbs lighted up (for greater visual appeal, they were of four different colors). The
subject's task was to try to press the particular button whose
bulb was going to light up. When he succeeded, that was
considered a hit. If he failed, one of the three other lights
went on, and that was a miss.

The subject's choice of a button to press has no influence on which light will go on, at least no obvious one within our normal understanding of physical processes. The selection of a light is made by a series of events inside the
apparatus, isolated from any identifiable control by the subject. An electronic number-generator is cycling very rapidly among the numbers 1, 2, 3, and 4, corresponding to potential illumination of bulbs 1, 2, 3, and 4, and altering an
electronic counter accordingly. After a button is pushed, the
connection between number generator and counter is severed,
so that the counter stands still, whenever a Geiger tube in
the apparatus sends out an impulse. The Geiger tube is activated by electrons emitted from a bit of the radioactive
element strontium-90, so placed that the tube is activated
on the average about 10 times per second, at intervals
which according to quantum theory are randomly variable in
length.

When a button is pushed, the light that will go on is
the one whose number appears in the electronic counter at
the next activation of the Geiger tube. The selection of a
light is thus determined by the exact time the strontium-90
emits an electron toward the tube, and should be random
and thus unpredictable. Schmidt tested randomness (with re-

spect to frequency of each light and of each combination of
two successive lights) by running the machine automatically
and testing the output against statistical expectation. He
found no evidence of departure from randomness.

Now what happens if someone sits down to this machine and tries to predict the theoretically unpredictable,
hoping to press the right button more than 25 per cent of
the time? With most people, what happens is just what most
of us would expect; they press the correct button about 25
per cent of the time. That's what happened to me through
some thousands of trials. That's what happened with most
of the hundred or so subjects Schmidt first observed working
with this device.

Among his hundred-odd subjects, including some whose
participation was especially sought because of their psychic
reputation, Schmidt found five persons who deviated significantly from the 25 per cent score. Their success, quantitatively, may not seem very impressive. The best performance averaged only about 27.5 per cent correct. But
this, and the slightly lower scores of others, were maintained consistently through so many thousands of trials, that
the possibility of their arising by random fluctuation may be
altogether dismissed.

I had an opportunity to borrow one of these machines
and use it with nine Yale undergraduates who had volunteered
because of an interest in psi phenomena and who thus might
be presumed especially likely to have some psychic ability.
Each had just 1000 trials, and seven showed no significant
departure from a 25 per cent performance. One student,
however, made the right guess on 294 trials out of the
1000; an outcome so extreme it might be expected by chance
to appear in about one of every 500 persons so tested. A
second student had a much higher and more significant score
on the first 100 trials (41 out of 100 correct, to be expected
by chance in about one of every 2500 persons so tested), but
then fell close to 25 per cent. These observations, though
as evidence of psi unimpressive in comparison with Schmidt's,
did--because of their occurring in these particular persons--
strengthen my judgment that performance on these machines
is at times an example of what we call psi.

I had also been led toward the same judgment by observing Bill Delmore, the law student responsible for my
active interest in parapsychology. I happened to be present

when he first saw one of these machines. Hearing an account of its operation, he said, "Oh, I think I can do that," and proceeded immediately to punch the correct button 30 per cent of the time or more. This statement is subject to the inaccuracies of memory, since no permanent record was being made. But his performance in subsequent weeks was recorded and has been described in an article by E. F. Kelly and B. K. Kanthamani (1972). Delmore was able to score well not only in a statistical sense but absolutely, averaging over 30 per cent correct in long stretches.

Some time after developing this machine, Schmidt (1973) turned his attention to what have been called "fast PK machines." Psi scoring on the four-button machine, if it occurs, might be achieved in either of two ways, almost equally impossible according to our usual ways of thinking. One would be by precognition, if for instance the subject can with some probability greater than 0.25 anticipate which light will come on at the exact instant he is going to press a button, and chooses his button in the light of that knowledge. The other would be by psychokinesis, or PK, if the subject can by pressing a particular button increase the chances that the corresponding light will come on. If the subject is given no choice about which button to push, but instead is instructed to press repeatedly a particular one, it may be tempting to classify a success as psychokinesis, and some subjects can score significantly with this procedure. Actually, though, as long as the subject can choose his button he might be scoring by precognition.

Schmidt realized that the possibility of precognition could be better controlled, in order to isolate psychokinesis for study, by building a different kind of machine. This machine would go along making choices without any button-pressing or other signal from the subject, and all the subject would do is just try to influence the machine by his thoughts. With this kind of machine, not requiring any muscular response from the subject, it also becomes possible to have the successive trials closer together, to have the machine make many choices per second while the subject steadily tries to influence them.

In experiments with one of Schmidt's new fast PK machines, the subject sits facing a dial with a recording needle which when at rest points directly up. It records the output of a device which generates random numbers ($+1$ or -1) many times per second. The needle is moved toward the right, let us say, when a preponderance of + 1's are generated, toward the left when a preponderance of -1's are generated. The task of the subject is to try, by thought alone, to keep the needle on one side more than on the other.

Taking his cue from the findings of earlier research, Schmidt tries to facilitate psi by giving the subject some choice and thus encouraging a feeling of freedom and spontaneity. Specifically, he offers each subject a choice between the visual feedback I have described and auditory feedback, where the subject wears headphones and + 1's are represented by clicks in one ear, -1's by clicks in the other ear. Moreover, he generally allows the subject to choose his own goal, right or left, in either form of feedback. (The experimenter can then adjust the machine so that each type of number equally often corresponds to the subject's chosen goal.)

Psi processes seem to be elicited more readily with these procedures than with the older techniques of parapsychological research. Schmidt tried out a fast PK machine with about 20 subjects, and from these picked out four persons for the first intensive trial. Each of these four then proceeded to achieve a score of at least 51 per cent, compared with the 50 per cent expected by chance and actually obtained (to a close approximation) in long periods when the machine was running by itself. The pooled results of these four subjects exceeded the expected 50 per cent by an amount which, though small in absolute value, would be expected by chance only once in 10,000 such experiments.

In a further experiment, Schmidt used 10 subjects; here, too, they were selected from about 20 persons who had taken part in preliminary trials. Of the 10, only one failed in the subsequent sessions to score above 50 per cent and that one scored only slightly below. In this longer second experiment, the chance that the overall deviation from 50 per cent could have been random rather than resulting from some real process is so remote that there is no need for it to be precisely stated (it is something like 10^{-12}).

The fast PK machines are too new to have been used very extensively as yet, but they clearly offer the possibility that a new and highly objective method may be widely applicable in the study of this seemingly subjective side of human life.

Already, in his first published paper on the fast PK machines, Schmidt (1973) is beginning to fulfill this prospect of scientific usefulness. He reports an exploration of how scoring rate varies with the speed at which numbers are being generated. With 30 numbers produced per second, 51.6 per cent of them were in the direction the subject was trying for. With the numbers produced 10 times as fast, 300 per second, the success rate dropped to 50.4 per cent. This is a difference worth noticing because of the very large number of trials, and it suggests for the higher speed a success rate one-fourth that at the slower speed. Since the effect, large though it is in the pooled data, did not appear in every subject, we can't tell yet whether it will be found generally or only under certain conditions. But it clearly indicates the possibility of experimental study of various factors influencing score in this PK task; through such study we might eventually approach some understanding of the processes involved. Of special importance is the possibility that the fast PK machines may permit indentifying short time intervals during which a subject is clearly exhibiting psi; this would be a great boon to physiological research in parapsychology.

These new electronic devices may be slow to reach their full use. Equipment for recording in detail what the machines and their users do, necessary for full scientific study of performance with them, is unfortunately beyond the means of most researchers in parapsychology since for the most part--unlike their colleagues investigating other topics --they must finance their own research with no help from government and little help from other sources. And some of the machines require considerable expense and skill to build and maintain. But some of the machines themselves, for those capable of electronic work, are not costly, and Schmidt has recently designed a special PK machine that, once built, forms a single compact unit not requiring much attention.

The Problem of Repeatability

Impressive though the evidence for psi appears to many people, it has always suffered from one serious flaw. Unlike other areas of experimental study, paranormal phenomena have never been the subject of any kind of dependably repeatable experiment. Never has the parapsychologist been able to say confidently to the doubter, "Come to my laboratory tomorrow at 2:00 p.m. and I will show you psi processes at work. "

For some of its research, of course, parapsychology must always accept this unsatisfactory state of affairs. The student of earthquakes or of tornadoes must likewise build his science partly on observations he somehow manages to make, or comes by at second hand, about events that are rare and not at his command. But no one who sees photographs of a stricken town doubts the reality of tornadoes, nor the desirability of improving our knowledge about them. Psi phenomena leave no such unmistakable traces, and the need for studying them will not be universally acknowledged unless their reality is known to be demonstrable at first hand to any doubter.

Will this ever be possible? Psi phenomena may, of course, be of such a nature that no procedure will ever be adequate to guarantee their occurrence at a particular time and place. Schmidt's findings, however, pose the possibility that a few selected subjects may, using his instruments, be able to demonstrate psi in a stable and dependable manner.

In another line of experimentation in recent years there has been a suggestion that similar stability might become available with unselected subjects. Here, as at so many other points in our attempt to understand human beings --but more surprisingly here--it is experimental work with lower animals that offers special promise. The promise lies in a specific line of work with rodents begun several years ago by a French zoologist, a professor at the Sorbonne, who as a parapsychologist uses a pseudonym, Pierre Duval (Duval and Montredon, 1968). The central feature was inspired by research some years ago with cats by two American parapsychologists, Karlis Osis and Esther Foster (1953). This feature is the separation of certain trials, termed "random-behavior trials," as ones on which the normal factors strongly influencing the animal's behavior seem to be inactive or in a state of balance, so that the weak influence of paranormal factors has more opportunity to be effective and detectable.

The experiments following this paradigm are surveyed by Dr. Morris in his paper in this volume. The appearance of dependable replicability was greatly exaggerated for a while by the numerous experiments of one investigator who was later found to have fabricated data in at least one ex-

periment and may have done so in all. The experiments
carried out by others suggest by themselves, however, the
possibility that with further study a dependably repeatable
experiment might be developed. Though no definite conclusion is justified at present, there is a potential challenge of
great import here. If dependably repeatable techniques are
eventually found, by explorations in either this or other directions, the status of parapsychology will obviously be radically changed.

The most direct reason for the change, of course,
would be just that psi phenomena could then be demonstrated
at will for all who chose to look. A still more important
influence on attitudes toward parapsychology, in my estima-
tion, would be the accumulating and interlocking research
that would naturally follow upon availability of suitable methods. Up to now, lacking dependable ways of bringing psi
into the laboratory, few scientists have chosen to devote
time to what might be a fruitless quest; if a dependably repeatable technique is available, we can expect a great increase in the number and variety of studies aimed at understanding psi phenomena. This increase in research should
in turn multiply the challenges, confirmations, and hints for
further study that each piece of research provides for others.
The history of science suggests that we are likely then to
see parapsychological research beginning to fall into general
patterns of findings, pointing to new sets of possible relationships which can in turn be verified.

Some of the patterns which might in time be solidly
verified would surely be ones we have no way of anticipating
now; others may be patterns that can already be tentatively
seen. For example, the animal research suggests that psi
occurs especially when an organism is oriented toward a
goal, and is somewhat active, but is not strongly controlled
by external stimuli or by its own prior responses. Psi
sensitivity could be instrumental in guiding action toward
the goal. Moreover, if we compare this series of animal
experiments with the general record of psychical research
on unselected human subjects, the suggestion emerges that
psychic functions are much more easily and generally elicited in animals than in human beings. If this is confirmed,
should it be taken at its face value? Or is it an incidental
product of the fact that the animal experiments use a technique in which psi could play a more important instrumental
role than it generally could for human subjects studied by
techniques standard in the past? Such a question produces

its own suggestions for systematic research on conditions influencing psi processes in human beings. Rex Stanford (1974a, 1974b) has shown, indeed, that numerous findings from human laboratory research and from study of spontaneous events yield a very important suggestion of this sort that badly needs to be followed up--the suggestion that both ESP and PK may operate in the service of goals most especially when one is unaware of their possibility.

Anti-Scientism

Increasingly, then, parapsychology challenges the complacency of the many scientists who feel certain that paranormal phenomena cannot occur. Many people in our society have an interest in the paranormal as part of an interest in occult traditions. For them, one of the conspicuous facts about the scientific establishment is that in consistently expressing toward the paranormal a contemptuous disregard, it has been a poor guide to adventurous seekers of knowledge wandering in the frontier. This fact joins with other reasons for anti-scientism in encouraging some to dream of giving up altogether the scientific tradition, embracing instead the occult tradition. I need not enlarge upon the personal and social disasters that would follow if our society as a whole tried seriously to follow this path. Few of us, I believe, would wish to renounce for our grandchildren the freedom from polio, diphtheria, and malaria that most of our children have enjoyed. What there is a need to enlarge on is the probability that even a less thoroughgoing, a more private and personal, even a not-too-serious affirmative answer may be seriously hampering to individual growth whether or not it has a broad social effect. Not only science, but clear thinking in general, is work. And any activity that interrupts the pleasant meanderings of our mind by slamming us up against reality can be hard work. Tennyson provides us a parallel in his account of Ulysses' sailors, tired of their long effort to return to home and a normal life, and entrapped in the land of the Lotus-eaters.

> Thro' every hollow cave and alley lone
> Round and round the spicy downs the yellow Lotos-
>   dust is blown.
> We have had enough of action, and of motion we,
> Roll'd to starboard, roll'd to larboard, when the
>   surge was seething free,

Where the wallowing monster spouted his foam-
fountains in the sea.
Let us swear an oath, and keep it with an equal mind,
In the hollow Lotos-land to live and lie reclined
On the hills like Gods together, careless of mankind.

To say that occult beliefs, and only they, offer to se-
duce us from our engagement with reality into a life of
dreams would be too broad a statement. However realistic
the general enterprise of science, for example, for some
scientists its personal functions include the facilitation of escape from many of the realistic demands of ordinary social
life. And however unrealistic systems of occult belief may
be, they provide many people with access to their daily
bread. So let us be more specific in our complaints. What
doubts or reservations should we have about the role in our
society, and in our personal life, of belief in the paranormal
and in the occult?

One of the most important reservations has to do with
the quantitative reasoning and judgments of probability that
are inevitably involved--even if they appear only implicitly
and despite every effort to avoid them--in thought and discussion about psi phenomena and occult beliefs. The central
finding of parapsychology, that there are very significant
consistencies for which we have yet no explanation, are certainly not a product of statistical fallacies. Most of the
parapsychological research I have read handles statistical
inference as competently as most of the other psychological
research I have read. But parapsychological topics, and especially other topics deriving from the occult tradition, are
often written about by persons other than scientific researchers, and these other writers often use or cite statistical or
other quantitative reasoning with utter lack of care.

Let me give an example, even though it borders on
numerology rather than parapsychology. In a book widely
sold on paperback stands, The Morning of the Magicians, by
Louis Pauwels and Jacques Bergier (1971), there is a passage about the wonderful mathematical mind of an Indian
named Ramanujan. Now Ramanujan may indeed have had a
wonderful mathematical mind, but I am thinking of the minds
of Pauwels and Bergier and others associated with their
book. For here is the way they present a story to illustrate the wonders of Ramanujan's skill and absorption with
numbers:

On all who came in contact with him he made
an extraordinary impression. He lived in a world
of numbers. Hardy went to see him in hospital
and told him he had taken a taxi. Ramanujan
asked what its number was: 1729. 'What a wonderful number,' he exclaimed; 'it is the lowest
number than can be expressed in two ways as the
sum of two cubes!'

For it is a fact that 1729 equals $10^3 + 9^3$, and
also $12^3 + 1^3$. It took Hardy six months to demonstrate this; and the same problem has not yet
been solved at the fourth power [p361-2].

Pauwels and Bergier seem to be saying that it took
someone six months to prove that summing the cubes of 10
and 9 yields the same number as summing the cubes of 12
and 1. Since one minute seems a fair outside limit for
proving that proposition, that surely can't be what they
meant to say. They must have meant that it took Hardy six
months to prove that no number smaller than 1729 shares
this property of being the sum of two different sets of cubes.
I decided to check the plausibility of their statement about
Hardy's difficulty, confident I could easily spare the necessary time. Sitting down in a quiet room with paper, pencil,
and what I could summon up of arithmetic skill surviving
from my rigorous training in a West Texas grade school
back in the 1920s, I set out to prove that no lower number
shares this property of the number 1729. I am sure that
when I was still in the sixth grade I could have done better;
but even now a rigorous proof--not by algebra but just by
disproving arithmetically all possible instances--took only
11 minutes.

It could be that Pauwels and Bergier are just having
fun with their readers and really know that if this demonstration took Hardy six months it can only be because he
waited half a year to get started. But I doubt it. It is
consonant with the quality of reasoning in the rest of the
book to suppose that this passage is meant quite seriously.
Yet the original writing of the book had as some possible
guarantee of care the fact that there were two authors, so
locating misstatements did not even at that point require
self-criticism. The original French publishers must have
had readers and editors who could have caught such gross
errors; so might the successive British and American editors, and in between was the mind of the translator. But,
no; this conspicuous piece of shoddy reasoning is still there

in my American copy published 11 years after the original.
We might hope, of course, that its presence would serve the
useful purpose of alerting a reader that the quality of thought
might be low in passages whose defects are less testable.
But I fear such works may most often be read with an un-
critical attitude which makes unlikely the discovery of even
the most egregious errors.

Confronted with such a passage as I have cited, every
reader has the knowledge with which to detect error. When
it comes to the misuse of statistics, the situation is different and the careless writer is more culpable. An instance
of this: I have happened across two reports of research
which purport to show that there is some substance in one
or more beliefs derived from astrology. I have not searched
out such studies; these are just the two I have happened
across. They are both shot through with fallacious statistical reasoning. One that--as a careful reading indicates--
shows in fact nothing whatever, appeared in a student publication, and I believe is by a student, and I refrain from
publicizing by citation the errors of someone I hope will
learn to do better. The other is in the collected works of
one of the great figures of psychology, Carl Jung (1969,
p459-84). One of his errors was pointed out to Jung between editions and he acknowledged it in a footnote. He apparently did not realize, and if his editors realized they did
not see fit to caution the reader, that the errors are more
numerous and serious. Reassessing properly the data provided by Jung would require some knowledge not only of statistics but also of astrology; so I cannot positively assert,
though I strongly suspect, that here too the data in fact show
nothing whatever. What I am sure of is that a reader can be
seriously misled if he assumes toward some of these passages the attitude of respect he may have developed in ad-
miration of other aspects of Jung's work; even admiring
Jung's frankness here about his own errors is no guarantee
against being led to repeat them.

Thinking About Randomness

One development within psychology itself gives added
heat to the passionate feelings with which some oppose all
invitation to think about the paranormal, fearing a corrupting
influence on our already meager capacity for clear thinking.
This development is more obviously pertinent to evaluating
strange experiences in everyday life than to judging experi-

mental evidence for psi phenomena, but is of real cautionary value even for the latter task. It is our increased awareness of the profound untrustworthiness of many of our commonsense judgments of randomness and improbability.

Parapsychology arose partly, under the name of psychical research, from consideration of occurrences that seemed very unlikely to have arisen by chance--for example, someone in England having a vision of an old but not often thought-of friend in India on just the day that friend was meeting a sudden death. Skeptics, after allowing for the possibility that many such incidents have come to seem strange mostly through the exaggerations of recall and retelling, are inclined to attribute the rest to "chance." Most of us, I suppose, have occasional vivid thoughts of old friends. Old friends, like oneself, being human, must sometime die. The two occurrences must in some instances coincide in time without any causal connection between them. To the extent we are convinced of the correctness of experimental evidence for psi, we are likely to relax our skepticism about whether any causal connection underlies such occurrences. Reports of strange incidents in everyday life thus feed into experimental parapsychology but then gain reciprocal support from it. If this support is unwarranted, and encourages people to misunderstand events they are experiencing, one may feel parapsychology to be having a bad effect on the quality of our thinking even if its experimental findings are themselves perfectly valid.

Any experimenter in parapsychology, or indeed in any branch of study where one is concerned with sequences of randomly determined events, is likely to be struck by the serious misjudgments made on even very simple issues of randomness. I was recently doing a class experiment in which two kinds of stimuli were placed in a series according to the sequence of even and odd numbers in a random-number table. To my surprise, one student seriously proposed that the table was biased, was not genuinely random, because runs of as many as five successive stimuli of one kind had occurred. No recondite mathematics are needed to figure out that about one of every 16 stimuli, on the average, should be the start of a run of at least five of a kind. My student was obviously in the grip of some conception of randomness incompatible with what precise reasoning would have quickly led him to.

Recent studies by two psychologists at Hebrew Uni-

versity (Tversky and Kahneman, 1971) have shown that serious deficiencies in reasoning about randomness are found not
only in people who lack technical training. Psychologists,
as a part of their education and professional work, are highly trained in reasoning about randomness. Yet Tversky and
Kahneman found they could readily pose problems that fellow
psychologists, as research subjects, would respond to with
the same kinds of errors common to many laymen. In research with high school and college students, they have isolated some of the typical reasoning which brings about these
errors.

One principle (Kahneman and Tversky, 1972) is that
of representativeness: we judge more probable something
that seems to resemble the pool of possible events from
which it is drawn. This is the principle that misled my
student into believing the random numbers were not random;
knowing that in the whole table even and odd numbers occur
about equally often, he thought it improbable that even a
small sample drawn from it could be so unrepresentative of
the whole as to contain only even numbers. He would also
have considered improbable a sample in which the two possibilities alternated regularly, for this would not echo the
chaotic arrangement in the total sequence. Kahneman and
Tversky found many of their student subjects believed that
if they tossed a coin six times the sequence HHHHTH was
less likely to occur than the sequence HTTHTH, where in
fact of course each of these, along with every other possible
sequence of outcomes is equally likely. The principle of
representativeness often leads us to find great significance
in seemingly meaningful coincidences, unable to believe they
could have occurred at random as part of the large reservoir of unconnected events necessarily occurring simultane-
ously at any time.

A second principle isolated by Tversky and Kahneman
(1973) is what they call availability, or ease of calling to
mind. We ascribe greater reality to, and thus judge more
likely to occur, events we can easily recall, picture, or
imagine than those not easily brought to mind. This pervasive mode of thought is a major source, they argue, of illusory belief in correlations which do not exist. I have found
myself the victim of this process while acting as my own
subject with one of Helmut Schmidt's fast PK machines.
The machine counts rapidly from 1 up, offering a brief visual display of each number as it goes along, and it is kept
going or is stopped by a random process inside, which the

subject tries to influence. The probability of stopping at each count may be set in advance as either 1/16, 1/32, 1/64, or 1/128. Sometimes when I mentally commanded the machine to stop, it stopped immediately. This was a very impressive occurrence, much more easily recalled than the numerous instances when I commanded just as decisively and the machine went right on. Were it not for a background of actual experience in science, I might have had difficulty persuading myself that the test of whether I could influence the machine must await final calculations on a mass of accumulated data, and that I could not trust the feelings rooted in my own immediate experience.

I could not, I believe, give too strong an impression of the extent to which Tversky and Kahneman find these principles of representativeness and availability to dominate reasoning about randomness and probability even in educated persons who have all the intellectual equipment with which they could instead reason soundly and precisely. Some critics of parapsychology may hope that in these new insights into common errors of reasoning will be found some weightier arguments against the general findings of parapsychology than have been provided by previous mathematical critiques. In that hope I think they will be disappointed, for the techniques of statistical reasoning used by parapsychologists in formulating those findings are the same as those used by other scientists for the same purposes; the principal difference in their application is that parapsychologists are accustomed, because of the implausibility of their findings, to employing more stringent criteria for rejecting the hypothesis of random origin and to reporting precisely the high or very high significance levels that sometimes are reached. The valuable critique that emerges from these new insights is applicable, though, to the everyday reasoning of all of us. Misjudgments about randomness are especially likely, I would guess, in those who have some paranormal gift whose occasional real operation may invite relaxation of more rigorous modes of thought, and in those lured to similar relaxation by a personal desire to find rational justification for irrational beliefs. Parapsychologists, too, may be lured to similar mistakes when they make judgments where judgments cannot be rationally justified--not in the careful statistical reasoning they employ in interpreting the overall results of an experiment, but in the informal judgments they may make about what is happening at any moment along the way. In order to understand psi phenomena, they would like to be able to recognize unmistakably when they are confronted with an instance and when they are confronted by a random event. The logic of statistical reasoning is limited in what it can do to meet this need, and the often fallacious "psycho-logic" of all humanity (see, e.g., Abelson, 1968) readily takes over.

Recent experiments by an American psychologist, Ellen Langer (in press) help us see why these studies of everyday reasoning about chance occurrences have a special pertinence for parapsychology. The focus of her research, done entirely out of the context of parapsychology, is on people's reactions to situations over which they have no control, and whose outcome is instead determined by chance. When will people act as though their own skills would deter-mine the outcome, and when will they act in ways appropri-ate to the true irrelevance of their skills? The general idea guiding Langer's research is that to the extent the chance event is surrounded by circumstances akin to those surround-ing skill-determined events, responses appropriate to skill-determined events are more likely to be made. She did several separate experiments to test specific implications of this idea--doing one, for example, with bettors at a race track and others with ticket buyers in small but genuine lot-teries developed for the research. Within each experiment, she varied some aspect of similarity to skill situations. The similarity always pertained to the surrounding circum-stances, never to the heart of the matter; the events were of a sort where the outcome would clearly depend upon chance rather than skill. In one experiment, competitive interests and expectations of success were varied by intro-ducing a seemingly competent or incompetent rival. In an-other, opportunity for personal decision was varied. In an-other, familiarity with the materials was varied. Finally, in two experiments the degree of active involvement, in-cluding time for thought, was varied. In each instance, the condition similar to what is standard in skill situations--competition, personal decision, familiarity, active involve-ment--increased the tendency to act as though skill were in-volved, to act as though the person himself could influence the chance outcomes. The effects were impressive and some-times very decidedly against the person's realistic interests. While Langer's research was entirely about the overt be-havior of her subjects, we may imagine that an inquiry about their beliefs would probably show an accompanying variation.

Now all of the specific conditions leading Langer's subjects toward unrealistic appraisal of chance situations as skill-determined are conditions present to a high degree in many ESP experiments, especially those done with exceptional subjects. The subject is likely to view the situation as highly competitive, he is constantly making personal decisions, he is likely to be very familiar with the materials and procedures and very actively involved. Langer's findings should give to any novice in parapsychology a strong expectation that his subjects will greatly exaggerate the extent to which their own powers are determining the events. These findings might well lead parapsychologists to predict "psi-missing" as a psychological reality in some subjects, even if they had no knowledge at all about whether there is any evidence for it as an objective reality.

Langer and Roth (in press) have done a further experiment in a situation especially close to that of subjects in many parapsychological experiments. In college students' trying to guess the outcome of coin tosses, development of an illusory sense of control--that is, an illusion of skilled prediction rather than chance--was found to be favored by having many successes early rather than late in the sequence of trials. In this experiment, the sequence of successes and failures was secretly manipulated by the experimenter. In (unmanipulated) parapsychological experiments, similar variations among subjects' experiences arise at random or through the operation of psi skills, and the occurrences early in an experiment may establish attitudes which are then maintained through the experiment or even afterward. Analogous circumstances arise, too, in the spontaneous occurrences of real or illusory psi phenomena.

The general study of human thought, then, may help us a great deal in understanding the thought processes surrounding the occurrence of psi phenomena. It is the non-psi aspects that are especially illuminated; but this is needed as one step along the way to illuminating also the psi aspects. With the help of this research we may at once become more sympathetic with some of the difficulties the psychic's gifts create for him and more able ourselves to distinguish truly paranormal performance from the self-deceptive appearance of psychic skill.

The research on everyday thought processes supplements research carried out long ago on the fallibility of eyewitness accounts of events (see, e.g., Wigmore, 1931). In experiments prompted by considering the trustworthiness of evidence presented in courts of law, psychologists staged

dramatic episodes in front of their classes and then asked
those present to write full accounts of what they had wit-
nessed or to answer specific questions about it. The startling extent of variation and contradiction among the accounts
provides us with a sound basis for not completely trusting
our own best memory of what we see and hear. Now we
have a basis for mistrusting also some of our important
judgments about events, especially about whether personal
skill is involved or whether the events may have arisen by
chance. Neither of these sources of doubt justifies a nihil-
istic despair about the capacity of human beings to know;
they show only that special techniques of recording and veri-
fying, such as those developed by science and mathematics,
offer us a more radical improvement than we generally
recognize.

It is fortunate, I think, that some of these new insights should have been gained at just a period when they
may be especially needed; if I am right in judging that the
positive findings of parapsychology have been gaining, and
will continue to gain, widespread recognition, we will sorely
need all the cautionary devices we can find in order to help
people place the facts about psi in proper perspective. We
must not over-generalize what facts there are, uncritically
accepting the variety of self-deceptions to which we could
then be readily tempted.

Tolerating Uncertainty

Yet there is an opposite danger of narrowing our
view so that we look only at knowledge that is already thoroughly substantiated by the strictest criteria of evidence and
of coherence with the rest of our knowledge. If we are too
concerned about ever giving even tentative consideration to
an idea that might turn out to be false, we could miss a
great many ideas of presently uncertain validity that may
eventually turn out to be true. Perhaps we should absorb
a lesson from the history of general psychology, which has,
I think, suffered from the narrowness of vision brought on
by the rigidity of its methodological blinders.

Tversky and Kahneman's principle (1973) of availability helps us in understanding this narrowness of vision.
Consider, for example, the extreme attitude one of the leading experimental psychologists, Donald Hebb, has displayed
toward parapsychology. Commenting on parapsychology in

1951, Hebb put forth what amounts to almost an explicit statement of the principle of availability: "Personally, I do not
accept ESP for a moment, because it does not make sense.
My external criteria, both of physics and of physiology, say
that ESP is not a fact despite the behavioral evidence that
has been reported" (p45). He went on to imply that this was
the only reason for rejecting the evidence for ESP, that the
other objections he had encountered seemed to him not valid.
In a recent address Hebb (1974) has returned briefly to this
theme; he is now more moderate in his dismissal of parapsychology. He relies partly on asserting "that the supporting evidence falls far short of what would be needed to
establish such obviously important propositions" as telepathy
and life after death, an assertion that seems more accurate
to me than his sweeping endorsement of the evidence for
ESP in 1951. He also seems to retreat somewhat from his
earlier position, in declining to assert that telepathy is in-
conceivable. Yet the basic source of his opposition seems
still to be that hypothetical processes are completely unavailable to his imagination if he can not reconcile them immediately with his present version of a scientific view of the
world. The principle of availability thus seems to sum up
the origins of his evaluation of evidence that, while not establishing any particular process, does certainly seem to me
to indicate very strongly some gaps in our present scientific
understanding. Careful reading of Hebb's recent paragraph
suggests to me, moreover, that the unavailability of this
idea to his imagination leads to a distortion of reasoning; as
in some other critics, his comments on this field seem to
depart from the lucidity and rationality that characterize his
writing on other topics.

In the experiments of Tversky and Kahneman, the low
availability that leads to judgments of improbability for certain ideas derives from such factors as their low incidence
in prior experience or the inconspicuousness of their occurrence. In Hebb's reasoning, too, lack of personal experience with the data of parapsychology may play some part.
But a distinctive source of low availability in Hebb derives
from his total trust in one set of principles as the absolute
criterion of what to expect. If those principles say the
probability of a particular event is zero, that event becomes
absolutely unavailable to one thinking about what is possible.
If my assessment of the observational evidence is correct,
the several statements Hebb has made about parapsychology
seem to provide a classic instance of distortion of judgment
by reliance on availability. Whether my assessment is

correct, or whether Hebb's reasoning illustrates the positive value the same conservative principle has in guarding us against too easy departure from accustomed thought, of course remains for future resolution.

For the present, however, I would reject Hebb's total trust in the adequacy of our present principles of physics and physiology. Great though the doubts those principles suggest about the seemingly paranormal, these doubts may not be justified; some strange events may occur much as they appear to. The advances of laboratory research in parapsychology must greatly weaken the justification for holding anything to be absolutely impossible. We are in a period where we need a maximum of tolerance for uncertainty. We need to consider that what seems impossible may actually be real; yet we need to continue doubting it enough to guarantee careful and constructive research. To believe strongly in all the hidden possibilities, in order to resolve these uncertainties, is reversion to a medieval domination of all life by religious faith; to reject absolutely all occult claims, holding them in the name of science to be absolutely impossible, is equally an abandonment of the scientific approach. To advance our knowledge of these matters, what we most need is to frankly recognize and accept the uncertainty of our present knowledge.

The need to tolerate uncertainty is especially clear when we consider attempts at theoretical explanation of psi phenomena. Evidence of strange facts often leads people to conclude that they have evidence for the first theory that comes to mind explaining it. If a medium, seeming to speak with the voice of a dead person, utters what appears to be a message from the deceased, the sitter is tempted to take this as conclusive evidence of personal survival after death. The temptation to leap from fact to interpretation is so strong that it has taken some time for wide appreciation of the fact that the science of parapsychology itself suggests alternative theories that might explain the same facts without any assumption of personal survival after death.

More generally, some people are willing to believe that parapsychology establishes the external reality of mind, soul, or spirit, and that this conclusion provides sufficient understanding. I can sympathize with eagerness to believe that the universe is more "human" and more concerned for humanity than we fear it may be, and for one greatly concerned with this issue the findings of parapsychology may offer some comfort. It does not seem to me, though, that the support it provides is very solid. It is a long way from discovery of a phenomenon to arriving at an adequate understanding of it, and the outcome of the search can not be confidently foreseen. We may eventually arrive at an understanding of paranormal phenomena that is just as dependent on physics and chemistry as is our understanding of color perception.

Whether we attain understanding of psi phenomena through the physical sciences or the human sciences, or some new blend of both, however, I think we may speed its attainment by willingness to consider outlandish theories. Events as incredible as some we must consider may just possibly require equally incredible theories.

Some of the theories that have been proposed are indeed strange. Jung has put forth a principle of synchronicity and Arthur Koestler has espoused the same general notion in his book, The Roots of Coincidence (1972). My inclination is to feel this theory says nothing, that it just offers us new words with which to admit our lack of understanding. But Koestler has now joined with two scientists in writing another book, The Challenge of Chance (Hardy, Harvie, and Koestler, 1974), which aims to give this theory an observational meaning; I don't think they have succeeded very well on their first try, but perhaps they will the next time.

Lawrence LeShan (1974) in working toward a general theory of the paranormal, proceeds from a view of physics vastly different from that adopted by Donald Hebb. LeShan sees similarities among the theoretical physicist, the mystic, and the psychic in their consciousness and mode of understanding the world. Where Jung and Koestler challenge our ordinary conceptions of randomness, LeShan especially challenges our conception of time, with its sharp distinctions among past, present, and future.

Other theories propose distinctive kinds of force, as in W. G. Roll's conception (1966) of psi-fields, and the integrated consideration of theory of the paranormal and theory about other kinds of force fields. Colleagues from mathematics and electrical engineering have worked with Roll on a quantitative analysis of the movements of objects in poltergeist cases he has been able to witness (Roll, Burdick, and Joines, 1973). Such analyses might eventually give clear observational meaning to the concept of psi-fields.

All these theories are bold affronts to our present conceptions of the world and an easy response is to dismiss them as entirely out of contact with reality. Yet in one or more of these seemingly fantastic theories may lie the roots of future understanding.

In matters of both theory and fact, then, I think we need to be set for a great diversity of ideas. But for clear thinking and real progress we must recognize the equally wide variation of these ideas in their relation to the verified evidence upon which science must depend. There may be great gain in listening seriously to accounts of paranormal phenomena associated with Eastern religions; conceivably, though it seems very unlikely to me, it might even be useful to consider seriously some of the principles set down in astrological tradition. But failing to distinguish sharply between the present evidence for either of these and the evidence for scientific generalizations, whether those of parapsychology or of other branches of science, can only lead to muddled thinking.

To those who are perfectly convinced, on whatever grounds, of the reality and importance of psi phenomena, an attempt to take a broad and open scientific view must seem at times tedious, unnecessary, perhaps entirely inappropriate. The scientist looks from afar at where psi is said to be and sees nothing, yet quivers as he approaches on tiptoe; at the first glimpse of something there, he retreats in dismay, only to be intrigued once again into another timid approach. This inept flirtation between science and psi goes on decade after decade. If the discoveries of J. B. Rhine in the early 1930s were the first touch of hand on hand, we are only about now reaching the stage of the first kiss. My own research efforts in parapsychology have for me, like the general relation between science and psi, this back-and-forth movement whose adequate representation would call for all the skills of a choreographer and ballet company.

Participation in this encounter can jar anyone into unaccustomed modes of thought. In my case, though I am inclined to very prosaic and factual ways of thinking, I am led to suppose that myth might provide a better way of summarizing the developing relation between science and psi. Science as Cupid, perhaps, considering himself a superior order of being and yet entranced by Psyche. There would have to be at least one reversal of the old myth; now it is

Psyche's face that must not be seen by the lover. And if in time our future science, in its love of Psyche, creates so much light as to see the bare beauty of her face, what then? Must they vanish from each other's sight, never to meet again? We would not want them to settle down to an old-fashioned marriage, each changed by permanent commitment to the other; science has too many duties unrelated to psi, and psychic skills have other potentialities than contributing to scientific knowledge. But perhaps we could hope for a modern domestic liaison in which science and psi accept each other fully for a while in a spirit of exploration and growth.

REFERENCES

Abelson, R. P. "Psychological Implication." In R. P. Abelson et al. (eds.), Theories of Cognitive Consistency: A Sourcebook (Chicago: Rand McNally, 1968), p112-39.

Child, I. L. Humanistic Psychology and the Research Tradition: Their Several Virtues. New York: Wiley, 1973.

Duval, P., and Montredon, E. "ESP Experiments with Mice." Journal of Parapsychology, 32 (1968), 153-66.

Hardy, A., Harvie, R., and Koestler, A. The Challenge of Chance: Experiments and Speculations. New York: Random House, 1974.

Hebb, D. O. "The Role of Neurological Ideas in Psychology." Journal of Personality, 20 (1951), 39-55.

_____. "What Psychology Is About." American Psychologist, 29 (1974), 71-9.

Honorton, C. "State of Awareness Factors in Psi Activation." Journal of the American Society for Psychical Research, 68 (1974), 246-56.

Jung, C. G. The Structure and Dynamics of the Psyche. (Collected Works, vol. 8.) Princeton, N.J.: Princeton University Press, 1969.

Kahneman, D., and Tversky, A. "Subjective Probability: A Judgment of Representativeness." Cognitive Psychology, 3 (1972), 430-54.

Kanthamani, B. K., and Rao, K. R. "Personality Characteristics of ESP Subjects; V. Graphic Expansiveness and ESP." Journal of Parapsychology, 37 (1973), 119-29.

Kelly, E. F., and Kanthamani, B. K. "A Subject's Efforts Toward Voluntary Control." Journal of Parapsychology, 36 (1972), 185-97.

Koestler, A. The Roots of Coincidence. New York: Random House, 1972.

Langer, E. J. "The Illusion of Control." Journal of Personality and Social Psychology, in press.
_____ and Roth, J. "Heads I Win, Tails It's Chance: The Illusion of Control as a Function of the Sequence of Outcomes in a Purely Chance Task." Journal of Personality and Social Psychology, in press.
LeShan, L. The Medium, the Mystic, and the Physicist: Toward a General Theory of the Paranormal. New York: Viking Press, 1974.
Moss, T. "ESP Effects in 'Artists' Contrasted with 'Non-Artists'." Journal of Parapsychology, 33 (1969), 57-69.
_____ and Gengerelli, J. A. "Telepathy and Emotional Stimuli: A Controlled Experiment." Journal of Abnormal Psychology, 72 (1967) 341-8.
_____ and _____. "ESP Effects Generated by Affective States." Journal of Parapsychology, 32 (1968), 90-100.
Osis, K., and Foster, E. B. "A Test of ESP in Cats." Journal of Parapsychology, 17 (1953), 168-86.
Pauwels, L., and Bergier, J. The Morning of the Magicians. New York: Avon, 1971.
Roll, W. G. "Token Object Matching Tests: A Third Series." Journal of the American Society for Psychical Research, 60 (1966), 363-79.
_____, Burdick, D. S., and Joines, W. T. "Radial and Tangential Forces in the Miami Poltergeist." Journal of the American Society for Psychical Research, 67 (1973), 267-81.
Schmeidler, G. R., and McConnell, R. A. ESP and Personality Patterns. Westport, Conn.: Greenwood Press, 1973 (first published in 1958).
Schmidt, H. "Anomalous Prediction of Quantum Processes by Some Human Subjects." Boeing Scientific Research Laboratories Document D1-82-0821, February, 1969. (a)
_____. "Precognition of a Quantum Process." Journal of Parapsychology, 33 (1969), 99-108. (b)
_____. "Clairvoyance Tests with a Machine." Journal of Parapsychology, 33 (1969), 300-6. (c)
_____. "Quantum-Mechanical Random-Number Generator." Journal of Applied Physics, 41 (1970), 462-8.
_____. "A Quantum Process in Psi Testing." In J. B. Rhine (ed.), Progress in Parapsychology (Durham, N.C.: Parapsychology Press, 1971), p28-35.
_____. "PK Tests with a High-Speed Random Number Generator." Journal of Parapsychology, 37 (1973), 105-18.
Stanford, R. G. "An Experimentally Testable Model for Spontaneous Psi Events. I. Extrasensory Events."

Journal of the American Society for Psychical Research, 68 (1974), 34-57. (a)

_____. "An Experimentally Testable Model for Spontaneous Psi Events. II. Psychokinetic Events." Journal of the American Society for Psychical Research, 68 (1974), 321-56. (b)

Tversky, A., and Kahneman, D. "Belief in the Law of Small Numbers." Psychological Bulletin, 76 (1971), 105-110.

_____ and _____. "Availability: A Heuristic for Judging Frequency and Probability." Cognitive Psychology, 5 (1973), 207-32.

Ullman, M., and Krippner, S., with A. Vaughan. Dream Telepathy. New York: Macmillan, 1973.

Wigmore, J. H. The Principles of Judicial Proof; or, The Process of Proof as Given by Logic, Psychology, and General Experience and Illustrated in Judicial Trials. Boston: Little, Brown, 1931.

Gertrude R. Schmeidler

THE RELATION BETWEEN
PSYCHOLOGY AND PARAPSYCHOLOGY

Introduction

The relation between psychology and parapsychology breaks into four parts: methods, content, theory, and possible applications. The parts shape up differently. Parapsychology's methods use rigorous controls that some other areas of psychology might well take as a model. Parapsychology's content on the one hand is startling in its demonstration of what seems to be a paradox and on the other hand is so consistent with a variety of psychological findings that it meshes neatly and thereby enriches and expands them. The theory is little developed, but it carries the potential for major advances. And the range of possible applications extends from simple techniques sharing basic similarities with those already in use to the possibility of a new model for human relationships and ethical values.

Parapsychology studies extrasensory perception (ESP), the intake of information by some method as yet unknown (and which therefore seems impossible). It studies psychokinesis (PK), the output of response without the use of known effectors (which therefore also seem impossible). It includes within its theoretical purview--and therefore should be studying--the possibility of the separation of conscious events from body events and hence the possibility of a surviving consciousness after bodily death. Its findings lead into theory, but only if its methods are good will its findings be worth attention. This paper will therefore discuss methodology first; next, the data obtained with good methods; then, their theoretical implications for psychology; and finally, their possible applications.

122

METHODOLOGY

Extrasensory Perception

Like most other topics, ESP is partly defined in a negative way. Just as learning is progressive change in behavior not due to maturation alone, and perception is response to a stimulus not wholly determined by response bias, so ESP is response to "targets" (stimuli) not due to sensory cues or to inference. It therefore requires targets which cannot be sensorially apprehended or inferred.

The standard procedure of ESP experimentation involves some half dozen steps. First, of course, the experimenter must decide on his target population. This may be the conventional five ESP symbols, or a set of words, a set of pictures, the 12 standard positions on the face of a clock, or any other content which is convenient or interesting.

Next the experimenter ensures that the target order will be random. There are several acceptable ways of doing this, and I will mention only a handful. He may use some machine like the ones that Schmidt (1969) has invented where the chance timing of decay in a radioactive element determines target sequence. He may assign (or may have an assistant assign) a digit or a combination of digits to each target, then enter a random number table at random and follow its order in making a written record of the target sequence. If he uses cards as targets, he may resort to the old method of repeated careful shuffling followed by two cuts with a knife blade. He may put target items into a container, arrange to have them thoroughly mixed, and use some device which permits only one to emerge at any time. He may program a computer to select a random or pseudorandom sequence. Many other methods are equally acceptable.

The experimenter must also ensure that a record of the targets is made without knowledge of the subject's responses. If he uses a machine, the machine may print the targets or keep an internal record of them. If he uses a random number table or cards, he or an assistant must record the sequence either before the subject responds to it or (if later) without knowledge of how the subject responded. In other words, targets must be recorded blind (a precaution not always followed in some other kinds of psychological research).

He must ensure that the targets are concealed. A standard method with cards or a written list is to keep the targets in a place separate from where the experiment is conducted, or to put them into an opaque container. A common practice which permits the subject to feel he is close to his own target material but still keeps proper control is to write out the target list, wrap it on both sides with aluminum foil, insert the assembly into a manila envelope, and staple it closed. Where a "telepathy" technique is used (ordinarily a "GESP" technique, which permits either telepathy or clairvoyance) so that the targets must be known to some individual while another is trying to respond to them, a good procedure is to have the responder (the "percipient") in one room with a closed door, the sender (the "agent") in another distant room, and only then permit the agent to examine the target. If timing of a series of targets is to be synchronized in this kind of a GESP experiment, communication of times should not be from agent to percipient, but should be either a signal which both can hear or a one-way signal from the percipient.

There is an important additional control for concealment which is standard procedure in parapsychology but is often neglected in other psychological research. The target must be concealed not only from the subject, but also from everyone in normal contact with the subject, so that inadvertent clues cannot be given.

Another step is to ensure that the subject's responses are recorded blind, without knowledge of the target. Responses may be punched into a machine, or written by the subject, or written by the blind experimenter, or taped and recorded by a typist who is ignorant of target order, etc. (Often, as in much of the research with nonsense syllables, this precaution too is neglected in psychological investigations.)

Thereafter the steps are the routines of good experimental procedure. The data should be scored blind; should be checked blind; should be evaluated by standard statistical methods; and all data should be reported. A distinction should be made between hypotheses stated before the data were obtained and post-facto analyses. It is my impression that parapsychologists tend to be more careful about these routines than do psychologists in many other specialties; but of course individuals vary.

Psychokinesis

PK, which represents "action at a distance," is investigated by so many widely different techniques that it is difficult to generalize about them. I will describe a sample.

For a time, PK was studied primarily with dice. Here two difficulties are especially prominent: the dice may be imperfect and the subject may control the throw by his muscular skill. Each is readily handled. To control for the imperfection of any die, the subject must try an equal number of times to have each of its six faces turn up. Inequalities or biases thus average out.

Experts on dice tell us that it is difficult to control which face will appear after one bounce, very difficult after two, and impossible or almost impossible after three bounces. Parapsychologists therefore use devices which make the dice bounce many times, for example by having them released into a chute made of corrugated plywood. Further precautions are probably only a matter of gilding the lily, but are likely to include putting the dice into the release box with the same face up for all "throws," having an automatic release mechanism, enclosing the whole assembly in glass.

A variant of this throw method is the placement test, in which small objects such as cubes are put into a release mechanism placed over the medial line of a table. The subject hopes an equal number of times that the objects will fall to the left or to the right of the middle line. Again, with this procedure mechanical inequalities average out so as to give no spurious advantage for the data as a whole.

With these or similar methods, where counterbalancing ensures target equality, recording accuracy may be open to question. Rigorously careful researchers can photograph the outcome of each response and have a blind judge tally the results. An alternative rigorous method is to conceal the target and require the subject to hope that the dice will fall the "right" way, without knowledge of what the "right" way is. Here a subject's recording of his own data is properly blind. A common method, less rigorous than is desired but still better than the methods of many psychological experiments, has two independent records of each throw, perhaps made by subject and experimenter or by two experimenters. Records are then compared and discrepancies are checked out.

Modern research increasingly makes use of electronic devices invented by Schmidt or similar to his, where radio-active elements determine the output and the machines have been carefully calibrated so that the expected output is known. The subject attempts to change the output in a specified direction. Automated recording ensures against error.

When PK on stable systems is investigated, the problems are somewhat different and the solutions are usually easier. In studying effects on temperature, for example, a thermistor can be insulated and its changes registered on a polygraph so that a properly blind record is made; and counterbalanced attempts to make the thermistor hotter or to make it colder can control for physical irregularities.

Other Problems of Parapsychology

No rigorous research design has yet been proposed to investigate such problems as whether consciousness can exist apart from the body. Findings from the loose designs are debatable, and will not be discussed here.

THE FINDINGS

The major finding from psi (i.e., from ESP and PK) research is that ESP and PK occur. There seems by now to be unequivocal evidence for each, and the evidence is especially strong because it is contributed by investigators in different laboratories who work with different methods.

Most early studies merely tried to find whether or not ESP and PK occurred and therefore tested only the null hypothesis that results would be within the range of chance expectation. The null hypothesis had to be rejected after a large number of experiments with well-controlled conditions had found ESP scores that were fantastically, almost numbingly greater than chance expectation, with odds of 10^{-35} and 10^{-70} (Soal and Bateman, 1954), or 10^{-22} in a single one of the many successful experiments performed in the Duke University Parapsychology Laboratory (Pratt, Rhine, Smith, Stuart and Greenwood, 1940/1966). These data seemed barren to many ("empty correlations," in Boring's words). They were relevant to psychology only in showing that humans had potentialities beyond those ordinarily listed in the introductory psychology texts.

Later studies attempted to fill these "empty" correlations. Typically, the investigation examined the relation between psi scores and a single other variable, such as serial position, specific content, or the subject's mood or attitude. Where a clearcut difference in ESP or PK score was shown to relate to a change in the independent variable, the results served both to reject the null hypothesis in respect to the occurrence of ESP or PK and also to give meaningful information about how psi abilities function. It is only these later investigations that will be discussed below.

Individual Differences

The general population. The best working hypothesis about the distribution of psi ability is that it follows a skewed normal curve, with a low mean and a wide range. Some few individuals have been carefully tested over a period of years and have shown a high scoring rate during this extended period (Pratt, 1973; Soal and Bateman, 1954). The evidence for a general distribution of low psi ability comes from dozens of experiments with unselected subjects who were tested under two conditions or were divided on the basis of some independent variable. Where the data show a significant difference between conditions, and a detailed examination makes clear that this result is not due to a few "star" subjects, we infer that the ability is general.

No consistent relations have been found to the usual demographic variables such as race, age, or sex. High ESP scores have been reported for many races and for a wide age range. Some experiments show higher scores for males and others for females; presumably the differences are due to experimenter effects or special situational demands.

Two of these general relations, birth order and somatotype, need further examination. Eastman (1966), replicating in New York a larger study in England (Green, 1965), found (as did the prior one) that first borns had higher ESP scores than later borns. Somatotype was studied in a single but large experiment (Bhadra, 1965) and showed lower ESP scores for extreme ectomorphs than for others; but the data come from an Indian population biased toward ectomorphy and the problem needs study with other groups.

Personality. Personality studies have given a richer yield and their data seem to converge on the generalization that higher ESP scores come from relaxed, outgoing, receptive, and cooperative individuals while lower scores come from withdrawn, hostile, or negativistic ones. Often the higher scores are significantly above chance expectation ("psi-hitting") and the lower ones are significantly below chance expectation ("psi-missing"). Psi-missing implies use of ESP to avoid the target.

A long series of attitude studies exemplifies the findings. Palmer (1971) summarizes research beginning in the 1940s to test the "sheep-goat" hypothesis: that subjects who accept the possibility of ESP success under the conditions of the experiment tend to have higher ESP scores than those who reject this possibility. In the original study the sheep, open to possible ESP success, scored somewhat above chance expectation; the goats who rejected ESP under these conditions and thus presumably had a negative attitude toward the experiment, scored somewhat below chance. Of the 17 experiments which meet Palmer's criteria for grouping together, 13 showed a sheep vs. goat tendency in the predicted direction (and six of them gave significant differences ranging from P = .05 to P = .00001), while four showed an insignificant tendency in the opposite direction. Palmer lists seven other experiments of similar type; here four (one of which was significant) showed the difference predicted by the hypothesis, two showed no difference, and one showed an insignificant contrary trend. The spread of data approximates what would be expected from the mean difference reported in the original research. The hypothesis is clearly consonant with our original generalization about personality.

A long list of studies converge upon this general concept, though they use different techniques and terms. For example, children referred to a school psychologist for diagnostic testing were categorized, and those diagnosed as "withdrawn" had significantly lower ESP scores than the others both in an exploratory and in a confirmatory study (Shields, 1962). Kragh's Defense Mechanism Test showed the expected negative correlation between defensiveness and ESP score in each of two series (Johnson and Kanthamani, 1967). Rorschachs scored for barrier minus penetration significantly confirmed the hypothesis that barrier scores would be relatively higher in subjects with chance ESP means and low variances than in subjects with high means and high variances (Schmeidler and LeShan, 1970). Honor-

ton (1972) categorized subjects according to the frequency of
their dream recall and found higher ESP scores for those
who reported that they recalled many dreams than for those
who recalled few or none.   Moriarty and Murphy (1967) hypothesized that children classed as more open and more
creative would have higher ESP scores than the others, and
found a nonsignificant difference in the predicted direction.
Moss (1969) predicted and found significantly higher scores
in artists, a group expected to be both receptive and outgoing, than in non-artists.   It seems, at the risk of over-
generalization, as if all these studies are investigating the
same continuum, with one pole marked as defensiveness,
withdrawal, barrier, or repression, and the other pole as
openness.   Viewed in this way, all the studies give convergent results.

Eysenck (1967) has summarized a large number of
studies which indicate higher ESP scores for extraverts than
for introverts.   Later studies have tended to confirm this
as a general though a weak trend.   An overlapping concept
gives similar results: when tendencies toward expansiveness versus compressiveness are judged from individuals'
drawings, Humphrey (1946) found that expansives had higher
scores on a clairvoyance test (but not on a telepathy test).
The finding of higher clairvoyance scores was replicated in
some later studies, though a good many others failed to confirm it.   Recently Kanthamani and Rao (1973) strongly confirmed it when they used the size of House-Tree-Person
drawings as their measure of expansiveness (P = .0001).
Carpenter and Carpenter (1967) made an analysis which may
help explain the inconsistent results of different experimenters.   When subjects were asked to role-play an expansive
or constrictive attitude, the variance of the constrictive
score was markedly low for the first half of the runs, but
in the second half rose to the level of the expansive attitude.
It may be that compressive or introvert subjects score well
only if they have "warmed up" to the experiment.   If so,
experimenters who start testing without adequate warm-up
time will find a scoring difference between expansive and
compressive groups, while those who succeed in encouraging
all their subjects to adopt a freely responsive attitude (or
who tend to make all their subjects feel constricted) will not
find the difference.

Anxiety or level of arousal is expected to follow the
Yerkes-Dodson law of an inverted U in relation to performance, with optimum effects in the mid-range.   Most inves-

tigators who study anxiety and ESP scores report a relation between them, but few describe the general level of arousal. It is therefore difficult to know whether or not the results are orderly. A provocative example comes from what most parapsychologists would class as a pilot study: Duane and Behrendt (1965) took simultaneous EEG recordings from identical twins separated from each other. Two pairs showed alpha bursts at the same time and the authors report that only these pairs were familiar with the procedure and at ease in it; the many other pairs who did not show this simultaneity were anxious and apprehensive. Conversely, Nielsen and Freeman (1965) reported that subjects with higher anxiety scores had higher ESP scores; but until we know whether their subjects regarded the ESP tests as agreeable or as anxiety-provoking, we cannot judge whether the findings are consonant with Duane and Behrendt's report. A sophisticated experiment by Carpenter (1971) gives a neat pattern of interaction. His subjects called ESP cards, but did not know that erotic pictures were taped to some of the cards. The erotic pictures would presumably be arousing. Carpenter also administered the Taylor Manifest Anxiety Scale, and found--as would be predicted by the Yerkes-Dodson law--that high anxious subjects had higher scores on the neutral targets while moderate and low anxiety subjects had higher scores on the erotic targets. Another experiment which gives us more information also is consistent with expectation. Sailaja and Rao (1973) tested subjects just before an anxiety-arousing interview and later when the anxiety was relieved, and found lower ESP scores before the examination.

If ESP is similar to other psychological functions, the value that a subject places on the ESP test should affect his score. Buzby (1967) asked subjects whether the test was of vital interest or only of casual interest to them, and found that vital interest was associated with higher variance in precognition (though not in clairvoyance) scores. This is reminiscent of the higher variance often found in subjects whom Beloff and Bate (1970) call "super-sheep," those who state that they are certain their ESP ability will result in high scores. Typically their scores vary widely so that the variance, but not the hit rate, is high. In a more neutral setting and presenting ESP in an intellectual context, Schmeidler (1952) found that subjects with higher theoretical values had higher ESP scores. Replication of this value pattern would be expected only if the context of the ESP test was the same.

Intra-Individual Differences

The differential effect. One of the best established findings in parapsychology is what Rao (1965) first called the preferential effect and later the differential effect. If subjects take two types of ESP test (speaking or writing, responding to symbols or to self-selected words, etc.) and state which they prefer, there is likely to be a significant difference in scoring between the preferred and the nonpreferred task. Typically, as would be expected, the preferred method or target has higher scoring. However, when psi-missing indicates that the whole experiment is aversive the effect tends to reverse, as with a double negative, and the preferred task typically shows more psi-missing while the nonpreferred is nearer to chance, or even shows psi-hitting. In 1965 Rao could cite dozens of experiments which demonstrated this intrasubject effect and since then many more have been performed, both by him and his coworkers and by others. The effect implies a lack of conscious control of the psi process, an implication supported by much other research. I shall cite in detail only one neat fairly recent example.

In a PK experiment, Stanford (1969) required all subjects to use two PK techniques with dice. One technique was to visualize the face which they hoped would turn up; the other was to give associations to the number which they hoped would turn up. Later (to control for the experimenter effect) he gave a word-association test from which subjects were categorized as tending toward visual or toward associative thinking. The data showed the expected interaction, with the visualizers doing better in the visual condition and the associaters in the associative condition. The correlation of PK difference scores with association scores was +.53. Here we have not only a demonstration of the differential effect, but also an analysis of the individual differences which relate to differential success and failure.

Mood. From experiments where self-reported moods are compared with ESP or PK scores, the clearest generalization is that each experimenter is likely to replicate his own findings. Nielsen (1970) has twice found that subjects in extreme moods, whether pleasant or unpleasant, are more likely to make high ESP scores than are subjects in moderate moods. Fisk and West (1956), however, in a mass ESP experiment, found higher scores for subjects in a pleasurable mood than in an unpleasurable one, as did Feather and Rhine (1969) in one part of a PK experiment where Feather acted as the only subject. André (1972) found no effect of mood. Rogers (1967) has repeatedly found higher ESP variance in the early part of the run, where the subject's mood is one of more eager interest, than in the latter part where the mood is one of boredom. Carpenter (1969) in each of three experiments found higher variance for subjects in a moderately positive or an extremely negative mood than for other subjects. The results are confusing.

In an attempt to clarify this confusion, the hypothesis was stated that any group tested and retested under uniform conditions is likely to be self-consistent in its own pattern of ESP in relation to mood and attitude, even though different groups will not necessarily show the same pattern. Two reports described results which tended to support this hypothesis (see Schmeidler and Craig, 1972). The data suggest, for example, that in a competitive group the mood favorable for ESP might combine high egotism and low anxiety, but that in a cooperative group the favorable mood might combine social affection, concentration, and surgency. To the extent that experimenters arouse different feelings in their subjects the moods relating to ESP success might also differ, which could account for the apparent contradictions in the results of the earlier studies.

State of consciousness. When an experimenter tries to induce a particular mood or state of consciousness in his subjects, results are clearer. Perhaps the best examples are reported by Braud and Braud (1973, 1974), who gave instructions for progressive relaxation (similar in many ways to meditation instructions). They found extraordinarily high ESP success in a series of sessions with different subjects-- except for one session where a group was hastily put together in order to demonstrate the effect to a reporter and where we may speculate that the subjects' knowledge that they were on display prevented full relaxation. An impressive series of reports also comes from Honorton and his associates (see Honorton, Drucker, and Hermon, 1973). Subjects were trained to report on a four-point scale the extent to which their states of consciousness differed from their usual ones and it was repeatedly found that those reporting a marked change in consciousness had higher ESP scores. Somewhat similar results are reported by Osis and Bokert (1971), who tried to train subjects in meditation, asked for self-reports, performed a factor analysis, and found that the strongest relation to a complicated ESP measure came from subjects who scored themselves as more open and self-transcending. Breitstein (1972) attempted to teach his subjects to meditate and found higher scores immediately after meditation than at any other time; but in a follow-up study found only suggestive data following the same trend. (The weakness of the follow-up data was largely due to the inclusion of one subject with pronounced psi-missing: an experienced meditator who disapproved of the research project, consented reluctantly to join it, and reported falling asleep at times when he should have made his ESP calls.)

Few subjects who are adept at meditation have been tested, but two other studies are worth mention. Green (1971) reported that Swami Rama agreed to try to move by PK a stationary object mounted on a pivot. After prolonged preparations, he succeeded in two out of three trials in moving the object through about 10° of arc each time. Schmidt and Pantas (1972) report that Pantas, who was experienced in Zen, had an extraordinarily high scoring rate in a long series of trials using electronic machines which could test for either precognition or PK. When these results are taken in conjunction with those of Breitstein and of Braud and Braud, they imply that changed states of consciousness facilitate ESP and PK success only if there is good rapport.

Honorton and Krippner's review (1969) of research on hypnosis and ESP indicates that hypnosis will under some conditions make for effective ESP scoring. Out of the 13 experiments listed in which a comparison was made of ESP in the hypnotic and the waking state, nine showed a significant advantage with hypnosis, two showed a significant decrement with hypnosis, and two failed to show a significant difference. A few more recent experiments confirm this trend. Comparison of successful and unsuccessful attempts to increase ESP scores hypnotically indicates that direct suggestion for high scores is ineffective or even counterproductive, whereas suggestions that the subject enter a relaxed but open state, receptive to ESP impressions, is likely to be associated with a high rate of ESP scoring. These suggestions seem almost identical with those that the Brauds (1973, 1974) used for relaxation.

Perceptual deprivation and perceptual overload may well produce altered states of consciousness, but little ESP or PK research has been done with them. Honorton, Drucker, and Hermon (1973) report no overall effect from a short

deprivation period and unpublished research from my laboratory supports this general negative conclusion. It is of
course possible that with preselected subjects and facilitating
suggestions, deprivation or partial deprivation will help the
subject enter an appropriately altered state. Krippner,
Honorton, Ullman, Masters, and Houston (1971) describe successful ESP results when a telepathic agent was subjected to
"sensory bombardment"; but they do not report a control for
the effect of suggestion.

Hallucinogens have often been informally reported to
result in ESP impressions, but no fully documented study of
them gives conclusive results.

Dreams, or hypnagogic states, have also frequently
been considered occasions for spontaneous ESP. For this
contention there is now sound experimental support from a
long series of extremely careful dream studies (Ullman and
Krippner with Vaughan, 1973) where significant evidence of
dream telepathy has been found in nine out of their total of
12 formal experiments. There has been no control, however, that permits comparison of dream accuracy with waking accuracy when the experimental demands are controlled;
ie. e., when the subject does not realize that to make the
experiment a success, his waking images should be less effective than his dream images. We therefore do not yet
know if the dream state is more conducive to ESP than is a
well-motivated waking state.

Confidence: recognition of ESP. Introspections about
an ESP experience sometimes report a qualitative difference
between dreams or waking impressions that carry ESP information and other dreams or impressions; a quality which
makes the person say, "I knew...." Sometimes, however,
the confidence is misplaced; i.e., there are false positives.
(There are also false negatives; see, below, the section on
Lack of Recognition of ESP.) Several experiments have investigated this quality by asking the subject to report his
level of confidence in a particular call or in an entire run
or session. Most but not all of these experiments show a
higher scoring rate when the subject reports more confidence, especially if the subject is restricted in the number
of high confidence ratings he may give. Two interpretations
of these findings are (a) that some special introspective
quality accompanies ESP, or (b) that the subject is being
given a new and more interesting task: to have ESP about
his own ESP. Some experimenters build this higher accu-

racy of confidence calls into their experimental design, and
decide before the data are collected that they will hypothesize high ESP scores for only those calls that the subject
checks. This was done by McCollam and Honorton (1973),
and by Fahler and Osis (1966) who with preselected hypnotic
subjects found that the checked calls were more accurate
than the unchecked (P = .00000002).

Serial effects. When ESP or PK data are analyzed
to see where the hits occurred, it is common to find most
of them at the beginning of a run or of a session, sometimes
with an upswing at the end. This decline or U curve is
reminiscent of serial position effects in other repetitive tasks
and is usually attributed to the subject's having more interest
at the beginning of any run, more boredom as it progresses,
and sometimes a renewed motivational spurt at the very end
(similar to what factories report after the four o'clock
slump). The inference is supported by findings on variance.
Experimenters used to hail this internal pattern as evidence
of ESP or PK (Pratt, 1949), but now that they no longer need
to demonstrate the existence of psi, they are more likely to
try to avoid the middle decline by shortening the task.

Response bias. Investigators ordinarily try to mini-
mize response bias by using targets that are similar in associative value and affect, or by warning subjects against it,
etc.; and they depend on counterbalancing or on statistical
treatment to keep it from contaminating their findings. Ingenious recent experiments, however, have studied its operation instead of treating it as a nuisance and have found provocative results. Stanford (1966) examined in two experiments the special situation of "closed" decks of ESP cards,
where the subjects knew that there would be five of each
symbol within the deck. Subjects typically called freely at
first, then tried to balance the remaining responses. Stanford found that in the first 10 calls, variance of hits was
normal; but in the latter calls, variance was low. (This,
like other research showing low variance, poses a mystery:
how can the subject use his ESP to have fewer high scores
and also fewer low scores than would be expected by chance?)

Subsequent ingenious experiments explored response
bias further and concurred on a finding which may be of
major theoretical importance. Stanford (1967) reviewed pri-
or work which indicated that ESP calls on the less preferred
targets had higher scores than on the more preferred and
conducted an experiment with 50 target choices that confirmed

the prior work. (The difference between hits on low-frequency and hits on high-frequency targets was significant at P = . 00005.) Kreitler and Kreitler (1972, 1973), in a series of brilliant experiments, rediscovered the effect and strongly confirmed it. They found ESP hits in response to telepathic messages to be higher for those subliminal stimuli that were far below threshold than for those only a little below; to be higher for autokinetic movement in the nonpreferred direction than in the preferred; and to be higher for infrequent themes or words in TAT stories than for frequent ones. They conclude that "ESP information is communicated through a lowly-attended channel different from that of usual perception and attains attentional effectiveness when conflicting with stimulation of similar strength" (Kreitler and Kreitler, 1973, p163).

Interpersonal Relations

Between experimenter and subject. From the earliest days of psychical research, what we now call the experimenter effect was often noted; some sitters were likely to find better results than others at mediumistic sittings. In early research at Rhine's laboratory at Duke, a similar effect was found with ESP calls: two experimenters who were meticulous in following the same formal procedure predicted and found that one would elicit significantly higher ESP scores than the other (Pratt and Price, 1938). Similar effects have appeared repeatedly (Osis and Dean, 1964) and the general interpretation is that an experimenter who is more distant or shy or ill at ease will find lower ESP scores than one who is more outgoing and more comfortable with the procedure.

One of the most striking of these experiments was by West and Fisk (1953). One experimenter, who had had prior success in eliciting high scores in ESP experiments, was the only one to have contact with the subjects. All contact was by mail and subjects were not informed that there was a second experimenter. Half the targets were prepared by the experimenter with prior success and half by an experimenter with prior failure in eliciting high scores. The concealed targets prepared by the one whose earlier ESP work had shown good scores yielded significant hits above chance (P = . 001), while the concealed targets prepared by the other gave chance scores. This implies a curiously subtle effect of ESP.

A somewhat similar finding appeared in a series of experiments-by-letter where there was no face-to-face contact between experimenters and subjects. Initial results came from a session when the coexperimenter was sick, but nevertheless conscientiously laid out the targets at the assigned time. Targets were laid out face down and he never knew what they were. Scores from the day he was sick were so much lower than when he was well that the effect of experimenter mood was examined in later experiments in the series. In the final experiment (Osis and Carlson, 1972) subjects were informed that Osis would be the experimenter and no subject knew that a coexperimenter would be there with him. Both Osis and his coexperimenter recorded their moods and the subjects' scores varied with the moods of the coexperimenter.

Rao (1968) published an account of what seems to be a similar effect: instances where high scores were associated with an inadvertent error in experimental procedure. In all cases the subjects' responses showed an interesting correspondence to the errors. Rao is conservative in interpreting the results of these laboratory accidents, and leaves open the question whether the obtained results are only coincidental, whether they show subjects' response to the special situation, or whether they show experimenters' ESP response to the subjects' data, resulting in the experimenter's making an ESP-guided mistake to satisfy his needs.

Experimenter effects of the more conventional sort were demonstrated by Anderson and White (see White and Angstadt, 1965). Anderson and White prepared and concealed targets and instructional materials to cooperative high school teachers. The teachers administered the ESP test to their own classes, but did not know the targets. Data were evaluated according to two scores: the teachers' feeling about each of the pupils, and the pupils' feeling about their teacher, each scored objectively from a question or questionnaire. ESP scores were higher for pupils who gave a favorable response to the teacher than for other pupils ($P = .000003$) and they were higher for pupils to whom the teacher gave a favorable response than for other pupils ($P = .0001$). They were overwhelmingly higher when both pupils' and teacher's responses were favorable ($P = .00000001$). Similar methods used by other experimenters often failed to support these findings, but sometimes (e.g., Nash, 1968) succeeded. Since Anderson was an outstandingly persuasive and effective teacher, the interpretation of the partial failure to replicate is presumably that Anderson's selection and indoctrination of the cooperating teachers developed in them a mood of interest and involvement that other experimenters often failed to develop in their cooperating teachers.

Between pairs of subjects. A different kind of interpersonal effect was studied by Kanthamani (1966) in an unreplicated experiment. Subjects were same-sexed pairs of high school friends. Kanthamani presented the ESP task to them as a competitive game that each would try to win by having more successes. She gave them some practice tries, then made a private record of which was the dominant and which the submissive member of the pair. ESP scores in the subsequent formal test were above chance expectation for the dominant friend and below chance expectation for the submissive friend. This implies that the subjects were using ESP to produce the psi-hitting or psi-missing that satisfied their interpersonal needs.

Several experiments examined telepathy (GESP) between pairs of twins, engaged couples, or other pairs expected to have a close relationship. Some experimenters found markedly higher scores within these pairs than within pairs of strangers; but other experimenters did not. Perhaps the special quality of the experimental situation can, when it is aversive, override interpersonal feelings. An interesting and informative account of interpersonal relations is the series of anecdotes by Schwarz (1971) about his own family, where interplay between parents and children, and the effect of other events such as the death of a relative or the anticipation of Christmas, are carefully traced for their relation to ESP.

One more experiment should be cited in this context (Schmeidler, 1961). Rorschachs of students who had not met were analyzed in pairs, and the prediction made either that a pair would be congenial when they met, or else that they would be hostile or reserved. The pairs were brought together, introduced, given instructions, then one was taken to a separated room to act as agent in telepathy (GESP) tests using prerandomized stimuli. Results showed significantly lower scores for pairs predicted to be hostile or reserved. However, when the percipient believed conditions were the same, but the agent was instructed (a) not to look at the targets and (b) to hope the percipient would fail, results flip-flopped and the pairs predicted to be hostile or reserved made significantly higher scores. This seems another example of a double negative resulting in a positive.

Within groups of subjects. Warcollier (1948) reported that when a group of friendly psychics tried to respond to a distant target, they often seemed instead to respond to each others' impressions.

Weisinger (1973) tested 325 schoolboys and found that their ESP responses resembled those of their most popular classmates, but avoided the responses of the least popular ones. A minor study along the same lines (Schmeidler and Goldberg, 1974) examined interplay in a mixed group consisting of a psychic, some of his friends whom he judged to have psychic ability, and also some control subjects. The psychic's friends showed significantly more correspondence to his responses when he was right than when he was wrong, but the control subjects did not.

Cognition

Intelligence. Positive correlations have been reported between IQ and ESP score for children or college students tested at school (Humphrey, 1945), but the relation must have been suspect from the first since a very early study (Bond, 1937) reported high ESP scores from a class of retarded children. Since some preschool and young school children show high ESP scores when tested under friendly conditions, mental age seems not to relate to ESP success. The implication is that the positive relations obtained between IQ and ESP hits are spurious, and that the contaminating factor is that brighter students tend to be happier than others in most classrooms and therefore to participate more readily in its tasks, including ESP tasks. This implication has recently been supported by scattered reports of no correlation between IQ and ESP. We should note also the significantly low ESP scores found in the write-in test whose subjects were members of Mensa, an intellectual organization where high IQ is a requisite for membership (Brier, 1967).

School achievement. Anderson (1959) reported a positive relation between school grades and ESP score when ESP tests were administered by the class teachers. This lends itself to the same interpretation as the positive correlations with IQ. When I examined my own students' grades to find if the relation existed, I found it only for students with a high need for achievement, i. e., only among students for whom grades were presumably important.

Memory. Feather (1967) reported rank order correlations ranging from + .28 to + .66 between ESP score and
recall for lists of ESP symbols (presented as a learning
task). The study has not been replicated and includes no
controls for differences in motivation, which might have accounted for the similarity of scores on the two tasks.

Learning. Schmidt (1969) and Targ and Hurt (1971)
used machines that give immediate feedback and permit quick
responses, so that many trials can be made in a single session. Each reports a subject who improved in ESP performance. If all subjects improved, the data would imply
learning; but most do not. Schmidt interprets the improvement as a function of motivation. In many prior experiments and some subsequent ones, relatively quick feedback
was given by the experimenter. Most show no evidence of
learning. A recent series first claimed and then disclaimed
it (McCollam and Honorton, 1973). In the earlier experiments of the series there was a yoked control group that received false feedback and thus as many positive reinforce-
ments as the experimental group. The control group showed
no improvement. In the first two experiments of the series
the experimental group improved in the accuracy of their
confidence statements about correct calls, but in the third
experiment one experimental group improved, but one showed no
change, and one became worse. The group with improvement had the least feedback and the authors concluded that
the data do not support the hypothesis of discriminative
learning.

Tart (1966) offers an interesting explanation of subjects' apparent failure to learn. Since the likelihood of
chance success is 1/4 with the Schmidt and Targ machines,
and 1/5 with ESP cards, five or six chance successes will
probably on average be reinforced in a standard length run.
Since few subjects average better than one additional correct
call in a series of this length, feedback is on average likely
to reinforce about five accidental successes for every ESP
success. Feedback thus should teach the subjects to give
chance rather than ESP responses.

Lack of recognition of ESP. In some half dozen experiments, subjects have been given ESP tests while they
believed they were responding to subliminal stimuli or a
memory task. Most but not all of these experiments showed
significantly high scores, as in Kreitler and Kreitler (1972,
1973). Two other recent ones will be described. Johnson

(1973) gave a short answer final examination to his classes. With an appropriate cover story, he taped below the answer blanks a concealed set of correct answers to half the questions. Approximately half of each class had these concealed answers for one set of questions, half for the others. His subjects were wholly unsuspicious. Significantly higher scores were assigned by a blind judge to the questions with concealed answers beneath them. Stanford (1974, p40-1), in an ingenious experiment, presented to his subjects what was ostensibly a memory task for material so long and detailed that they could not remember all of it. Some of the "memory" questions dealt with items that could have been, but were not, initially presented. He scored these latter answers for ESP and found significantly high results, which he interpreted to mean that we may often use ESP unwittingly in our daily life when we think we are relying upon memory or inference, or that we are acting on impulse.

Lack of awareness of ESP or PK specifics. In many experiments subjects have obtained high scores although they did not know where the ESP target was or what it was (whether a card or only a symbol representing the card, a picture, or a thought about the picture) or did not know how to produce the PK (e.g., whether a tumbling die should be given a turn to the left or to the right). Two of these reports will be cited.

In an experiment by Schmidt and Pantas (1972), success was signaled to the subject by a light. The subject's task was to keep the light coming on by pushing the "right" button on a console in front of him. He was not informed that his console was sometimes attached to circuitry which scored precognition and sometimes switched to circuitry which scored PK. Subjects scored significantly high in both conditions with no awareness that they were succeeding on two different tasks.

In a precognition experiment (Schmeidler, 1964), subjects called the five ESP symbols and five colors. The experimenter coded the calls into digits for computer scoring. The computer was programmed to select pseudorandom targets, score them against the subjects' calls, and print out the calls and total number of hits, but not print out the targets. Subjects were not aware of these arrangements, but scored significantly high. They were consciously trying to identify the symbols or colors, but their scores showed that they had identified internal computer changes. Their psi seemed to be goal oriented rather than means oriented, as was true also in the Schmidt and Pantas experiment.

Information processing. A hint about the answer to the problem of how information is processed comes from Child and Kelly (1973), who used a pretested subject for ESP card guessing with imbalanced decks: decks with 9, 7, 5, 3, 1, of the various symbols. The subject not only made more hits than would be expected by chance, but also on incorrect calls tended to adjust his call frequency to the target frequency without being aware that he was doing so. Apparently the holistic pattern of imbalance was registered and processed, aside from precise information about each card.

THEORETICAL IMPLICATIONS FOR PSYCHOLOGY

Personality and Social Psychology

Personality findings in parapsychology fit neatly into psychological theory. The higher scores of receptive, open, and cooperative subjects compared to withdrawn, defensive, or negativistic subjects; the effect of anxiety and arousal; and the patterns of interpersonal relations tend to confirm conventional psychological expectations of how these factors affect performance on any non-ESP task. Some of the research also provides a few new minor insights that converge upon these expectations. There is no theoretical conflict here, merely enlargement and enrichment of other personality and social findings.

One major extension of existing theory deserves comment. ESP research has shown that potential personal relationships can affect task performance even when the subject does not know the other person and is unaware that the other person is involved. This markedly extends our concept of effective human relations and has broad implications for social psychology.

Cognition. The finding that performance can be effective without knowledge of the specifics of the task is not an unfamiliar one in psychology, though too often it is brushed under the rug. Sherrington said long ago that the spinal cord thinks in movements, not in muscles. We know that a person can tie his shoelaces well even though he cannot report his sequence of movements. Imageless thought posed the same issue: a person can give a correct answer to a difficult problem before he has consciously spelled out the reasoning behind his answer. Parapsychological data add further examples that seem coordinate with these, where-in a subject succeeds at a task without awareness of what the task demands. The suggestion from parapsychology is that he responds to the meaning, to the general pattern, to some holistic grasp of generalities. It raises the old question of the meaning of "meaning," and may be of service to psychology in restating the problem so forcefully that we know we need to confront it.

A further problem raised by parapsychology perhaps belongs rather to physics or to physiology than to psychology. It is the question of how ESP information is transmitted to the subject and how PK from him is transmitted. If it is included in the list of theoretical issues relevant to psychology, it can be useful to us only as a reminder that there are perceptual and response potentialities that need to be explored.

Altered states of consciousness. There is convergent evidence from many research projects that ESP is more likely to be effective in a relaxed but motivated state reminiscent of meditation or hypnosis than with a critical, reality-oriented attitude. This opens the possibility that different modes of perception dominate response in the "altered" and in the normal state. LeShan (1974) proposes a bold statement of this position: that there are not only different modes of perceiving reality but also that there are different kinds of reality to be perceived. He contrasts the everyday world of solid objects located in three-dimensional space and having a unidirectional flow of time, with the physicists' view of energy flux and perhaps of bidirectional time flow. This second view seems astonishingly similar to reports from psychics and from many mystics--so similar that when modern physicists put their concepts into words, their statements are indistinguishable from those of mystics and psychics. (I tested this out on my graduate classes, and LeShan was right, at least as far as my classes and I were concerned. We were likely to attribute quotations from Einstein, Eddington, and Oppenheimer to mystics or psychics, and vice versa.) It is common to say that there are different levels of reality; but it would be a major theoretical contribution to cognitive psychology if we could demonstrate that altering our conscious state permits a shift from perceiving one level of reality to perceiving another.

Suppose that we take this as a working hypothesis and try to examine it. A question which immediately arises is how we can shift from one perceptual framework to another. Here the introspections of psychics (White, 1964) offer a set of clues: relaxation and a kind of purposeful concentration, "stilling the mind," and waiting; the rejection of personal associations; the incursion of some idea that does not have the feel of a personal association; followed by a feeling of release. All this is astonishingly like the descriptions of the creative process that have been extracted from intro-spective reports. It also overlaps with at least two sets of the experimental findings reported above: the high ESP scores of subjects in certain relaxed and "altered" states and the high ESP scores when ESP messages are inconsistent with response bias. The hypothesis deserves further study.

POSSIBLE APPLICATIONS

The characteristic that makes psi so elusive in the laboratory, its sensitivity to mood and to interpersonal influences, may be one that makes it especially useful for diagnostic testing of interpersonal relations. I will propose a research application and a clinical application; each suggests many other possibilities.

In a study of a group's interactions, verbal reports and questionnaires are likely to give less useful information than such behavioral measures as body lean, eye contacts, speech subtleties, or perhaps even chair placement. These latter are hard to measure objectively; ESP scores are easier. An ESP test in which various members act as percipients may show that a person will make high ESP scores with one sender, chance scores with another, and below-chance scores with a third. These could be interpreted as measures of his feelings of closeness or withdrawal to the various agents; other more refined measures (such as variance or displacement) are also available. Later tests of the same type could indicate whether the feelings have been stable or have shifted. In the clinic, a similar measure might (in the absence of other information) indicate which of the available therapists has elicited a more forthcoming response from a child, or how one person's feelings shift, perhaps without his being conscious of it, according to some change in another's behavior.

There is a different, broader way in which the theory of psi may ultimately affect practical affairs. In our private ethical codes, we are accustomed to thinking that outward behavior is morally important because it can help or hurt others, but that our thoughts are private and socially irrelevant: that they can be hurtful without doing others harm, or helpful without doing them good. Religious codes often state otherwise ("as a man thinketh in his heart, so is he") but the nonreligious person may well believe that ethics demand only good or at least nonhurtful actions. Data from parapsychology, however, show that hidden feelings can directly influence others and therefore seem to demand a revision of the nonreligious ethical requirements.

REFERENCES

Anderson, M. "The Relationship Between Level of ESP Scoring and Student Class Grade." Journal of Parapsychology, 23 (1959), 1-18.

André, E. "Confirmation of PK Action on Electronic Equipment." Journal of Parapsychology, 36 (1972), 283-93.

Beloff, J., and Bate, D. "Research Report for the Year 1968-69." Journal of the Society for Psychical Research, 45 (1970), 297-301.

Bhadra, B. R. Unpublished doctoral dissertation, Sri Venkateswara University, Tirupati, India, 1965.

Bond, E. M. "General Extrasensory Perception with a Group of Fourth and Fifth Grade Retarded Children." Journal of Parapsychology, 1 (1937), 114-22.

Braud, L. W., and Braud, W. G. "Further Studies of Relaxation as a Psi-Conducive State." Journal of the American Society for Psychical Research, 68 (1974), 229-45.

Braud, W. G., and Braud, L. W. "Preliminary Explorations of Psi-Conducive States: Progressive Muscular Relaxation." Journal of the American Society for Psychical Research, 67 (1973), 26-46.

Breitstein, H. Unpublished master's thesis, City College of the City University of New York, 1972.

Brier, B. "A Correspondence ESP Experiment with High-I. Q. Subjects." Journal of Parapsychology, 31 (1967), 143-8.

Buzby, D. E. "Subject Attitude and Score Variance on ESP Tests." Journal of Parapsychology, 31 (1967), 43-50.

Carpenter, J. C. "Further Study on a Mood Adjective Check List and ESP Run-Score Variance." Journal of

Parapsychology, 33 (1969), 48-56.
_____ "The Differential Effect and Hidden Target Differences Consisting of Erotic and Neutral Stimuli. " Journal of the American Society for Psychical Research, 65 (1971), 204-14.
_____ and Carpenter, J. C. "Decline of Variability of ESP Scoring Across a Period of Effort. " Journal of Parapsychology, 31 (1967), 179-91.

Child, I. L. , and Kelly, E. F. "ESP with Unbalanced Decks: A Study of the Process in an Exceptional Subject. " Journal of Parapsychology, 37 (1973), 278-97.

Duane, T. D. , and Behrendt, R. "Extrasensory Electroencephalographic Induction Between Identical Twins. " Science, 150, no. 3694 (1965), 367.

Eastman, M. Unpublished master's thesis, City College of the City University of New York, 1966.

Eysenck, H. J. "Personality and Extra-Sensory Perception." Journal of the Society for Psychical Research, 44 (1967) 55-71.

Fahler, J. , and Osis, K. "Checking for Awareness of Hits in a Precognition Experiment with Hypnotized Subjects. " Journal of the American Society for Psychical Research, 60 (1966), 340-6.

Feather, S. R. "A Quantitative Comparison of Memory and Psi. " Journal of Parapsychology, 31 (1967), 93-8.
_____ and Rhine, L. E. "PK Experiments with Same and Different Targets. " Journal of Parapsychology, 33 (1969), 213-27.

Fisk, G. W. , and West, D. J. "ESP and Mood: Report of a 'Mass' Experiment. " Journal of the Society for Psychical Research, 38 (1956), 320-9.

Green, C. E. "The Effect of Birth Order and Family Size on Extrasensory Perception. " Journal of the Society for Psychical Research, 43 (1965), 181-91.

Green, E. Report to the Third Interdisciplinary Conference on the Voluntary Control of Internal States, Council Grove, Kansas, 1971.

Honorton, C. "Reported Frequency of Dream Recall and ESP. " Journal of the American Society for Psychical Research, 66 (1972), 369-74.
_____, Drucker, S. A. , and Hermon, H. C. "Shifts in Subjective State and ESP Under Conditions of Partial Sensory Deprivation: A Preliminary Study. " Journal of the American Society for Psychical Research, 67 (1973), 191-6.

          and Krippner, S.   "Hypnosis and ESP Performance:
    A Review of the Experimental Literature. " Journal of
    the American Society for Psychical Research, 63 (1969),
    214-52.
Humphrey, B. M.   "ESP and Intelligence. " Journal of Para-
    psychology, 9 (1945), 7-16.
          .   "Success in ESP as Related to Form of Response
    Drawings: I. Clairvoyance Experiments. " Journal of
    Parapsychology, 10 (1946), 78-106.
Johnson, M.   "A New Technique of Testing ESP in a Real-
    Life, High-Motivational Context. " Journal of Parapsy-
    chology, 37 (1973), 210-7.
          and Kanthamani, B. K.   "The Defense Mechanism
    Test as a Predictor of ESP Scoring Direction. " Journal
    of Parapsychology, 31 (1967), 99-110.
Kanthamani, B. K.   "ESP and Social Stimulus. " Journal of
    Parapsychology, 30 (1966), 31-8.
          and Rao, K. R.   "Personality Characteristics of
    ESP Subjects: V. Graphic Expansiveness and ESP. "
    Journal of Parapsychology, 37 (1973), 119-29.
Kreitler, H. , and Kreitler, S.   "Does Extrasensory Percep-
    tion Affect Psychological Experiments?" Journal of Para-
    psychology, 36 (1972), 1-45.
          and   .   "Subliminal Perception and Extra-
    sensory Perception. " Journal of Parapsychology, 37
    (1973), 163-88.
Krippner, S. , Honorton, C. , Ullman, M. , Masters, R. ,
    and Houston, J.   "A Long-Distance 'Sensory Bombard-
    ment' Study of ESP in Dreams. " The Journal of the
    American Society for Psychical Research, 65 (1971),
    468-75.
LeShan, L.   The Medium, the Mystic, and the Physicist:
    Toward a General Theory of the Paranormal.   New York:
    Viking Press, 1974.
McCollam, E. , and Honorton, C.   "Effects of Feedback on
    Discrimination Between Correct and Incorrect ESP Re-
    sponses: A Further Replication and Extension. " Jour-
    nal of the American Society for Psychical Research, 67
    (1973), 77-85.
Moriarty, A. , and Murphy, G.   "An Experimental Study of
    ESP Potential and Its Relationship to Creativity in a
    Group of Normal Children. " Journal of the American
    Society for Psychical Research, 61 (1967), 326-38.
Moss, T.   "ESP Effects in 'Artists' Contrasted with 'Non-
    Artists'. " Journal of Parapsychology, 33 (1969), 57-69.

Nash, C. B. "Comparison of ESP Run Score Averages of Groups Liked and Disliked by the Experimenter." Journal of the American Society for Psychical Research, 62 (1968), 411-4.

Nielsen, W. "Relationships Between Precognition Scoring Level and Mood." Journal of Parapsychology, 34 (1970), 93-116.

_____ and Freeman, J. "Consistency of Relationship Between ESP and Emotional Variables." Journal of Parapsychology, 29 (1965), 75-88.

Osis, K., and Bokert, E. "ESP and Changed States of Consciousness Induced by Meditation." Journal of the American Society for Psychical Research, 65 (1971), 17-65.

_____ and Carlson, M. L. "The ESP Channel--Open or Closed?" Journal of the American Society for Psychical Research, 66 (1972), 310-9.

_____ and Dean, D. "The Effect of Experimenter Differences and Subjects' Belief Level Upon ESP Scores." Journal of the American Society for Psychical Research, 58 (1964), 158-85.

Palmer, J. "Scoring in ESP Tests as a Function of Belief in ESP. I. The Sheep-Goat Effect." Journal of the American Society for Psychical Research, 65 (1971), 373-408.

Pratt, J. G. "The Meaning of Performance Curves in ESP and PK Test Data." Journal of Parapsychology, 13 (1949), 9-23.

_____. "A Decade of Research with a Selected ESP Subject: An Overview and Reappraisal of the Work with Pavel Stepanek." Proceedings of the American Society for Psychical Research, 30 (1973), 1-78.

_____ and Price, M. M. "The Experimenter-Subject Relationship in Tests for ESP." Journal of Parapsychology, 2 (1938), 84-94.

_____, Rhine, J. B., Smith, B. M., Stuart, C. E., and Greenwood, J. A. Extrasensory Perception After Sixty Years. Boston: Branden Press, 1966 (first published in 1940).

Rao, K. R. "The Bidirectionality of Psi." Journal of Parapsychology, 29 (1965), 230-50.

_____. "Spontaneous ESP in Laboratory Tests: The Error Phenomenon." Journal of the American Society for Psychical Research, 62 (1968), 63-72.

Rogers, D. P. "An Analysis for Internal Cancellation Effects on Some Low-Variance ESP Runs." Journal of Parapsychology, 31 (1967), 192-8.

Sailaja, P., and Rao, K. R. Experimental Studies of the

Differential Effect in Life Setting. New York: Parapsychology Foundation, 1973. (Parapsychological Monographs, no. 13.)

Schmeidler, G. R. "Personal Values and ESP Scores." Journal of Abnormal and Social Psychology, 47 (1952), 757-61.

_____. "Evidence for Two Kinds of Telepathy." International Journal of Parapsychology, 3 (1961), 5-48.

_____. "An Experiment on Precognitive Clairvoyance." Journal of Parapsychology, 28 (1964), 1-27.

_____ and Craig, J. G. "Moods and ESP Scores in Group Testing." Journal of the American Society for Psychical Research, 66 (1972), 280-7.

_____ and Goldberg, J. "Evidence for Selective Telepathy in Group Psychometry." In W. G. Roll, R. L. Morris, and J. D. Morris (eds.), Research in Parapsychology 1973 (Metuchen, N. J.: Scarecrow Press, 1974), p103-6.

_____ and LeShan, L. "An Aspect of Body Image Related to ESP Scores." Journal of the American Society for Psychical Research, 64 (1970), 211-8.

Schmidt, H. "Precognition of a Quantum Process." Journal of Parapsychology, 33 (1969), 99-108.

_____ and Pantas, L. "Psi Tests With Internally Different Machines." Journal of Parapsychology, 36 (1972), 222-32.

Schwarz, B. E. Parent-Child Telepathy. New York: Garrett Publications, 1971.

Shields, E. "Comparison of Children's Guessing Ability (ESP) with Personality Characteristics." Journal of Parapsychology, 26 (1962), 200-10.

Soal, S. G., and Bateman, F. Modern Experiments in Telepathy. New Haven, Conn.: Yale University Press, 1954.

Stanford, R. G. "The Effect of Restriction of Calling Upon Run-Score Variance." Journal of Parapsychology, 30 (1966), 160-71.

_____. "Response Bias and the Correctness of ESP Test Responses." Journal of Parapsychology, 31 (1967), 280-9.

_____. "Associative Activation of the Unconscious' and 'Visualization' as Methods for Influencing the PK Target." Journal of the American Society for Psychical Research, 63 (1969), 338-51.

_____. "An Experimentally Testable Model for Spontaneous Psi Events. I. Extrasensory Events." Journal of the American Society for Psychical Research, 68 (1974),

34-57.

Targ, R. , and Hurt, D. B. "Learning Clairvoyance and Precognition with an ESP Teaching Machine. " Proceedings of the Parapsychological Association, 8 (1971), 9-11.

Tart, C. T. "Card Guessing Tests: Learning Paradigm or Extinction Paradigm?" Journal of the American Society for Psychical Research, 60 (1966), 46-55.

Ullman, M. , and Krippner, S. , with A. Vaughan. Dream Telepathy. New York: Macmillan, 1973.

Warcollier, R. Mind to Mind. New York: Creative Age Press, 1948.

Weisinger, C. "Two ESP Experiments in the Classroom. " Journal of Parapsychology, 37 (1973), 76-7 (abstract).

West, D. J. , and Fisk, G. W. "A Dual ESP Experiment with Clock Cards. " Journal of the Society for Psychical Research, 37 (1953), 185-97.

White, R. A. "A Comparison of Old and New Methods of Response to Targets in ESP Experiments. Journal of the American Society for Psychical Research, 58 (1964), 21-56.

_____ and Angstadt, J. "A Review of Results and New Experiments Bearing on Teacher-Selection Methods in the Anderson-White High School Experiments. " Journal of the American Society for Psychical Research, 59 (1965), 56-84.

Robert L. Van de Castle

SOME POSSIBLE ANTHROPOLOGICAL CONTRIBUTIONS
TO THE STUDY OF PARAPSYCHOLOGY

The historical development of parapsychology has been
characterized by efforts to progress from an initial collection of anecdotal reports to a later careful, systematic investigation in the laboratory setting.   Through collecting
anecdotes, it becomes possible to survey the range and
variety of phenomena that might possess a possible paranormal origin and to examine cases for detection of similar
features that might lead to the construction of hypotheses to
account for these similarities.   To date, considerable anecdotal evidence dealing with possible psychic occurrences has
been collected from individuals in the United States and in
Great Britain.   An excellent collection of such anecdotal
material from subjects in Western society is provided in
Louisa Rhine's book, Hidden Channels of the Mind (1961).

Although parapsychology has made significant strides
in terms of receiving greater acceptance by the scientific and
academic communities, it still suffers from a lack of suitable
theoretical models and from our inability to specify the conditions that could lead to a reasonable approximation of a
repeatable experiment.   Perhaps one of the difficulties lies
in the fact that we have centered our investigative efforts
too narrowly upon members of our own culture.   One is reminded of the story about the inebriated individual who was
busily engaged in searching the sidewalk underneath a street
light.   After observing his frantic activities for several
minutes, someone approached him and asked what he was
doing.   The drunk explained that he was looking for a key
he had lost.   When asked if he were sure that he had lost
it in that area, the drunk explained that he had lost his key
in a nearby alley but that it was too dark to see there so he
decided it would be easier to look under the lamppost.   Few

parapsychologists have ventured away from the well-illuminated sidewalks of our cities or from the ready availability of our undergraduate populations to explore what types of psi events may exist in other settings or what levels of psi ability may be present among non-Western subjects.

It has been estimated that 4000 to 5000 human societies existed during the last century. Nature's laboratory has thus provided us with a rich diversity of variables such as genetic patterns, diet, child-rearing practices, forms of family organization, religious rituals, and usage of mind-altering drugs. These are only a few of the large number of factors upon which various cultures could be contrasted. It would be impossible to duplicate such sampling differences within our own culture and in our present state of ignorance it would be premature to dismiss any of these variables as being irrelevant. Darwin's theory of evolution would never have been propounded had he remained in England; perhaps parapsychologists might discover the psychic equivalent of what the Galapagos Islands represented for Darwin if they also were to journey off to distant lands and observe at first hand how psi products can be shaped by environmental and cultural influences.

The lack of investigation of non-Western societies by parapsychologists would not be so unfortunate if useful accounts about possible paranormal phenomena were being provided by anthropologists. Anthropologists, however, because of their own cultural myopia, have generally failed to consider the possibility that genuine paranormal events might be possible. Although thousands of anthropologists have engaged in field studies of non-Western societies, only a few reports are available in which the anthropologist was willing to consider that a paranormal basis might underlie some of the unusual phenomena he observed. Typical of the view held by most contemporary anthropologists would be the following statement found in a standard reference book on magical practices (Middleton and Winter, 1963): "They are termed magical from the point of view of the anthropologist because there are no grounds in terms of Western science for believing them able to accomplish the ends claimed for them" (p13). Consistent with such an orientation, many anthropologists consider witch doctors or shamans to be psychotics, and native practitioners of magic as charlatans who resort to shabby sleight-of-hand tricks to produce their puzzling feats.

Magic does come in for some consideration by anthropologists as a means of sustaining social institutions.
Witchcraft is thus viewed as a mechanism for expressing
intragroup hostility and jealousy since such accusations are
generally leveled toward the more economically advantaged
or socially alienated members of a group. Harrington and
Whiting (1972) provide a good review of how anthropologists
account for supernatural beliefs through the socialization process. Among some of the examples they cite are that societies high in the overall indulgence of infants tend not to
fear ghosts at funerals, that societies characterized by severe weaning practices believe that sickness is caused by the
ingestion of magically poisoned food, and that love magic is
more common in societies where strong anxieties about sexual socialization are present.

An important factor that has hindered the focusing
of greater attention upon possible paranormal events in the
non-Western societies by both anthropologists and parapsychologists is that no comprehensive review is available of
ethnographic material that contains presumptive evidence of
psi components at work. The best source that I know of in
English is the book by de Vesme (1931), although it suffers
from a lack of criticality and no effort is made to evaluate
the evidence offered. Several accounts are found in a book
by Lang (1900), and Oesterreich (1966) has three chapters
dealing with possession cases and shamanism. Rose (1956)
has collected several anecdotal accounts concerning the psychic abilities of Australian aborigines and St. Clair (1971)
offers many firsthand observations concerning healing, divination, and psychokinesis among spiritist groups in Brazil.
Probably the best foreign-language review is that provided in
Italian by de Martino (1942, 1943-46), but Zorab (1957) also
lists several other non-English titles in his Bibliography of
Parapsychology.

Perhaps it would be useful at this point to give a
few examples of the types of accounts that have been given
by some authors.

Rose (1956) describes how three different individuals seemed to be aware that a tribal member had died on a
particular day. One of them described his feelings as follows:

> I'm sure something happened to me when Billie
> Combo died, and I'm sure it was caused by his

death. I was on the station here at Woodenbong
that day. Suddenly I felt dopey--it was as if a
cloud came over my mind. I couldn't think; I was
depressed and upset.

When I went to lie down, my wife asked me
what was wrong. I said, 'I don't know but it's
serious.' She said, 'Is it one of our people,
Walter?' I said, 'No,' because if it had been one
of our people, that is, someone related closely to
us your way or by the totem, I would have seen
my totem rooster I always see when one of us dies.
The rooster is the one that tells me of such things.

But I had this strange feeling just the same
[p130-1].

The deceased Billy Combo was a cousin of this person, but
was not a totem relative.

An older woman who was described as generally
cheerful reported that a heavy feeling had come over her the
day that Billie died. Her words were "It comes awful heavy,
that feeling. When I had it last week, I knew one of my
people was gone. It was a feeling full of death. All our
people know it" (p131).

The third individual was reported to know the identity
of the deceased because he and Billie both had the crow totem. He claimed that he was given the information by a
black crow that appeared to him in a vision. Rose comments that this belief of a spirit totem appearing to a clan
member when a totemic relative dies is widely held among
tribalized aborigines.

The methods used for eliciting psi information vary
greatly. In his book, With Graciela to the Head-Hunters,
Boeldke (1958) described a Quechua who specialized in telling
the future from the smoke of his cigar and gave an instance
of an accurate but unexpected prediction with this method.
Boeldke also relates an instance where a clairvoyant attached to his party of tribesmen was consulted because a
group they were to have met failed to turn up. The clairvoyant mixed some cocoa leaves with lime and with a tree
bark called chamayo which he chewed, then spat the mixture
into his hand and shook it. When he opened his hand the
practitioner examined the pattern and stated that the others
would never reach them and that the main party should stop
and force its way through the jungle and it would then meet

the other party before nightfall. He predicted that one of the
men would have an injured leg and another would have a hurt
back.   The Indians insisted on following this advice and
Boeldke claimed that everything turned out as it had been
foretold.

   A lengthier anecdote was first told by William Stead
in the April 1895 issue of Borderland.   An account is described in de Vesme (1931).   The account involves an Eng-
lishman who was hunting with a compatriot and a Boer 400
miles north of Pretoria.   They met a Kafir medicine man
whom they asked to tell their fortunes.   The witch-doctor
agreed to throw his "dol ossen" which consisted of a collection of objects made of glass, crockery, bone, stone, iron,
etc., that were cast upon the ground.   He first threw for
one of the group and said that this man had been across the
big waters to white man's country two or three years ago.
While there, the witch-doctor continued, this man had fallen
in love and was going to marry a young woman but that she
had died.   The diviner said that at the present time he was
engaged to another woman in Pretoria but that marriage would
never take place because her father would find fault with this
man's economic condition.   This man had been in Europe at
the time mentioned, had become engaged to a German girl
who died three months before their marriage date, and was
currently engaged to a woman in Pretoria.   Just as the past
and present details were correct, so too was the future prediction as four months later his fiancée's father broke off
the engagement because he disapproved of this man's financial position.

   When the witch-doctor threw his bones for Stead, he
initially refused to offer any interpretation and did not do so
until pressured after the third throw.   He then said that
Stead lived a half hour's journey by foot from "Proot Dorp,"
was married, and that the youngest of his two daughters,
who was 18 months old, was critically ill, and that his wife
was distraught because Stead would not return in time to
see his daughter again.   Unable to dismiss the matter lightly,
Stead took out his notebook and noted the day, time, and
words uttered by the witch-doctor and had his companion initial the account.   When Stead reached home six weeks later,
his wife confirmed that their youngest daughter had been so
ill that the doctors had given up on her and that on the day
of the bone-throwing, the wife repeatedly kept verbalizing
her concern that Stead would not return in time to see his
daughter again.

In addition to the reports involving ESP abilities, anecdotes concerning apparent PK powers are also available. The following description of his encounter with Edu, a high priest of the Umbanda cult in Brazil, has been provided by St. Clair (1971):

> He fingered a necklace of cowrie shells that was in front of him on the desk and watched as I got my tape recorder into position. 'I would prefer it if you didn't use that machine,' he said. 'Let's just converse.'
> I told him that I wanted to get his exact words on tape. That it was important for a foreign journalist to capture exact phrases because so many Brazilian reporters just made up their own quotes. Still he said he wished that I would put the recorder away. I argued that in such an important project as I was writing, he would want to have his exact words on paper. Finally he shut his eyes, remained silent for a few seconds and then, looking at the machine, said, 'Turn it on.'
> Delighted, I pushed the button and the reels started to turn. But to my dismay the tape came gushing up out of the box like plastic spaghetti! I slammed at the stop button but it did no good. Soon his desk was a pile of forever-ruined tape. 'This has never happened before,' I sputtered.
> 'You see?' he said with his soft voice and an even softer smile. 'Yemanjá didn't want you to use that machine either' [p185].

Other impressive anecdotes could be added to this brief selection (Van de Castle, 1974a), but the mere multiplication of examples would not carry much persuasive weight unless there were also some supportive empirical evidence available. The literature, to date, has been very sparse, but it does offer encouraging data that psi can be demonstrated with non-Western subjects under adequately controlled testing conditions.

Foster (1943) found significant above-chance scores in a clairvoyance test administered to 50 Plains Indian children at an Indian school in Manitoba. Ronald Rose (1956) and his wife Lyndon used standard ESP cards for individual tests of slightly over 50 Australian aborigines. Their overall deviation of 545 hits above chance expectation for the 665 runs administered was statistically significant at a very low P value.

I have been engaged in a long-term testing program with Cuna Indian adolescents from the San Blas Islands of Panama. Groups of about 25 junior high school students have been tested at a time. A total of 461 subjects, each of whom completed two GESP runs, had been tested by 1972. I served as agent for all sessions and the testing stimuli consisted of cards containing colored pictures of objects familiar to this culture: a jaguar, shark, conch shell, canoe, and propeller airplane. The overall results were almost exactly at the chance level, but a significant sex difference in favor of the girls was found. A total of 56 girls had been tested during two or more consecutive years and the correlation coefficient of +.30 between successive yearly scores was marginally significant (P < .05). The correlation coefficient of +.10 for the 174 boys tested during successive years was not significant, but the combined coefficient of +.15 for the two sexes combined was significant at less than the .05 level.

The most interesting finding was one involving dreams. Each student was requested to write in Spanish his most recent dream. These dreams were translated by Mac Chapin, an anthropologist who has lived among the Cunas for several years. The results are presented in more detail elsewhere (Van de Castle, 1974b), but two general patterns of dream content were found to be associated with above-chance ESP scores. One pattern involved the presence of aggressive, sexual, and animal imagery. This constellation seems to represent a form of "primary process" mentation in which censorship is minimal and the dreamer is open to the expression of his instinctual drives. The other dream pattern involved the presence of parents and certain relatives. Since the traditional values of the Cunas emphasize the traits of friendliness and cooperation, I have interpreted this pattern as one of identification with the main representatives of the cultural traditions, the extended family members, and such a dreamer seems thereby to have assimilated the Cuna qualities of helpfulness and hospitality.

The highest ESP scores were obtained by those who manifested elements of both the dream patterns described above. Thus the individual who seemed comfortable and unthreatened by his impulse life and who had incorporated the traditional tribal values of friendly cooperation was the subject who most often achieved ESP success. Although such a constellation seems consistent with the personality dynamics often attributed to successful ESP performers in our own society, its generalizability will not be known until similar dream studies have been carried out on a non-Cuna population.

Any investigator who works with subjects from another culture must, of course, always be flexible in attempting to adapt the testing situation to fit the particular preferences and skills of the native practitioner. A good example of such a practice was shown by the staff of the Psychical Research Foundation when working with Lalsingh Harribance. Harribance is a native of Trinidad who achieved considerable local fame for his ability to give psychic readings in a face-to-face situation. When tested with the standard ESP cards his results were unimpressive, but when he was confronted with the task of identifying the sex of persons shown in concealed photographs, he obtained highly significant results (Roll and Klein, 1972; Stump, Roll and Roll, 1970).

The techniques used for divination vary widely among native practitioners and there is probably no single method that would prove to be superior to any other. The important element, whether studying the arrangement of "bones" or the formation of curling smoke, appears to be that it provides a stimulus upon which the practitioner can fixate his attention and gradually narrow down his center of concentration. It is also important that there be some cultural acceptance of the procedure and that the practitioner believe in its efficacy. It is unlikely that an African witch-doctor would be very successful in reading tea leaves or that a sensitive in Boston would scrutinize the entrails of a freshly disembowled animal before making her predictions.

When it comes to the question of drugs, however, a different situation may prevail. Just as modern medicine has made extensive use of drugs such as curare and rauwolfia that were pharmaceutical agents employed by native healers, the possibility exists that some of the hallucinogenic substances ingested by tribal clairvoyants may prove to be psi-facilitative in our own culture. Dr. William McGovern (1927) an assistant curator of South American ethnology for the Field Museum of Natural History, provided the following report about natives of an Amazon village who had been drinking Banisteriopsi caapi (also called yage and ayahuasca).

> Curiously enough, certain of the Indians fell into a particularly deep state of trance, in which they possessed what appeared to be telepathic powers.

Two or three of the men described in great detail
what was going on in malokas hundreds of miles
away, many of which they had never visited, and
the inhabitants of which they had never seen, but
which seemed to tally exactly with what I knew of
the places and peoples concerned.   More extraordinary still, on this particular evening, the local
medicine-man told me that the chief of a certain
tribe on the faraway Pira Parana had suddenly
died.   I entered this statement in my diary and
many weeks later, when we came to the tribe in
question, I found that the witch-doctor's statement
had been true in every detail.   Possibly all these
cases were mere coincidences [p263].

Another account involves a Brazilian colonel named
Morales who was on a military mission in 1932 up the head-
waters territory of the Amazon near Eastern Peru.   He ingested some yage and asserted that

he heard the music of an orchestra playing in what
was apparently American surroundings.   He says
he also became conscious of the death of his sister
in a house far away from where he was located.
The house was in Rio de Janeiro some 2,900
miles distant, as the crow flies, from the remote
village where he then was.   A month later, a run-
ner brought him a letter ... telling him that his
sister had died about the time Morales had drunk
the infusion of the yage plant [Wilkins, 1948, p22].

A more recent description of the effects of ayahuasca
has been provided by the anthropologist, Kenneth Kensinger
(1973):

The Cashinahua drink ayahuasca in order to
learn about things, persons, and events removed
from them by time and/or space which could affect either the society as a whole or its individual
members.   Hallucinations generally involve scenes
which are a part of the Cashinahua's daily experience.   However, informants have described hallucinations about places far removed both geographi-
cally and from their own experience.   Several informants who have never been to or seen pictures
of Pucallpa, the large town at the Ucayali River
terminus of the Central Highway, have described

> their visits under the influence of ayahuasca to the
> town with sufficient detail for me to be able to
> recognize specific shops and sights. On the day
> following one ayahuasca party six of nine men in-
> formed me of seeing the death of my chai, my
> 'mother's father.' This occurred two days before
> I was informed by radio of his death [p12-3].

Since the parapsychological literature has been increasingly stressing that ESP scoring levels are generally
enhanced during altered states of consciousness (ASCs), one
could advance an argument that our culture is probably the
most unlikely to yield many cases of psi. From the cradle
onward, all forms of institutional authority are directed
toward ensuring that members will not be tempted to engage
in the pursuit of ASCs. Severe penalties in the forms of
fines and prison sentences are meted out to those deviants
who willfully pursue the paths of pleasure promised by ASC
adherents. Yet ASC is considered a desirable goal in most
non-Western societies. Bourguignon (1972) examined the data
available on 488 non-Western societies and found there was
some institutionalized form of dissociation present in 89 per
cent of these societies.

If a strong relationship between ASCs and psi does
exist, then it seems only logical that an investigator should
seek out those settings where ASCs would be frequently encountered so that he could better study the nature of this relationship. I hope that some of my fellow parapsychologists
will rise to this clarion call and vacate those comfortable
armchairs and start outfitting themselves for some prospec-
tive jungle safaris.

REFERENCES

Boeldke, A. With Graciela to the Head-Hunters. London:
    Barrie, 1958.
Bourguignon, E. "Dreams and Altered States of Conscious-
    ness in Anthropological Research." In F. L. Hsu (ed.),
    Psychological Anthropology, 2d ed. (Cambridge, Mass.:
    Schenkman, 1972), p403-34.
de Martino, E. "Percezione Estrasensoriale e Magismo
    Etnologico." Studi e Materiale di Storia delle Religi-
    one, 18 (1942), 1-20; (1943-1946), 31-84.
de Vesme, C. A History of Experimental Spiritualism,
    trans. by S. de Brath. Vol. 1. Primitive Man.

London: Rider, 1931.

Foster, A. A. "ESP Tests with American Indian Children. " Journal of Parapsychology, (1943), 94-103.

Harrington, C. , and Whiting, J. W. M. "Socialization Process and Personality. " In F. L. Hsu (ed.), Psychological Anthropology, 2d ed. (Cambridge, Mass. : Schenkman, 1972), p469-508.

Kensinger, K. M. "Banisteriopsis Usage Among the Peruvian Cashinahua. " In M. J. Harner (ed.), Hallucinogens and Shamanism (New York: Oxford University Press, 1973), p9-14.

Lang, A. The Making of Religion. London: Longmans, Green, 1900.

McGovern, W. M. Jungle Paths and Inca Ruins. New York: Grosset and Dunlap, 1927.

Middleton, J. F. , and Winter, E. H. (eds.). Witchcraft and Sorcery in East Africa. London: Routledge and Kegan Paul, 1963.

Oesterreich, T. K. Possession: Demonical and Other Among Primitive Races, in Antiquity, the Middle Ages, and Modern Times, trans. by D. Ibberson. Secaucus, N. J. : University Books, 1966.

Rhine, L. E. Hidden Channels of the Mind. New York: Sloane, 1961.

Roll, W. G. , and Klein, J. "Further Forced-Choice ESP Experiments with Lalsingh Harribance. " Journal of the American Society for Psychical Research, 66 (1972), 103-12.

Rose, R. Living Magic. Chicago: Rand McNally, 1956.

St. Clair, D. Drum and Candle. New York: Doubleday, 1971.

Stead, W. T. In Borderland (April 1895), 154.

Stump, J. P. , Roll, W. G. , and Roll, M. "Some Exploratory Forced-Choice ESP Experiments with Lalsingh Harribance. " Journal of the American Society for Psychical Research, 64 (1970), 421-31.

Van de Castle, R. L. "Anthropology and Psychic Research." In E. D. Mitchell et al. , Psychic Exploration, ed. by J. White (New York: Putnam's, 1974), p269-87. (a)

_____ . "An Investigation of Psi Abilities Among the Cuna Indians of Panama. " In A. Angoff and D. Barth (eds.), Parapsychology and Anthropology (New York: Parapsychology Foundation, 1974), p80-97. (b)

Wilkins, H. T. Devil Trees and Plants of Africa, Asia and South America. Girard, Kan. : Haldeman-Julius, 1948.

Zorab, G. Bibliography of Parapsychology. New York: Parapsychology Foundation, 1957.

Lawrence LeShan

WHAT IT FEELS LIKE TO BE A PARAPSYCHOLOGIST

The other papers in this volume concern the research
being done by parapsychologists today. I would like to shift
the emphasis here and focus on what it feels like to work in
this area. Perhaps this will be useful in adding to the understanding of the present position in parapsychology and of
the situation and motivation of those of us who work actively in this difficult and intriguing field.

Ours is a strange, crucial, and disturbing science.
If you are in close contact with it, you are likely to find it
upsetting both intellectually and emotionally. On every level
it is full of paradoxes.

The data fly in the face of common sense. By definition, paranormal events are occurrences that cannot happen, but do. They are fascinating and "mind-blowing" at
first and then, as William James pointed out, they tend to
become dull and boring on repetition. They are exciting and
stimulating and one would suppose that they would remain in
the memory and become exaggerated and more colorful with
time. The opposite is true, however; since the early part
of this century we have had clear evidence, as first noted
by F. W. H. Myers, that paranormal experiences tend to
slip out of the mind as time passes.

The methodology in parapsychology is extremely
tough-minded and rigorous. Because of the impossible nature of the data and the extremely critical attitude of scientists generally, it has had to develop in this direction until
the experiments could emulate Caesar's wife and be above
suspicion. Paradoxically, however, the field is constantly
accused of a lack of scientific rigor in its research.

162

The amount of data demonstrating the existence of paranormal occurrences is very large--so large that, it is sometimes said, with only a tenth of the evidence now in hand, the facts would be accepted as proven in any other field of science. Yet parapsychology is frequently accused of having no scientific facts to back its claims.

Parapsychology is the study of paranormal events, but it is deeply committed to the idea that there is no such thing as a paranormal event: that all events come under natural law and are therefore normal. (This, however, is qualified somewhat by the concept that some events are more normal than others. Beethoven's Ninth Symphony is not a paranormal event, but it is certainly not very normal!)

Both critics of parapsychology and its over-zealous believers frequently seem to lose all critical judgment when they cross what W. F. Prince (1930) called the "enchanted boundary" which separates this field from others. They behave in ways they never would in their own areas of specialization. In our field they either reject tight scientific data out of hand or else are only too ready to believe enthusiastically in what Jule Eisenbud has called "fact-free theories." Just as many of our critics act as if they had completely closed minds to any possible facts or data existing or being discovered, so do many believers appear to have no critical judgment whatever. There are a great many of the latter who, in Carlyle's bitter words, "hunger and thirst to be bamboozled." They regard disproofs with a completely unbelieving eye and go happily on to the next subject of extravagant belief.

Work in this field calls for walking a fine line between openness to new ideas and kooky acceptance of everything. It is a difficult tightrope to walk and all of us find ourselves slipping off it, first on one side and then on the other. At times we find ourselves accepting nonproven ideas and as we recover from that, we find ourselves in the position of Petrarch when he wrote "So much do I fear to become entangled in error that I throw myself into the embrace of doubt instead of truth." Since I came into parapsychology 10 years ago, I have had to eat more of my words than in all the rest of my life and to constantly try to guard against the error that John Levy, Executive Director of the Association for Humanistic Psychology, once warned me of: the error of believing my prejudices to be valid.

The data of parapsychology obviously have tremendous philosophical implications, but most parapsychologists tend to avoid philosophy as if it were the plague. It is a field that needs metaphysical daring, but researchers tend to ignore metaphysics. In the most "far out" area of scientific research today, there seems little question of the truth of the assertion of H. H. Price (1939) that "it will be the timidity of our hypotheses, and not their extravagance, which will provoke the derision of posterity" (p341). Psi abilities give us clear indications of a larger and a more complete concept of what it means to be a human being, but we parapsychologists keep trying to cram these abilities back into the old concepts. We keep trying to stick to "common sense" in spite of Humphry Osmond's statement (1959, p74) that science is composed of "uncommon sense." Most of our attempts at scientific explanation and hypothesis-making are carefully tailored to fit the model of 19th-century physics and not the science of the 20th century.

At a time of great public interest in this area, the number of people working in it is unbelievably small: there are probably fewer than 30 full-time researchers in the entire world. With the large public interest growing to the degree that new "psi" magazines (not scientific journals, but popular magazines) proliferate steadily, financial support for research is at such a minimum that researchers and laboratories spend a good deal of their time trying to raise enough funds to survive on a hand-to-mouth basis.

We are constantly faced with the dilemma that it is very easy to design experiments demonstrating the existence of psi and very difficult to design experiments that will tell us anything new about it. With the tremendous accumulation of data now available, it is pointless to continue to "prove" the existence of psi. (When there are four or five zeros to the right of the decimal point in a probability value, adding a few more zeros is not very useful.) Unfortunately, we have fairly few ideas as to how to progress further; few new ideas on how psi operates. If challenged to present a bold new research program, many professional parapsychologists would have little to say.

Part of the problem is that we cannot assume that the psi abilities we are specifically testing in our subjects are those that they are actually using. We must be constantly aware that they may be using entirely different forms of psi to obtain the results which appear, that the experimenters also may be using psi abilities (including the judges in double-blind studies), and that any experiment in this field, no matter how tightly designed, has a host of potential unknown variables.

We who work in this field have much specific information about psi, as is reported in the rest of this book. This information belies everything we were raised to believe and everything that our culture believes about the way the universe works and what is the nature of humankind. This places a constant stress, a sort of psychological double-bind, double vision, on parapsychologists. We must live in a world operating on the everyday laws of what is regarded by our culture as common sense. At the same time we see these laws being circumvented by the data we work with. We regularly see individuals acquiring specific, concrete information through nonsensory channels. We see that neither time nor distance can block these channels; that there is no inverse-square law for space, and that precognition (which can be defined as an effect occurring before its cause) does happen. Since we parapsychologists--as well as other members of our culture--have built our ego structures in terms of a definite view of reality, we are constantly in a situation of extreme psychological stress. We are forbidden by our professional training and orientation to take the easy ways out of this dilemma that the rest of the society frequently takes. We cannot simply deny the evidence and attribute it to bad memory, "artifact," or chicanery. We cannot view the universe as operating according to "normal" laws with a few brightly colored bubbles of mystery, obeying a different set of laws, floating around in it and brightening up things for the story hour. We cannot ease our problem by declaring that "everything is related to everything else" in a soft-headed way of thinking and believe we have solved our problems. We are stuck with a paradox, facing it daily and having to live in a constantly contradictory situation. The stress factor among serious people working in this field is very high. It is perhaps no accident that parapsychologists have shown marked tendencies to lose crucial data, not follow up promising leads, and to exist only in small numbers. The criticism from colleagues in other sciences for being too soft-headed and from believers for being too closed-minded does not help the psychological situation. The lack of research funds and job opportunities further compounds the problems.

And yet it is, for us, the most rewarding field we

could be in. We work on the largest and most important problems we know of: what is the real nature of man and what is his relationship to others and to the rest of the universe? We deal scientifically, it seems to us, with the three questions that, according to Kant, it is the endeavor of philosophy to answer: "What can I know? What ought I to do? What dare I hope?" Behind all parapsychological research stands the hidden agenda of our profession. What happens to the personality at biological death? We know we stand at the spearhead, the forefront of science, in asking the great questions. Most of us would find any other profession dull indeed. Our field is best described by the words of G. N. M. Tyrrell (1945), one of our most perceptive parapsychologists, who defined it as "a subject which lies at the meeting place of religion, philosophy, and science, whose business it is to grasp all that can be grasped of the nature of human personality" (p317). Who would wish to be embarked on a lesser adventure?

REFERENCES

Osmond, H.   "A Call for Imaginative Theory. " International Journal of Parapsychology, 1 (1959), 69-83.

Price, H. H.   "Haunting and the 'Psychic Ether' Hypothesis; With Some Preliminary Reflections on the Present Condition and Possible Future of Psychical Research. " (Presidential Address.) Proceedings of the Society for Psychical Research, 45 (1939), 307-43.

Prince, W. F.   The Enchanted Boundary. Boston: Boston Society for Psychic Research, 1930.

Tyrrell, G. N. M.   Presidential Address. Proceedings of the Society for Psychical Research, 47 (1945), 301-19.

Part IV

PARAPSYCHOLOGY AND PSYCHIATRY

The relation of psychiatry and parapsychology is an important one from two quite different points of view: the theoretical and the applied. Its theoretical importance lies in the depth and intimacy of the psychiatrist's knowledge of his patients. In the course of many hours of treatment, a psychotherapist may well gain deeper insights into the on-going psychological processes of an individual than could a specialist in any other field. The psychiatrist who sees what patterns occur in one of his patients and then finds similar patterns in others may thus be in a better position than any other expert to generalize wisely. The concepts which psychiatrists give us may therefore be the most useful concepts about human behavior that we have.

However, we must not forget that the working psychiatrist's daily concerns are practical ones. How should he respond to this particular comment from his patient? What does the comment really mean? Does it reflect reality or only fantasy? What are the patient's present abilities, his potentialities, his defects and limitations? What intervention is needed? A host of such questions may arise, of which these of course are only a sample.

For some of the immediate, day-by-day concerns, parapsychology's data may be relevant. The clearest example comes if a patient complains that others can read his mind, inflict ideas or compulsions upon him, send him messages that do him harm but cannot be ignored, and so on. How much of such complaints is delusional?

If data from ESP and PK research had given only null results, the answer would be easy. All such complaints would then be classed as fantasies or hallucinations or delusions. But since in fact the data show that telepathic or other ESP information can come from outside, that even precognitive impressions may have a factual base, and that it is possible for a person, by wishing or willing, to cause direct changes in the outside world, the answer is more difficult. The patient's statements might or might not be reality-based. The psychiatrist will need to discriminate as keenly between the veridical and the delusional for this type of statement as for a patient's reports of parental mistreatment or of persecution by his associates. Parapsychology's affirmative findings open a Pandora's box for the psychiatrist.

From one point of view, or for some aspects of psychotherapy, the distinction is unimportant. If a patient feels that the weather is oppressive, this is his psychic reality and is all that needs to be known; it is irrelevant whether others consider the weather only pleasantly warm or whether they too complain of the high humidity and excessive heat. From this angle, then, reports of telepathic messages or of hurtful PK effects can be handled therapeutically without probing into their authenticity.

But for the therapist concerned with examining the relation between the patient's ideas and reality, it is important to learn whether or not there is a reality base for such impressions. Consider, for example, the patient who gives in his dream reports or in apparently random comments some specific, unique information about his therapist (or about another patient) that he could not have obtained normally and that is therefore presumably telepathic. Several psychiatrists, perhaps most notably (in addition to those whose articles follow) Dr. Jule Eisenbud (see his Psi and Psychoanalysis, New York: Grune and Stratton, 1970), have clearly shown that such authentic telepathic input should be interpreted as a special need for intimacy or perhaps for control. It can have important dynamic meaning, just as would unusually keen and accurate observation of the other person's appearance or behavior. It might, when it is information about the therapist that is obtained paranormally, give useful cues about transference patterns. It should not be ignored.

The articles in this section occasionally refer to such practical problems, but are far more concerned with conceptual ones. In the first, Dr. Montague Ullman writes briefly of the history of psychical research, emphasizing its relevance to issues in psychiatry. He continues with a long-er section on the recent past and then describes the present, including a brief report on the research in dream telepathy from his own laboratory. In a final unit, he even tries to predict the future. He discusses the difficulty of identifying a psychic event, uses case history material to describe "the telepathic maneuver," writes of the scientific resistance to psi, and suggests that more effective research can be per-formed when such resistance has lessened.

The second paper, by Dr. S David Kahn, analyzes both the cognitive and the emotional roots of scientific re-sistance to accepting psychic phenomena and suggests that the cognitive reasons will not dissipate until we have a re-peatable experiment. This sets the major theme of his pa-per: that we require a good model of psi, a wise general understanding of how it functions, before we can hope to de-sign a repeatable experiment. He cites two models. One is that psi appears occasionally, in a clear but erratic im-pression. This model is best tested with a technique like ESP cards, where each response is either right or wrong. The second model, which he follows F. W. H. Myers and Gardner Murphy in considering more plausible, is that psi input interacts constantly with other input into the stream of consciousness. The latter part of his rich and thoughtful paper suggests modern sophisticated research methods, in-cluding one that has given striking data in his own labora-tory, which according to the second model might yield the dependably repeatable results that parapsychology needs.

Dr. Berthold E. Schwarz in the third paper empha-sizes case histories which show the varying dynamics of psi events at different parts of the life cycle. The short report here is an excerpt from a more detailed, unpublished paper that leads, as did Dr. Schwarz's earlier work, to a broad-based thesis of the meaning of psychic events. His thesis is strikingly similar to the model of psi for which Dr. Kahn argues and does not conflict with the other papers in this section.

The concluding paper is by Dr. Jan Ehrenwald. As its subtitle states, it presents a neuropsychiatric model of psi phenomena; but it also does a great deal more. It de-scribes how this model can be reconciled with physical theories and it also examines what we could call the soci-ology of psi: the cultural factors that make parapsychologi-cal events and theories both attractive and threatening.

Interwoven are supporting data from the laboratory and from case records. Its lucid and systematic account packs a great deal into a small space. It could be taken as a summation of the preceding papers in this section, or indeed of the whole book.

Montague Ullman

PSYCHIATRY AND PARAPSYCHOLOGY: THE CONSUMMATION OF AN UNCERTAIN ROMANCE

This presentation will attempt to assess where we have been, where we are, and where we are likely to go with regard to the interrelationship between psychiatry and what was formerly called psychical research, now known in the West as parapsychology.

WHERE WE WERE

The Remote Past

Two recent review articles (Ullman, 1974a, 1974b) trace the history of the kinds of engagements and disengage-ments that occurred between the group of scholars that came together in the last two decades of the past century and the early years of this one and the medical men of the day who specialized in nervous disorders. The founders (in 1882) of the (British) Society for Psychical Research exhibited a live-ly interest in the exciting discoveries reported by those in-vestigators (Braid, Bernheim, Liébeault) who were trying to establish the validity and significance of hypnosis and the remarkable phenomena associated with it. Hypnosis was only one source of rapidly accumulating evidence that there are important unseen dimensions to human personality. Hysteria, multiple personality, and even paranoia were scrutinized and studied not only for the light they shed on the unconscious or subconscious, but also as to whether or not supranormal faculties played a role in the etiology and symptomatology of the various syndromes. T. Weir Mitchell, Morton Prince, and Pierre Janet lent their time and prestige to clinical in-vestigations of this kind whereas theoreticians like William James and F. W. H. Myers engaged in integrative efforts

171

designed to map out human personality on a scale ample
enough to accommodate the new yield of information concerning the range of man's psychical as well as psychological
abilities. Myers (1903) led the way with the publication of
his massive two-volume study, which not only summarized
data from a wide variety of sources but also outlined the
case for survival based on the evidence for the existence of
human faculties that could operate apart from and independent of the body. While Myers' survival thesis itself is
arguable, the book was for psychical research what Freud's
Interpretation of Dreams was for the future of psychoanalysis.
It brought together facts from diverse sources that had to be
looked at in their interconnectedness and to be housed in
some kind of unified theoretical structure. What both Myers
and Freud did was to study altered and deviant states of
consciousness in an effort to shed light on consciousness itself and its counterpart, the realm of the unconsciousness.

Therein the comparison ends; Myers died before he
could complete his book, while Freud's monumental volume
on dreams marked the beginning of his effort to bring the
new science of psychoanalysis into being. Just as Myers
took note of Freud's work, Freud took note of the existence
of psi phenomena and of the societies organized to deal seriously with them (Jones, 1957, v3). Freud, however, faced
the task of establishing the respectability of psychoanalysis
itself. His own intellectual honesty and curiosity led him to
flirt with the field by way of seriously entertaining the possibility that telepathy existed and that telepathically perceived
content might undergo transformation in the unconscious. He
came up against sharp opposition from his colleagues, notably Jones, and this undoubtedly tempered the extent of his
own engagement with the subject.

Freud and the generation of analysts that followed
sought to establish a scientific basis for both understanding
and treating mental illness. Part of the price that was paid
for sanitizing the subject matter of psychiatry was to dissect
it away from any occult connections. This was nowhere
more evident than in the responses of Freudian analysts to
any of their colleagues who showed an inclination to take the
subject of telepathy seriously. Their efforts were met with
pejorative psychoanalytic jargon to the effect that such thinking was regressive in character and evidence of an unre-
solved striving for omnipotence (Ullman, 1974a, 1974b).

The early thrust of psychiatric leadership in the field

of psychical research was thus aborted and what came into being in its stead was a movement analogous in its own way to what we have said about psychoanalysis. The approach to research in this area established by J. B. Rhine sought to transform what had been known as psychical research into the new science of parapsychology. Since science with a capital S requires quantification, laboratory controls, and repeatability, this was the order of the day. Psychical research in the course of becoming parapsychology was subjected to a process of objectification that, at least initially, obscured the subjective soil out of which it arose. This splitting of subject and object was unfortunately predicated on a dualistic framework that carried with it religious and idealistic overtones. From the point of view of history, what might have been twins--or at least siblings--were born and reared in separation from each other. Commenting on this, Weir Mitchell (1939) wrote:

> With the general adoption of analytical methods in the treatment of psychoneurotic illness the interrelations of psychical research and psychotherapeutics became less obvious, and at the present time we cannot say that the researches of one department of knowledge have much bearing on those of the other. But there will always remain some common ground--the realm of the unexplained--in which discoveries may be made in one field of investigation or the other. That there is a realm of the unexplained in the history of mental healing cannot be denied [p183].

All that follows bears witness to the slow but gradually increasing momentum of the effort to bring the person and his capacity for experiencing and existing in various states of consciousness back into the picture as we move further into the strange and puzzling world of the paranormal.

The Intermediate Past

A monograph of Wilhelm Stekel appeared in 1921 on the telepathic dream, a year before Freud's initial paper (1922) appeared. Stekel's emphasis on the role of strong emotions and the facilitating influence of sleep--along with Freud's emphasis on the possible interpretation and transformation of telepathic content in the dream--laid the groundwork, despite the desultory and controversial reports that characterized the psychoanalytic literature of the twenties and thirties, for the upsurge of interest in the forties. Ehrenwald (1942, 1948) and Eisenbud (1946, 1947) were the leading writers at the time, with supporting contributions from Meerloo (1964), Pedersen-Krag (1947), Servadio (1956), Ullman (1959), and others. A comparison of clinical material containing presumptively telepathic dreams led to a number of practical as well as theoretical formulations concerning the conditions for their occurrence, their dynamic significance, and the light they shed on underlying character structure. Much of what emerged validated the earlier speculations of Stekel, Freud, and the handful of others who were impressed with telepathic material coming up in the course of analysis. These contributions have been reviewed elsewhere (Ullman, 1974a, 1974b) and will be briefly summarized here and illustrated by clinical material from the author's experience. Eisenbud emphasized the way in which telepathy served unconscious needs and in general its connection with repressed material. He made explicit use of the telepathy hypothesis in his therapeutic work and argued that it both extended and validated psychoanalytic theory. There was general consensus among writers on the subject of the role of transferential and countertransferential factors as facilitating mechanisms for telepathic transfer, with the most frequently cited dynamism being the transitory withdrawal of interest or attention from the patient on the part of the analyst. Situations often arose, according to Eisenbud, in which more than one patient at a time was involved in a telepathic interchange. Fodor (1942) and Coleman (1958) also described telepathic effects spreading beyond the dyadic relationship of therapist and patient. Eisenbud pointed to an abundance of telepathic material from a wide range of patients, whereas Ullman and Ehrenwald found patients with obsessive and schizoid structures more likely to report dreams that appeared to be telepathic.

Ehrenwald carefully and methodically evolved a theoretical structure to help contain and articulate the variety of psi effects that occurred in the clinical setting and to relate these effects to the larger issues of psychopathology in general and schizophrenia in particular. His own views appear at the end of this Part IV.

Schwarz's views on psi likewise appear later in Part IV.

Ullman emphasized the frequency with which telepathic content appeared in dreams of patients whose affective ties to others were weak and tenuous and in whom the telepathic maneuver seemed to be a way of knowing about a significant figure without having to assume responsibility for knowing. It was as if an anonymous listening device had been perfected as a kind of psychic barometer to monitor the degree of trust and safety these patients could allow themselves to feel in the situation in which they found themselves. Intercurrent anxieties experienced by the analyst removing him momentarily from affective contact with the patient often triggered telepathic events. This is well illustrated in the clinical material offered below. In addition, Ullman felt that both need and interest on the part of the analyst favored the occurrence of telepathy in a way perhaps somewhat analogous to the formal experiments that reveal how experimenter bias pro and con can influence ESP results. Ullman also felt that once a psychotic reaction set in, this level of psi contact appeared to recede but the fact of its having existed as a real event in the life of the patient may have been in part responsible for the degree to which his overt symptomatology and his preoccupations center about thought-transference, reading the minds of others, having his own mind read or influenced by others, etc. Formal experiments with psychotics (e.g., West, 1952, Zorab, 1957) appear to support the thesis that psychotics have no special ESP ability, although Humphrey (1954) obtained highly significant results with a small group of schizophrenics.

Aside from the elucidation of the dynamics of psi in the clinical setting, an effort was made to define the criteria for assessing a dream as presumptively telepathic with regard to the life of the therapist. In essence these were: (a) that the crucial elements in the dream having a bearing on the life of the analyst be unusual, at least in regard to the frequency with which they were apt to turn up in dreams; (b) that a close temporal relationship exist between the dream and the corresponding events in the life of the therapist; (c) that the patient could have had no normal access to the significant information he incorporated into his dream, nor could he have inferred any of it from his day-to-day contact with the therapist; and (d) that the telepathic elements depicted in the patient's dream be dynamically meaningful in the context of the therapeutic exchanges going on at the time.

Despite these guidelines, the judgment as to whether

a dream of a patient is presumptively telepathic or not remains a subjective one and as such subject to debate and
differences of opinion, as has in fact been the case (Ellis,
1947). It is perhaps for this reason that the weight of
clinical evidence alone, even combined with the appeal of
such authority as Freud (in terms of interest) and Jung (1963)
(in terms of commitment), never exerted much influence in
changing to any recognizable extent the general lack of interest in and level of suspicion about psi events in the clinical setting. Despite these realities, the fact is that when
one is at the receiving end of a dream which fulfills all of
these criteria there is often the additional gut-level criterion
of experiencing something uncanny.

The following series of dreams of a patient undergo-
ing analysis illustrate some of the points under discussion.
The dreams which are to be considered occurred in the
course of a week in the analysis of a severely compulsive
and withdrawn individual. She was a 29-year-old college
teacher, the mother of one child, who entered into analysis
in October 1947 because of increasing estrangement from
her husband and general unsureness about what her feelings
were. Although possessed of high ideals of motherhood,
household responsibilities weighed heavily on her. Most of
her drive lay in the direction of an intense interest in the
history of music, the subject which she taught, as well as in
a lively interest in history in general. She looked back on
her marriage of eight years as having occurred in a spirit
of romantic rebellion. She was overwhelmed at first by the
brightness and precocity of her husband. The impact of his
aggressive, impulsive, and often erratic personality set the
stage for a gradual but pronounced withdrawal on her part
with increased reliance on interests outside the marriage.
She disparaged the feminine role and often felt extremely
competitive toward her husband. She felt blocked in terms
of using her specialized knowledge in any creative way and
was often intolerant and jealous of the creative efforts of
others, including her husband. Attitudes of rigid self-denial,
almost to the point of asceticism, operated compulsively,
interrupted sporadically by transient periods of excessive
self-indulgence in the form of short-lived but highly charged
extramarital affairs. In relation to her friends and colleagues
she characteristically assumed the role of confidante and father confessor, a role in which she was acutely aware of the
neurotic difficulties of others but totally at a loss in evaluating her own problems.

The family grouping included an older brother. The lines were quite sharply drawn, the mother maintaining a more affectionate relationship with the son while the patient remained the father's favorite. This favoritism, expressed as it was through over-protective and over-indulgent attitudes, gave rise to mixed and often confused feelings in the patient. The patient was bluntly derogatory in relation to her mother, whom she regarded as hypocritical and stupidly conventional. Following a stormy adolescence the shy, inhibited behavior she exhibited as a child gave way to a compulsive rebelliousness and the rejection of most of her former values. In college she had disdain for what she considered the more juvenile campus activities. She preferred to associate with older, more sophisticated girls. She was popular and always had an intimate circle of friends. In recalling this period of her life there were no clear feelings of happiness or unhappiness. The dominant feeling, then as in later years, seemed to be an intense, although somewhat curiously detached interest in and preoccupation with the many new intellectual horizons opening up to her. In short, she found life "interesting" but was more deeply touched by ideas than by people. Her interest soon centered in music and, more specifically, the history of musical forms. She achieved some recognition for her knowledge in the field and soon after her marriage obtained a teaching position on a college faculty.

The patient came to analysis with a defensive structure that was relatively intact. She experienced little overt anxiety and, aside from some underlying vague but persistent feelings of dread and foreboding, she felt at a loss as to where and how to tackle her problems. Early resistances took the form of subtle efforts to embroil the therapist in discussions of the theoretical aspects of the task at hand and attempts to maintain a thoroughly objective and detached view of her own problems. There was a fascination with the symbolism and form of her own neurosis along with a profound lack of awareness of herself and the implications of her illness. Hidden by compulsive self-effacement and retreat into anonymity, she had an unrelenting need to play a unique and ambitious role in life. In dreams depicting the analytic situation she was usually in the role of a passive onlooker with the analyst portrayed either as an all-powerful threatening figure or as weak and ineffectual. The underlying picture was that of extreme cynicism and despair, a blocking out of all assertive impulses, and profound withdrawal, precariously balanced by the exploitation to the fullest of rich intellectual

resources through which some feeling of mastery was maintained. As might be surmised, this push to intellectual
mastery, so outstanding a characteristic of her everyday activity, constituted the first real problem to be dealt with in
the analysis. This came out most glaringly in relation to
her handling of her own dreams, where almost a ruminative
delight occurred over their form and structure and the symbolism involved, all of which served as substitutes for any
genuine spontaneous reactions to the dream elements.
Handled in this autistic fashion, the dream lost its potential
to make the unknown more known. The more colorful and
imaginative the dream, the less real meaning it held for the
patient. At the time of the occurrence of the dreams to be
described below there had not yet been full clarification of
these attitudes. It was felt that before genuine interpretive
efforts could be successful, full awareness of these attitudes
would have to be established. This is a significant point,
inasmuch as the function of these attitudes, well concealed
behind a great interest in the dreams and a profusion of
them, was actually in a sense to detonate the dream in
terms of its analytic possibilities while at the same time
providing a relatively safe medium for the patient.

There was one loophole in her character armor which
did make for beginning analytic inroads. She had anxiety
lest someone discover the fact that she was under analysis.
This was practically the only anxiety she experienced. The
undue precautions she would be forced to take soon helped
make the patient aware of the irrational quality involved in
the reaction. This led to an opening up of basic attitudes
toward the analysis and a beginning awareness that she regarded it as a special confessional where her great need to
remain uninvolved and anonymous--the passive onlooker on
her dreams--could go unchallenged. In corroboration of this
there were disproportionate fear reactions over any slight
psychosomatic disturbances that occurred from time to time,
the fear being connected more with the possibility of their
occurrence than their actual significance. Although movement had been slow, the setting at the time of the occurrence of the telepathic dreams, approximately six months
after the inception of the treatment, was one in which a definite positive response had been elicited to the analysis, and
with this, a great real interest in herself and a spark of
real faith in the procedure.

First Dream. On Monday morning, April 26, 1948,
the patient presented the following dream which had occurred

on awakening the previous morning:

> I was at a music class. It was a practical music
> class, not one dealing with the history of music.
> The room was clear. It was large and dark. It
> seemed like an elementary school classroom with
> high ceilings. The only light came from above.
> You were the music teacher who came in to give
> the class (of girls) music criticism--as music
> teachers do. There was a sense of real help, not
> a sense of being lectured at. There were a few
> words here and there in re content of the work
> which was unclear, but the general feeling was
> one of being helpful, soothing and honest and
> gentle. And then I awakened.

Associations. The patient discussed two men, both
of whom stood in authority relations to her. The previous
session had been devoted to a discussion of certain secret
sources of satisfaction. Diaries were the first indirect and
hidden outlet. Clandestine sexual affairs and an intense
idealization of her own child also served this purpose. She
spoke of a rabbi she had seen recently--a man who was
very learned and had a great zest for life. Beneath the ad-
miration she professed was a subtle disparagement. Significantly, although she expected him to be very formidable he
proved to be rather kindly. His limitations had to be clearly defined by her so that he could be properly categorized.
She also spoke of a music teacher whom she likened to her
husband and described as an aggressive and impulsive individual. He, too, produced an overwhelming first impression
on her only to lead later to disillusionment. One feature
common to both men was their exhibitionism and need to im-
press others.

It was the first time that she had dreamt of the analyst in a kindly light. The contrast between this and the
derogatory thoughts that flooded her mind was quite striking.
She undoubtedly felt threatened, but at the same time some
relief at the encroachment in the previous session of affect-
laden material. In the dream there was a simple and genuine expression of gratitude to and appreciation of the teacher. The conscious derogatory associations seemed to crowd
in, in an effort to block off the recognition of these positive
attitudes.

Second Dream. During this session the patient pre-

sented a second dream which occurred on awakening the
same day. She said that she had had a very bad night and
had suffered from insomnia, a state of affairs most unusual
for her. She said she could not remember ever before being this unrelaxed at night:

> Mr. E. , who was some kind of instructor, came
> to the house to demonstrate a new camera gadget.
> His gestures were very clear. There were people
> in our living room. It was a meeting or a social
> group. He went to the hall closet and took out a
> large wooden box. He lifted up the cover and took
> out a camera (our own) very slowly and deliberate-
> ly. I was very conscious of him opening the
> closet door and of hoping that the closet would be
> neat so that I would not be embarrassed before my
> friends. I was conscious of the people's admira-
> tion of the box and the way the closet was kept.
> I said this was a box my husband had sent back
> from Germany. Then Mr. E. made his point by
> demonstration. He looked through what seemed to
> be a stereopticon lens (a very special kind of lens)
> into the street below. There was a factory or
> warehouse there and people were leaving to eat.
> They were white-collar workers rather than fac-
> tory workers. The picture was black and white
> and unusual because it was three-dimensional.
> The lens could make you see things miles away
> that could not be seen with the naked eye. He
> focused on a hatless man who was followed by many
> people. Mr. E. also compared this with the pic-
> ture of an inert figure, either a dead body or that
> of a drunk lying on the ground and the people pass-
> ing him by callously. Mr. E. demonstrated this
> great device. You could really see people's emo-
> tional reactions with it. The man was moved by
> what he saw. There was a slight twitching of his
> facial muscles and the people around him were re-
> acting to him.

Association. Mr. E. was identified with the analyst.
The patient said the gadget seemed to reflect more than
meets the eye. She had been working with slides on the
night before the occurrence of the dream, preparing to give
her course in the history of music. The idea of "seeing
more than meets the eye" she related to the analysis. She
then spoke about the anxiety she had had in bed, but could

not pin it to anything--there had been reluctance to come to the session which the patient explained on the basis of her son's illness. The dream itself was not clear in relation to her associations and no interpretation was given.

Before considering the telepathic possibilities I want to review my activities on the Sunday immediately preceding the day on which the two dreams were presented. I had been invited to present a paper on telepathy and analysis before a group of psychiatrists on May 6, 1948. The members of this group had a common interest in the subject and several previous papers had been read. Approximately two weeks after the May 6th meeting I was scheduled to present a case at a clinical seminar at the New York Medical College. I had decided to utilize material from the same patient for the two occasions, omitting the telepathic features in the later presentation. The patient, of course, had no inkling of either meeting.

I began the preparation for the paper on telepathy on Sunday, April 25, 1948, the Sunday alluded to above. In reviewing the case I noted that I had earmarked eight dreams scattered over the six-month interval since the inception of the patient's analysis as having telepathic possibilities. It was around these dreams that I hoped to base the presentation. It was a curious twist that it was just this patient who was so secretive in her approach to analysis whose dreams were to be brought out into the open. Personal facts had to be disguised sufficiently to prevent recognition without detracting from their cogency.

Several thoughts occupied my mind as I read over the material. Here was a field I had long been familiar with and interested in, but I had never before gotten down to the task of serious or recordable research efforts. It was also to be my first analytic presentation outside the sheltered academic atmosphere. Although there was common ground in terms of interest in the implications of parapsychology for psychiatry, my own analytic approach, strongly influenced by the "culturalists," differed markedly from those of my more orthodox colleagues. Two excellent and convincing papers had already been given before this group dealing with telepathic occurrences in patients under treatment. All of these ruminations contributed to a let-down feeling as I looked over the eight dreams I had on hand. Viewed at some distance from the time of their actual occurrence, they carried less emotional impact than they had at first. I had neglected to record in detail my own activities and introspections which might have had important corroborative value. The difficulties in convincingly eliminating chance and other possibilities seemed more formidable than ever.

On this first occasion of my actual evaluation of the dreams as a group, I noted that four of the eight dreams had occurred over weekends and were presented by the patient at her Monday session. She also had sessions on Wednesday and Friday. The telepathic feature of seven of the eight dreams seemed to be initiated by unusual occurrences in my own life. It may be that the weekend, providing greater opportunity for out of the routine events, made for the greater Monday frequency. At any rate, somewhat disappointed in the material I had collected, I had the hope, perhaps born out of some measure of desperation, that the Monday frequency would recur and that fresh material would be forthcoming for the presentation two weeks hence. The following day a series of dreams was initiated, two of which have already been given, which more than filled the bill, so much so that I discarded all eight of the dreams I had originally planned to discuss and limited my presentation solely to the dreams the patient brought to analysis during the first two sessions following the Sunday in question.

There was one other train of events occurring on that Sunday that I wish to establish. Before I began the preparation of the case I recalled an obligation to collect some data that I had, dealing with the early days of the New York Society for Medical History. I had these data in a closet that was made up of two separate divisions, one locked and the other unlocked. Not having the key with me I opened the unlocked section and looked for the papers, but without success. My eye did catch sight, however, of a large wooden box with many small built-in compartments. I had had this box made while stationed in France during World War II for the storage of microfilm and subsequently mailed it back home to my wife. I had not been at this closet for many months and the sight of the box brought back many memories.

Bearing in mind the account given of my own activities that Sunday, certain correlations with regard to the two dreams the patient presented the next day can now be brought to light. Although a prolific dreamer, she had presented no previous dreams involving lecturing, classrooms, or demon-

strations--this despite her own experience as a teacher.
Standing alone, the first dream is of no telepathic significance. Taken in conjunction with the second dream, however, we have a situation in which the following specific
points of correlation can be drawn:

(1) The setting of the first dream in a classroom and
the second in a living room. My concern with two pre-
sentations--one to be held in a classroom and the other
in a more informal and social atmosphere of a colleague's
waiting room.

(2) Both dreams involving a figure readily identifiable
as the analyst--in the one case as an instructor and in
the second case as a demonstrator.

(3) The temporal relationship of the two dreams to my
preparation the day before.

(4) In the second dream a closet was of importance to
the patient. A closet had been for a brief time the focus
of my own attention.

(5) The dream involved the removal of a large wooden
box from the closet. Seeing the wooden box in my own
closet gave rise to a transient reverie.

(6) The box was one the patient's husband had sent
back from Germany during the war. My box was one I
had sent back from France during the war.

(7) In the dream the box was associated with a camera
contained within. The box I had was used for storage of
microfilm.

(8) In the dream the demonstrator made his point by
means of a very special kind of lens--a stereopticon lens
(an image not too far removed from the contemplated
demonstration of the unique character of telepathic communication).

(9) In the dream, stress was placed on the unusual
quality of the picture--it was three-dimensional--one
could see things miles away--you could really see people's
emotional reactions (again an image very suggestive of
and a symbolic portrayal of the penetrating qualities of
telepathic perception).

These points of correlation suggested the reasonable possibility of telepathic factors operating in relation to the dreams. What made for even greater conviction was the light this hypothesis shed on certain aspects of the analytic situation at the time. The unexplained anxiety and insomnia may have stemmed from a telepathic sensing of the contemplated presentation, which would constitute an uncontrollable threat to her persistent and compulsive need for secrecy and concealment. One may speculate as to yet another source for the anxiety. One of the most rigid and deep-seated of her characterologic difficulties was the compulsion to yield uncritically to the needs of others with no effective efforts at self-assertion. In the particular situation at hand, unwittingly and unknowingly on both our parts, she was confronted with the very compelling need of mine, telepathically sensed, for more and better material and a reliance on her to come through with it. The dreams may then have been her effort to fill the bill and the anxiety with regard to them caused by a fear that she might fail. I might mention in this connection that in the following session two days later she reported a dream which was much more spectacular from a telepathic standpoint and at that time there were no traces of anxiety or distress.

In the first dream the portrayal of the analyst in a warm, friendly light, with implications of gratitude and good feeling, seemed rather significant inasmuch as it was the first time such feelings had come through in a dream. The explanation previously indicated did not seem enough to account for it. If telepathy did occur, some further speculations are in order. The needs of the actual analytic relationship constituted such an overwhelming threat to this patient's techniques of withdrawal that from the very beginning there was frustration, withdrawal, and smoldering resentment. At the one point where the analyst's needs were extracurricular, so to speak, and evolving out of strivings of his own that had no direct bearing on the welfare of the patient, it is here that a startling change occurred: she complies magnificently and for the first time the analyst is seen as a nonthreatening and friendly figure. In fact, the entire situation is exploited to the hilt and all the dramatic and exhibitionistic possibilities of the presentation situation are enjoyed to the fullest. Here successful compliance with my needs could be accomplished in absolute safety for the patient; the sordidness uncovered by the gadget described in the dream is for display before a group and not likely to be handled in the more personal and therefore more threatening analytic situation.

Third Dream. In introducing this dream, which occurred on Wednesday morning, April 28, 1948, the patient
stated:

> This morning I had a dream full of action. I was
> watching it like a movie. I was sitting on a park
> bench. Next to me is a tall, well-groomed dame,
> not pretty, kind of British, attractive and compe-
> tent. In her forties. She asked me whether I saw
> her sister come flying past. She [the sister] was
> seven feet tall. Then there was a sense of a long,
> skinny, bony--somewhat comical--body plunging
> through the air as I turned around. I stood on the
> opposite side of the street observing a hotel front.
> It had huge plate-glass windows. Very large and
> well-cleaned. I am trying to think of the family
> name of this woman. It was Brain or Braintree.
> There was a man, Basil Rathbone, who looked like
> her brother. He opened the window, but as he did
> it the upper part of the window fell, so that whether
> you raised it or lowered it you were imprisoned.
> At another window there was another sister with
> curly crisp hair, going through the same horrify-
> ing efforts at trying to get out. There was a pane
> of glass between that person and the outside.
> These people were trying to jump and were frus-
> trated. Possibly they were in danger of fire. Out
> of the entrance of the hotel I saw this blonde dame,
> well-groomed. As I looked over to a lower story
> window there was a child who was an exact repli-
> ca of this woman. This was the gimmick. They
> could be released because this woman showed that
> she was well equipped to care for the child. A
> policeman came and opened the window letting the
> child out, and the child effected the escape of the
> others. It was like a movie plot which somehow
> involved the whole family. Then the scene changed
> to a roadhouse. Basil Rathbone was the proprie-
> tor. He had imprisoned in his house an old man
> that he claimed was the bad guy. I knew he was
> a good guy. Then a young guy walks out and says
> 'My name is Rubins.' This has a liberating effect,
> as if I had been vindicated. The name seemed an
> anachronism, since the other names were more or
> less Victorian.

Associations. The patient spoke about a young musician friend of hers with white hair, and said the Rubins character reminded her of him:

> The dame reminds me of a Virginia Woolf character. She could be a sister of Basil Rathbone. He was the long, lean British character--the traditional villain. When I was younger I would seek out these movies. Virginia Woolf was my great love in literature. I feel this has nothing to do with me.

Further associations brought out her antipathy toward women who are well-groomed, women who accept a conventional feminine role. They are placed in the same category as her mother, as women who allow themselves to become decorative objects. She would rather die than be like that. She feels that her husband victimizes weak women.

In relation to her friends who are neurotic she often plays the role of the happy, normal girl.

The dream touched on her attitudes toward her child, attitudes which had previously been explored to a limited extent. It was as if she admired her child from a distance and secretly idealized him. Occasionally this facade broke down under the pressure of sporadic uncontrollable rages against the child and then guilt and anxiety would be released. How this fitted in with the dream was not clear and the accompanying associations were too shallow to permit of further interpretive work. The other features of the dream produced no further associations.

The following events in my own life are set down for consideration in the light of the patient's dream:

On the evening preceding the occurrence of the patient's dream (Tuesday) I had an appointment with Miss M., a friend of mine who occasionally acted as my secretary, to dictate the paper I planned to give. Some time back she had been a patient of mine for a brief period because of difficulties stemming from an underlying compulsive character structure. She had developed an interest in parapsychology, but had a very critical eye toward all alleged paranormal events and was skeptical and cautious in her approach to them.

Miss M. and I had supper together and then we

walked over to my office a few blocks away.   In doing so
we passed a movie theatre.   Being in an escapist mood I
half-jokingly, half-seriously, suggested leaving the work and
enjoying a good movie.   But Miss M. kept steadfastly to the
job at hand and added that as a rule she did not enjoy movies
anyway.   A few moments later we passed by an apartment
house and my eye was caught by the unusual front of the
structure.   The front was made up almost completely of two
huge panes of glass and the entire interior of the lobby was
visible.   It was so striking that I called Miss M.'s attention
to it.

At the office I proceeded first with the dictation of
another case--that of a very disturbed young woman in the
early months of pregnancy whose illness centered about potentially destructive trends toward herself and the unborn
child.   Later on in the evening Miss M. asked a question
pertaining to a situation such as this, namely, if the patient
went through with the pregnancy and had the child would
nature come to her rescue in the sense of actual motherhood's
causing her attitudes toward the child to change in a more
favorable direction.

I then proceeded with the dictation of the paper, again
wondering how material of this order would strike someone
whose interests ran along the more disciplined lines of laboratory investigation.

Next, I wish to establish the following facts relative
to Miss M.   The words tall, well-groomed, British, competent, and attractive all fit very closely.   Allowing for the
use of exaggeration in the dream--she was 5 feet 8 1/2
inches tall and was in her late twenties at the time, rather
than 7 feet tall and in her forties--the description is a fairly good one.   I asked someone who knew Miss M. casually
to submit a brief description of her to me in writing, without imparting my real motive for making the request.   The
following description was given:

> Miss M. is a slender person about 5' 8" tall,
> narrow-boned, with sharp clean lines, vivid color-
> ing with her red hair and bright lipstick, and a
> definite sense of style and distinctive form in
> dress and manner.   Her dark eyes are sharply
> bright, with a tense, penetrating look at times as
> if she had strong feelings about almost every stim-
> ulus confronting her, and her lips are often pursed

as she speaks, in a way suggesting both control,
caution, and reflectiveness about what she says.
But the rhythms of her speech are not even, as
this might suggest, but strongly punctuated or ca-
denced, with a marked rise and fall of inflection
and a colorful quality enriched by her low, sometimes throaty, generally resonant voice, and upper-
class enunciation. There are often quite sharp ac-
cents, even little explosions of speech, inter-
spersed with stretches that sound like music.

Other important facts in relation to Miss M. include
the following:

Miss M. 's sister did make a fatal suicidal leap from
her apartment window. This occurred very soon after
the termination of what was supposed to have been a successful three-year analysis.

Miss M. has often remarked how much I resemble her
brother.

Her sister was an ardent Virginia Woolf fan.

A man named H. , Miss M. 's fiancé, died at approximately the same time as her sister, of a brain tumor.
He was under analysis at the time and the tumor and its
manifestations had been overlooked and then interpreted
as purely psychogenic in origin.

Miss M. , when subsequently informed of the dream
at the time of its incorporation into my paper, wrote me as
follows:

This is terribly far-fetched, but the name
'Brain' makes me think of H. , who died at the
same time as my sister did, of a brain tumor.
He is, so to speak, my second reason for distrust-
ing analysis--for reasons you already know about
[an allusion to the unfortunate sequel to her sister's
analysis].

Thus, in the case of two people very close to Miss
M. , tragic outcomes occurred which were more than incidentally related to analysis. In a postscript to the above
note Miss M. adds:

P. S. Tuesday night I dreamed my cat jumped
out of a window in the fortieth story of a strange
building. It was awful and I told Dorothy [a friend]
about the dream Wednesday A. M. She reminded
me about this.

The striking feature about the patient's third dream is
that the majority of the dream elements seemed to have
more of a direct bearing on events relating to Miss M. and
myself than to herself. She was completely at a loss as to
how to deal with the dramatic events in the dream dealing
with the suicide, imprisonment, etc. Some of the tallying
points in this telepathic steal have already been alluded to.
Not resting content with a mere description of a person she
has never met, the patient goes on to probe two most intimate and painful areas and with unerring accuracy describes
the tragic fate of Miss M. 's sister and then struggles with
associations around the word "brain" in connection with this
woman and someone else close to her. Having successfully
established herself as a telepathic subject by virtue of the
first two dreams, she then goes on to compete more openly
and somewhat maliciously with a person whom I held in high
esteem. Her flagrant telepathic explosions make a mockery
of the caution and reserve that Miss M. displayed toward
parapsychological matters. All three characters in this
drama are depicted as trapped--the patient, Miss M. , and
myself. Identifying with the figure of the child, she indicates at one and the same time her own potential for escaping from the shackles of illness and makes use of it as an
expression of her own superiority over Miss M. , who not
only has no child of her own but who asks naive questions
about the mother-child relationship. The analyst is dealt
with in no more kindly fashion. I am depicted as a villain
whose liberating influence exists only by grace of my own
analysis. The name of the person I had locked up in my
house sounded suspiciously like the name of my analyst at
the time--Dr. Robbins. The patient's allusion to the name
Rubins as being anachronistic may stem from her awareness
that an event presented as synchronous should have been
separated in time, namely, my own analysis and hers. (The
likelihood here is that she came by the knowledge of Dr.
Robbins' name through normal channels.)

There were also similarities in the dreams of the
patient and Miss M. occurring that Tuesday evening: in both
cases bodies were hurtling through the air out of apartment
house windows. In Miss M. 's case, her own dream was so

vivid and disturbing that she went out of her way to relate it to a friend. There is one other bit of evidence in support of a telepathic rapport between Miss M. , the patient, and myself that centered about an incident occurring several months before. One evening my wife became quite ill in a rather sudden and abrupt fashion. The following morning both the patient and Miss M. had dreams depicting the illness and the setting in which it occurred.

At the end of the recital of the dream the patient unwittingly showed her hand. She stated quite bluntly: "All this has nothing to do with me." Although it has been my experience that patients often discredit dreams or feel blocked as far as associations go, this kind of definitive disavowal in someone who has worked effectively with dreams is not usual.

That this material may be significant from a parapsychological standpoint obviously rests on factors other than the determination of mathematical probability. That it is, is subjectively inferred from and supported by the following:

(1) The uniqueness of the dream elements involved--as in this case the idea of a third dimension, the stereopticon lens, the body flying through the air.

(2) The time interval in relation to the events in the therapist's life--in each of the dreams discussed, the reality events occurred during the day or evening preceding the dream.

(3) The number of points of correlation between the dream elements and the reality events.

There is one other factor which may prove valuable in the comparison of telepathic dreams with nontelepathic dreams and that centers about the differences in the patient's response. In this case the patient did more work with nontelepathic dreams; they were more meaningful to her. Telepathic dreams often stumped her and evoked characteristic remarks concerning their strangeness to her.

Fourth Dream (December 1, 1948). On another occasion, later that year, and within a week of the time I made another presentation to a psychiatric group, the patient presented another dream involving someone standing in relation to me giving an unusual demonstration.

This morning I underwent some kind of phenomenal feeling. I was sort of disturbed because I couldn't grasp it. It was a dream about my family. It was a flashback to a schoolroom situation. Barry [patient's brother, a physician] was writing meaningless script on the board like A and B, scattered like doodling. This ain't possible. Yes, this is significant. Here I've been taking for granted that everything is OK because the samples on the board are in my father's handwriting, but my father is dead. This is very significant. I must remember it. It was scraping rock bottom. I was standing on bricks. A pictorial translation of the figure of speech....

Associations. The patient spoke about a family situation:

It was quite an ordinary family situation. All were there although not seen. My brother and myself. The only thing I saw was Barry with a pointer like I use to demonstrate slides. He was teaching. Scribbles or doodles. The blackboard was similar to a negative [white instead of black]. The writing was black on white. It was analogous to Alan's [her child] scribbling. There were letters in combination. All I can remember was A, B. It was scattered. There was no pattern. Everything was going smoothly until I had a double-take. Of course there is something wrong. My father is dead. Then it occurred that this is important. I must remember this for the doctor.

Of significance in relation to possible psi functioning are the following: the setting itself in which the patient has the phenomenal feeling of dealing with something which she could not grasp; the correlation between the schoolroom in the dream and the presentation in the lecture-room at the college where my talk was given; the significance of the protagonist's being her brother, who is a physician; and the description of the script as meaningless and being like doodling, an image that ties in with the idea of telepathy as something apart from conscious effort, yet having to do with communication despite the strange and unfamiliar form in which it appears. The family is all there, although not seen. This may have reference to the fact that a case history touching on members of her family was presented. The

pointer was used by her brother, suggesting a demonstration
of some sort. The fact that the blackboard was opposite in
color to what would be expected and the writing was black
on white conveys the feeling of dealing with something in an
inside-out, or reverse, fashion. The telepathic maneuver
makes things on the "inside" apparent on the "outside" in a
manner that stands in contrast to ordinary communication.

It is my impression that the telepathic maneuver
comes into play in situations the demands of which allow for
no other type of contact, or make another type of contact
relatively less appropriate. This patient, suffering from an
obsessive-compulsive character structure and torn asunder
under the mass of contradictions that one only finds in the
obsessive personality--contradictions which did not leave her
free to express love or hate or any intermediary expressions
of either--was forced into this "extra dimensional" way of
operating from time to time in the analysis. To her it was
appropriate. The questions as to whether functioning at a
telepathic level is ever genuinely appropriate is an important
one. Perhaps the telepathic sensing of injury or death to
loved ones at a distance is an example of telepathy as an
appropriate function. Under those circumstances it may
serve as the only way of becoming aware of an important
reality. Regarded in this way, the regressive or atavistic
view of telepathy is held up to question. That it can appear
inappropriate, much as any neurotic mechanism is really inappropriate, there can be no doubt--as illustrated in the example given--but that this is the whole story is by no means
certain. Further speculations along these lines will have to
be held for the future.

Although the clinical situation, because of the inherent limitations of control and observation, cannot come up
with hard evidence for the reality of the telepathic dream,
it does present a unique and very special kind of opportunity
to get at the nature and quality of the human interaction going on at the time such events are presumed to occur. The
clinical situation differs from that of the characteristic objective crisis associated with telepathy, i. e. , one coming
about external to and apart from the subject. The transactions do not take place at the high pitch of arousal that accompanies such crises. Nevertheless, the fact remains that
the therapeutic situation is a stress situation in which the
therapist becomes both the stressor--i. e. , the one challenging an existing characterologic status quo--and the source of
relief, a supportive trustworthy significant figure. In a way

that is somewhat analogous to the major crises that characterize anecdotal accounts, therapy results in a succession of
mini-crises of an intrapersonal nature in relation to which
the person of the therapist plays a major role. Dynamically,
the telepathic maneuver appears to be deployed in the interest of transferential needs--i.e., idiosyncratically generated
feelings toward the therapist that are inappropriate in the
present context and hence have to be disowned--or they surface at times when the patient feels the impact of counter-
transference--i.e., the same kind of idiosyncratic and inappropriate feeling developing in the analyst toward the patient. It is conceivable that if further thought and observation were given to the operation of psi in the consulting
room, more could be learned of its spontaneous occurrence
under other circumstances. Although explorations of this
kind are possible since a much larger number of analysts
have experiences of this kind than one would be led to assume from the number of instances reported in the literature, the fact of the matter is that in practice this poses a
problem with regard to the degree of self-disclosure required of the therapist if the patient's telepathic thrusts into
his private life are to be fully and honestly explored. Material that goes beyond the level of discretion and comfort
simply won't get reported. This is particularly true in the
therapeutic situation where the telepathic maneuver, at least
in the beginning, tends to operate in the interest of maintaining distance, or tends to display hostile, suspicious, or
competitive aspects.

It is doubtful as to whether material of this kind,
despite the most rigorous kind of handling, can ever constitute a proof of the existence of telepathy. The very complexity of the situation involved, the intricacies of the relationships among the many factors brought into play, and the
difficulties of dealing with dream elements on a mathematical basis all bode ill for anyone venturing into this territory
armed with p values and chi squares. If the statistical
evaluations applied in incomparably simpler experimental
situations fail to convince, it seems unlikely that they would
be of much service here. Whatever conviction is generated
stems from the fuller interpretation the telepathic hypothesis often leads to.

The Recent Past

The greater general interest in the past few years in

parapsychology and the greater level of scientific interest it
has aroused have not in any discernible measure been reflected in any greater degree of professional activity in this
area on the part of most psychiatrists and psychoanalysts.
Eisenbud has remained actively engaged with the subject both
clinically and theoretically. His recent volume (1970) sums
up his clinical experiences with psi in the psychoanalytic
setting and his papers have been devoted to an analysis of
the nature of scientific resistance to the recognition of psi
events (1966-67, 1972). This has led him to interpret the
stance of scientists as generated defensively from the basic
incompatibility of psi with the scientific outlook. Eisenbud
(1972) postulates a kind of selective inattention to psi events
by the body of science as "the progressive need on man's
part to disavow the immense potentialities for good and evil
of his inner nature, and his need to get further away from
that early conception of causality which places him at the
center of things" (p41). What Eisenbud appears to be saying
is that it is the very ubiquitousness and power of psi that
appears to be frightening scientists off, holding up as it does
the spector of a return to the primitive's regressive preoccupation with the omnipotence of thought. Whether or not
Eisenbud's thesis is valid concerning the prevalence of psi
and the significant role it plays in the affairs of men as
well as in a more pervasive way helping to maintain an ecological balance among all living organisms, I think it is fair
to say that the scientific method as we know it has evolved
in the course of man's attempt to master nature as he has
come to understand nature outside and apart from himself.
We are only now beginning to forge the tools with which to
look at man in his relationship to nature, which in turn
means looking into man himself. We are apt to discover
psi as part of that nature and perhaps, as Eisenbud and
others have suggested, as part of a larger scheme of things.

Experimental Studies

Another significant development in recent years has
been the effort to induce dream telepathy experimentally in
the laboratory, making use of the rapid eye movement (REM)
monitoring technique to determine the onset and termination
of recurring dream sequences in the course of a night's
sleep. A full account of how this work came into being
and of the formal and informal experiments carried out in
the Division of Parapsychology and Psychophysics (formerly
the Dream Laboratory) of the Department of Psychiatry of

the Maimonides Medical Center in Brooklyn is given in a recently published volume (Ullman and Krippner, with Vaughan,
1973).

Methodology. The formal studies were conducted
either with single subjects over a period of several nights
or with a series of subjects each sleeping in the laboratory
for one night. The subjects were volunteers, some of whom
were selected on the basis of earlier successful performances
on screening nights. The subject's sleep was monitored
electroencephalographically and he was awakened at the estimated end of each REM period to report his dream. An
agent or sender spent the night in a separate room attempting telepathically to influence the subject's dreams by con-
centrating on the selected target picture at intervals throughout the night and particularly when signaled that a REM period for the subject had begun. The target, generally an art
print, was randomly selected by the agent from a pool of
targets in opaque, sealed containers after the subject was in
bed. Only the agent was aware of the target chosen for the
particular night and he remained in his room throughout the
night acoustically isolated from both subject and experimenter.
The dream protocols were transcribed from the taped reports. Copies of them, along with copies of the targets
used for any given experimental series, were given to three
independent judges who assessed correspondences on a blind
basis. The results were analyzed using either the Latin-
square analysis of variance technique or the application of
the binomial expansion theorem.

Results. From the summer of 1964 through the fall
of 1971, 12 formal experimental studies in dreams and telepathy were completed. Nine of these 12 studies yielded results that were statistically significant, supporting the telepathy hypothesis: (a) a twelve-night screening study for the
selection of future subjects (Ullman, Krippner, and Feldstein, 1966), (b) a seven-night study with one subject (Ullman et al., 1966), (c) an eight-night replication study with
the same subject (Ullman and Krippner, 1969), (d) an eight-
night study with a different subject (Krippner and Ullman,
1970), (e) a 16-session study utilizing hypnosis and dreams
(Krippner, 1968), (f) a 16-night study with four subjects involving differing target conditions (Krippner, Honorton, and
Ullman, 1972a), (g) a study involving hypnotically-induced
dreams (Honorton, 1972), (h) an eight-night study of precognitive dreams with a single subject (Krippner, Ullman, and
Honorton, 1971), and (i) a 16-night precognitive dream study

with the same subject (Krippner, Honorton, and Ullman, 1972b). Three studies yielded nonsignificant results: (j) another 12-night screening study (Ullman, 1969), (k) an eight-night study with a single subject (Ullman, 1969), and (l) a 16-night study with a single subject (Krippner, 1969).

Between the spring of 1964, when a standard proce-dure for monitoring the subject's sleep was adopted by the laboratory, and the end of 1969, 74 pilot sessions involving one or more agents and a single subject were completed. These pilot sessions were not part of any formal experi-mental series but were exploratory in nature, investigating potential subjects as well as possible useful techniques and procedures. Equally rigid precautions against sensory leak-age were taken with the pilot sessions as with the experi-mental sessions. If chance rather than telepathy had been operating, half of the 74 pilot sessions would have been "hits" and half would have been "misses." Instead, the judges awarded scores that produced 52 "hits" and 22 "misses." This distribution is statistically significant (Krippner, 1970).

There is empirical evidence suggesting that, in some instances at least, forms contained in the target material come through more clearly and recognizably than the con-tent itself and that this applies to more complex targets as well as simple targets where the form itself is the predomi-nant feature. There are two experimental techniques that may have a possible bearing upon the perceptual aspect of psi effects as this relates to similarities based on form. Each of these techniques limits information input, but in different ways. Tachistoscopic presentations limit exposure in time. Work with the stabilized retinal image limits in-formation ordinarily collected and maintained through the play of eye movements about an object under fixation.

There have been a number of experiments beginning with awakened interest in the Pötzl phenomenon demonstrat-ing that cues occurring outside of conscious awareness can produce perceptual illusions and fragmentation of the image. Similar effects are noted in connection with Evans' (1967a, 1967b) observations on fragmentation phenomena associated with binocular stabilization. He notes that under conditions of stabilization when a pattern disappears it does so in parts and the parts drop out in a nonrandom fashion. He talks of the hierarchy of the visual system and suggests, as an explanation of the fragmentation phenomena, that when the information supply is limited, as in stabilization experiments, not all levels of the hierarchy are activated. As a consequence, only parts of the pattern are seen to be corresponding to the level of the hierarchy reached. Evans also notes that characteristic stabilization will fragment after repeated tachistoscopic exposures.

The fragmentation of images noted by Warcollier (1938) and Sinclair (1962) in their efforts to effect the transfer of information at a distance resembles in remarkable ways the fragmentary percepts obtained through the two experimental strategies described, particularly with regard to the fragmentation of complex forms into simpler forms and the emergence of simple forms out of more complex imagery. On occasion similar forms emerged when similar targets were used by two different investigators. These findings suggest by implication that the neurophysiological pathways involved in the processing of psi effects may be the same as in normal visual perception.

WHERE WE ARE GOING

In trying to map general directions that may be realizable in the foreseeable future, perhaps the first question that arises is, "Is parapsychology a viable science?" The answer, I believe, is a qualified yes. Parapsychologists have set standards for themselves that match in rigor the application of the scientific method in other disciplines. The fact that this has not yet gained them the same measure of respectability and acceptance accorded those working in other areas hinges on the absence of a repeatable experiment. This situation, which has prevailed for such a very long time is, I am afraid, apt to continue for the simple reason that the problems raised are insoluble in the context of parapsychology as a separate discipline. Stated another way, the problems are not soluble in the same context--the field of parapsychology--in which they have surfaced. Their solution will rest not on the continued examination and measurement of these surface outcroppings, but on an examination of the complicated network of hidden underground connections weaving psi effects into the very fabric of natural events. Parapsychologists will have achieved their goal once other scientists take up the challenge. They can then dematerialize as parapsychologists and reappear as members of interdisciplinary teams addressing themselves to the specific remaining mysteries that still exist in all fields of human endeavor, but this time with the knowledge that psi effects may play a significant role in the unraveling of these mysteries. This situation is somewhat analogous to the one in which ethnic minorities find themselves. They have to adopt an independent stand initially to make the world aware of their special problems, but paradoxically the long-range solution to these problems rests not with the maintenance of this separateness, but with its dissolution in the interest of establishing a brotherhood of man.

There are signs on the horizon that this indeed is beginning to come about. Whether we like it or not, the momentum for parapsychological research is outstripping the efforts of the professional parapsychologists and moving more into the hands of interested parties and investigators ranging along a very broad continuum of competence and scientific integrity. Despite the obvious pitfalls and dangers, this is, to my way of thinking, not only a good thing, but a necessary one. It represents the first crude approximations of what, hopefully, ultimately will be a concerted, broad-based interdisciplinary effort, international in scope, to incorporate the reality of psi effects into man's ongoing effort to explore and understand the world in which he finds himself in the course of what appears to him to be his finite existence on earth. It is cause for celebration rather than resignation.

Does this imply that the professional corps of parapsychologists should push some kind of self-destruct button? By no means! Rather, as indicated below, they, being the ones who have the most specialized knowledge about these unique effects, must now join with their fellow scientists in the search for answers. The ground rules for the search, however, have become somewhat more elaborate. The observer has to be included as a participant in the hard as well as the soft sciences; the conditions for experimentation have to include the reality of psi interaction; and because we are now moving into areas where the mental and physical have come together we will need a variety of specialists working together to address themselves in interdisciplinary fashion to the problems in a single discipline.

Coming down to specifics, what might this mean in the case of psychiatry? What are some of the enduring mysteries and are they possibly psi-related? There is much about the major psychoses, particularly schizophrenia, that still eludes us. Ehrenwald (1948), working in the tradition of earlier psychical researchers, felt that psi events played a role in the genesis of at least some forms of schizophrenia (paranoia and catatonia).

Psi events, by their nature, appear to be able to exert a mental influence on energy systems at a distance as well as to transcend ordinary relations to space and time. I have elsewhere speculated on the possible relevance this might have with regard to psychosis (Ullman, 1952):

"To understand the unique quality of the telepathic dream, we have to be aware not only of what is unique about the dream itself, but also what is unique about the dreamer. Time seems to stand still for the schizophrenic. Perhaps it may be said that his psychosis begins at the point where this fiction becomes his reality. The ability to obviate the changing quality of experience, namely, its temporal aspect, can only be achieved by an overwhelming effort to break all ties with reality. But this obviating process, before it leads the individual to take the fatal leap into the state of absolute timelessness, omnipotence, and psychosis, may leave traces and side effects which indicate its existence and direction. Telepathic functioning may be just such an evidential side effect. If time and space are viewed as static, fixed, and rigid categories, much as containers in which events occur rather than as reflecting properties of matter, then the dynamism of telepathy has to be placed outside of time and space and of necessity outside of our reach.

"It seems to me, if I may be permitted a further brief excursion into philosophical speculation, that two preliminary steps may be postulated which, if valid, might help in coping with this difficulty. The first has to do with the implications of regarding time and space not as given categories, but rather as abstractions from our experience to express, in the case of the former, the element of change or unlikeness in our experience and, in the case of the latter, the element of sameness or likeness in our experience. Adjustment to experience through time and space as we know them while it represents the most human and most rewarding way of adjustment in terms of mastery over nature, does not shed light on how these aspects of experience are dealt with in the case of those who have forsaken human goals and needs. This may have some relevance to the situation in borderline psychotics who, in coming close to a total surrender of the possibility of fulfilling their human needs, experience at the same time a disruption of their ability to experience the temporal and spatial aspects of reality in a human way. Whatever deeper level is opened up as a result of this disruption is at this point a matter of conjecture. Telepathic functioning provides us with a glimpse, sufficient to confirm its existence, but too evanescent to reveal much information about it" (p12-3).

These thoughts were reemphasized two decades later (Ullman, 1973), when I suggested that

"we may have to reconceptualize our understanding of both of these psychoses [schizophrenia and manic-depressive psychosis] in terms of the spatial and temporal aspects of character organization. There has been some tendency in recent years to merge the two psychoses, but I think that symptomatically, temperamentally, and perhaps constitutionally they remain distinctive. The manic-depressive maintains affective ties to the world, but cannot modulate them. The schizophrenic deploys his affective capacities in the service of maintaining distance between himself and the world. The schizophrenic is future-oriented in terms of his unrelenting vulnerability to unpredictable threats to and assaults upon his isolation. The manic-depressive is past-oriented in the depressive phase, relating in terms of past failures, and present-oriented in the manic phase, relating in terms of a sense of unreal successes.

"Time plays a different role for each in still another way. Magical thinking and omnipotence of thought play a key role for the schizophrenic. Normal processes, extending in time, have to be bypassed to arrive at magical solutions. Real time, in a sense, doesn't exist for the schizophrenic. This is in contrast to the manic-depressive for whom time is either retarded or accelerated, depending on the phasic variation he is experiencing. In the depressive phase, there is a severe limitation in the contextual field and time is retarded. In the manic phase, there is a tremendous expanse in the contextual field and time is accelerated. In the depressive phase the past overshadows the present and the future, and in the manic phase the present overshadows both the past and the future. Is this difference

in orientation reflected in differences in ESP performance? Would precognition be more apt to be associated with schizophrenia, telepathy or clairvoyance
with the manic psychosis, and retrocognition with the
depressive psychosis? Would other but equally consistent relationships obtain where compensatory abilities
might play a role--i. e. , the schizophrenic sensing
things paranormally in the present in connection with
his excessive vigilance concerning the future?

"Space can be thought of as content, as context,
and in a certain sense as encompassing the qualities
of palpability, endurance, and sameness in contrast to
the qualities of impalpability, elusiveness, and change
associated with the concept of time. In this sense the
schizophrenic is time-oriented--the changing aspects
of reality are more important to him than the enduring ones, since it is change and not sameness nor
familiarity that evokes vigilance operations. For the
manic-depressive it is space, context, and sameness
that predominate over time and change, since the
manic-depressive does invest himself in his human
context but unfortunately as an expression of the fantasy either that it cannot change or that it is changing
too fast for him to keep up with.

"This differential weighting of space and time in
the two syndromes might provide potential clues for
further research efforts. Might it not be better to
seek effects in the psychological realm with schizoid
individuals and psychokinetic effects with those closer
to the manic-depressive end of the spectrum (and here
I would include hysterics)? In the first case we are
testing the limits of the schizophrenic's omnipotence
of thought, his need to know in the service of vigilance
operations, and his preoccupation with the temporal or
changing aspects of reality. In the second case we
are testing the limits of the individual whose interaction with the world [about him] is much more invested
in space, context, bodily and motoric involvement.

"I have not yet engaged in any systematic study,
but I have developed the clinical impression that from
a psychopathological point of view good ESP performers
as encountered in the clinical situation are on the
schizoid side. I haven't had the opportunity to study
sufficient [numbers of] PK performers, but I would

offer the speculation that they fall within the manic-
depressive or hysteric syndromes" (p111-3).

In some ways the task that confronts us now is to review the work of Myers in the context of current technological, theoretical, and conceptual trends. Myers' categories
(1903), in somewhat different language, deal with those aspects of human experience that are possibly psi related.
His categories include: Genius; Personality disorganization;
Sleep; Hypnosis; Sensory automatisms; Phantasms of the
dead; Motor automatisms; Trance, possession and ecstasy.
If we add to these drug- and nondrug-related explorations of
inner space, we encompass a good deal of what current investigators are concerned with. There have been remarkable
technological advances in areas likely to have some relevance
for psi research but that haven't been exploited in the interest of psi research or where only beginnings have been
made. Emotions are certainly important as mediators of
psi exchanges. An interesting technique has evolved to
translate into a visual form one's repertory of emotional
responses (Clynes, 1973). Might those with similar profiles
be better at psi exchanges? Biofeedback as perfected and
applied by the Greens (Green and Green, 1971), and Brown
(1974) holds out the promise of learning more about internal
processes by objectifying them through techniques of external display.

Lilly (1972) and Masters and Houston (1966) have been
exploring inner space using both drug- and nondrug-related
techniques. Lilly has been writing about it from a personal
and experiential point of view; Masters and Houston in terms
of strategies designed to liberate creative energies and release untapped potentials. Fischer (1971) describes himself
as a cartographer of inner space and has charted the major
changes of state along an arousal continuum. Ornstein
(1972) calls our attention to the way in which split-brain
preparation studies shed light on the dual nature of our information processing systems, the left hemisphere being related to language and the linear mode and the right hemisphere being related to holistic patterning in space and time.

Clinically, under the leadership of people like Maslow (1964), who talks about peak experiences, and Assagioli
(1965), the founder of "psychosynthesis," who talks of height
psychology as a modern-day contrast to the depth psychology
of old, man's extended faculties become the focus of the
therapist's interest rather than his pathological heritage.

Some of these concerns have crystallized as the movement known as "transpersonal psychology." Grof (1973), based on his extensive experience with the psychedelic effects of LSD, has made significant contributions to our understanding of the transpersonal experience.

Last, but not least, the explorations in the new territory are not without those scouts who, armed with the power of abstraction, the mastery of subatomic physics and the capacity to play with imaginary numbers and hypernumbers, are attempting to provide theoretical charts capable of both describing and predicting the properties and limits of subjective space; I refer to the work of Wigner (1962) and Bohm (1973) in physics and Musès (1972) in mathematics.

The early founders of the (British) Society for Psychical Research had a strong antipathy toward what they felt was the materialistic course science had charted for itself. William James (1896) expressed this sentiment:

> Through my slight participation in the investigations of the Society for Psychical Research, I have become acquainted with numbers of persons of this sort, for whom the very word Science has become a name of reproach, for reasons that I now both understand and respect. It is the intolerance of Science for such phenomena as we are studying, her peremptory denial either of their existence or of their significance except as proofs of man's absolute folly, that has set Science so apart from the common sympathies of the race. I confess that it is on this, its humanizing mission, that our Society's best claim to the gratitude of our generation seems to me to depend. We have restored continuity to history [p9].

Perhaps it has taken all this time--nearly a century --and the evolving of a counter culture, to turn science around so that we can begin to look through the other end of the microscope. The observer is now being observed and once that begins to occur, psi effects are no more mysterious than the existence of consciousness itself or the nature of the electron.

REFERENCES

Assagioli, R. Psychosynthesis. New York: Hobbs Dorman, 1965.

Bohm, D. "Fragmentation and Wholeness. " The Academy, 17 (1973), 18-25.

Brown, B. New Mind, New Body. New York: Harper & Row, 1974.

Clynes, M. "Sentics: Biocybernetics of Emotional Communication. " Annals of the New York Academy of Sciences, 220 (1973), 57-131.

Coleman, M. L. "The Paranormal Triangle in Analytic Supervision. " Psychoanalysis and Psychoanalytic Review, 45 (1958), 73-84.

Ehrenwald, J. "Telepathy in Dreams. " British Journal of Medical Psychology, 19 (1942), 313-23.

_____. Telepathy and Medical Psychology. New York: Norton, 1948.

Eisenbud, J. "Telepathy and the Problems of Psychoanalysis. " Psychoanalytic Quarterly, 15 (1946), 32-87.

_____. "The Dreams of Two Patients in Analysis Interpreted as a Telepathic Rêve à Deux. " Psychoanalytic Quarterly, 16 (1947), 39-60.

_____. "Why Psi?" Psychoanalytic Review, 33 (1966-67), 147-63.

_____. Psi and Psychoanalysis. New York: Grune & Stratton, 1970.

_____. "Some Notes on the Psychology of the Paranormal. " Journal of the American Society for Psychical Research, 66 (1972), 27-41.

Ellis, A. "Telepathy and Psychoanalysis: A Critique of Recent Findings. " Psychiatric Quarterly, 21 (1947), 607-59.

Evans, C. R. "Fragmentation Phenomena Associated with Binocular Stabilization. " British Journal of Physiological Optics, 24 (1967), 242-8. (a)

_____. "Further Studies of Pattern Perception and a Stabilised Retinal Image: The Use of Prolonged After-Images to Achieve Perfect Stabilisation. " British Journal of Psychology, 58 (1967), 315-27. (b)

Fischer, R. "A Cartography of the Ecstatic and Meditative States. " Science, 174 (1971), 897-904.

Fodor, N. "Telepathic Dreams. " American Imago, 3 (1942), 61-87.

Freud, S. "Dreams and Telepathy. " Imago, 8 (1922), 1-22.

Green, E. E. , and Green, A. M. "On the Meaning of

Transpersonal: Some Metaphysical Perspectives. "
Journal of Transpersonal Psychology, 3 (1971), 27-46.

Grof, S. Agony and Ecstasy in Psychiatric Treatment:
Theory and Practice of LSD Psychotherapy. Palo Alto,
Cal.: Science and Behavior Books, 1973.

Honorton, C. "Significant Factors in Hypnotically-Induced
Clairvoyant Dreams. " Journal of the American Society
for Psychical Research, 66 (1972), 86-102.

Humphrey, B. M. "ESP Tests with Mental Patients Before
and After Electroshock Treatment. " Journal of the Society for Psychical Research, 37 (1954), 259-66.

James, W. "Address by the President. " Proceedings of
the Society for Psychical Research, 12 (1896), 2-10.

Jones, E. The Life and Work of Sigmund Freud. New
York: Basic Books, 1957. 3 vols.

Jung, C. Memories, Dreams, Reflections. New York:
Pantheon, 1963.

Krippner, S. "An Experimental Study on Hypnosis and Telepathy. " American Journal of Clinical Hypnosis, 11
(1968), 45-54.
_____. "The Paranormal Dream and Man's Pliable Fu-
ture. " Psychoanalytic Review, 56 (1969), 28-43.
_____. "Electrophysiological Studies of ESP in Dreams:
Sex Differences in 74 Telepathy Sessions. " Journal of
the American Society for Psychical Research, 64 (1970),
277-85.
_____, Honorton, C., and Ullman, M. "Telepathic Trans-
mission of Art Prints in Sleep. " Proceedings 80th An-
nual Convention, American Psychological Association,
1972. (a)
_____, _____ and _____. "A Second Precognitive
Dream Study with Malcolm Bessent. " Journal of the
American Society for Psychical Research, 66 (1972),
269-79. (b)
_____ and Ullman, M. "Telepathy and Dreams: A Controlled Experiment with EEG-ECG Monitoring. " Journal
of Nervous and Mental Disease, 151 (1970), 394-403.
_____, _____ and Honorton, C. "A Precognitive
Dream Study with a Single Subject. " Journal of the
American Society for Psychical Research, 65 (1971),
192-203.

Lilly, J. C. The Center of the Cyclone. New York: Ju-
lian Press, 1972.

Maslow, A. H. Religious Values and Peak Experiences.
Columbus: Ohio State University Press, 1964.

Masters, R. E. L., and Houston, J. The Varieties of
Psychedelic Experience. New York: Holt, Rinehart

and Winston, 1966.

Meerloo, J. Hidden Communion. New York: Helix Press/ Garrett Publications, 1964.

Mitchell, T. W. "The Contributions of Psychical Research to Psychotherapeutics. " Proceedings of the Society for Psychical Research, 45 (1939), 175-86.

Musès, C. "The Exploration of Consciousness. " In C. Musès and A. Young (eds.), Consciousness and Reality (New York: Outerbridge & Lazard, 1972), p102-31.

Myers, F. W. H. Human Personality and Its Survival of Bodily Death. London: Longmans, Green, 1903. 2 vols.

Ornstein, R. E. The Psychology of Consciousness. San Francisco: W. H. Freeman, 1972.

Pedersen-Krag, G. "Telepathy and Repression. " Psychoanalytic Quarterly, 16 (1947), 61-8.

Servadio, E. "A Presumptively Telepathic-Precognitive Dream During Analysis. " International Journal of Psycho-Analysis, 37 (1956), 1-4.

Sinclair, U. Mental Radio, 2d rev. ed. Springfield, Ill. : Thomas, 1962.

Stekel, W. Der telepathische Traum. Berlin: Johannes Baum Verlag, 1921.

Ullman, M. "On the Nature of Resistance to Psi Phenomena. " Journal of the American Society for Psychical Research, 46 (1952), 11-3.

_____. "On the Occurrence of Telepathic Dreams. " Journal of the American Society for Psychical Research, 53 (1959), 50-61.

_____. "Telepathy and Dreams. " Experimental Medicine and Surgery, 27 (1969), 19-38.

_____. "Psi and Psychiatry: The Need for Restructuring Basic Concepts. " In W. G. Roll, R. L. Morris, and J. D. Morris (eds.), Research in Parapsychology 1972 (Metuchen, N. J. : Scarecrow Press, 1973), p110-3.

_____. "Psi and Psychiatry. " In E. D. Mitchell et al. , Psychic Exploration, ed. by J. White (New York: Putnam's, 1974), p247-67. (a)

_____. "Parapsychology and Psychiatry. " In A. Freedman and H. Kaplan (eds.), Comprehensive Textbook of Psychiatry, 2d ed. (Baltimore: Williams and Wilkins, 1974), v2, p2552-61. (b)

_____ and Krippner, S. "A Laboratory Approach to the Nocturnal Dimension of Paranormal Experience: Report of a Confirmatory Study Using the REM Monitoring Technique. " Biological Psychiatry, 1 (1969), 259-70.

_____, _____ and Feldstein, S. "Experimentally Induced Telepathic Dreams: Two Studies Using EEG-REM Monitoring Technique." International Journal of Neuropsychiatry, 2 (1966), 420-37.

_____ and _____, with A. Vaughan. Dream Telepathy. New York: Macmillan, 1973.

Warcollier, R. Experimental Telepathy. Boston: Boston Society for Psychic Research, 1938.

West, D. J. "ESP Tests with Psychotics." Journal of the Society for Psychical Research, 36 (1952), 619-23.

Wigner, E. P. "Remarks on the Mind-Body Question." In I. J. Good (ed.), The Scientist Speculates (New York: Basic Books, 1962), p284-301.

Zorab, G. "ESP Experiments with Psychotics." Journal of the Society for Psychical Research, 39 (1957), 162-4.

S David Kahn

"MYERS' PROBLEM" REVISITED

In the discussion to follow I wish first to identify and consider the strongly ambivalent attitudes toward parapsychology that are still prevalent in the scientific community after a hundred years of psychical research and which largely account for its continued lack of serious support. Second, I will suggest that this situation cannot be expected to change substantially until we achieve a clearly repeatable experiment. Third, I want to review and then question the adequacy of our present concepts of telepathy. Fourth, I will try to illustrate the continuing value of new theoretical models. And last, I will indicate how drawing on some neglected ideas of F. W. H. Myers--the leading 19th-century pioneer of modern parapsychology--might help us to develop a repeatable experiment when they are articulated with recent developments in the technology of signal detection and enhancement.

Doubt, Belief, and Repeatability

The year 1875 was in retrospect a propitious one for psychology. Darwin's Origin of Species had by then established the new scientific milieu. Wundt had just published his ground-breaking Principles of Physiological Psychology and was now being called to Leipzig where he would establish the world's first formal psychology laboratory. Our own William James had recently returned as an instructor in physiology at Harvard, where that year the first room was set aside for psychological experimentation in this country; he was soon to discover what was to become an abiding interest in psychical research. Freud had just turned 19.

The year 1875 was also a milepost for parapsychology, though it passed almost unnoticed. It saw the appearance of a paper on "mind-reading" by a Dr. T. A. McGraw (1875), a surgeon, in the Detroit Review of Medicine and Pharmacy, and this was soon followed by a lecture on the same topic by the physicist W. F. Barrett before the British Association at Glasgow (it is interesting to note, however, that the British Association refused to publish this lecture and it did not appear in print until 1883 (Barrett, 1882)). Here was the first appearance within the scientific establishment of the cautious suggestion that thought transference should be considered a suitable subject for inquiry. Within 10 years, formal societies were established in both England and America, though not under direct academic sponsorship. The roster of scientists who lent their name and efforts to these enterprises was impressive and enthusiasm and expectations ran high.

The Cambridge philosopher, Henry Sidgwick, one of the founders of the (British) Society for Psychical Research, told William James shortly before his (Sidgwick's) death that, although he had hoped for a "promptitude of result," "if anyone had told him at the outset that after 20 years he would be in the same identical state of doubt and balance that he started with, he would have deemed the prophecy incredible. It appeared impossible that that amount of handling evidence should bring so little finality of decision." James (1909/1960, p310), in reporting this the year before his death in 1910, added:

> My own experience has been similar to Sidgwick's.... I am theoretically no 'further' than I was at the beginning; and I confess that at times I have been tempted to believe that the Creator has eternally intended this department of nature to remain baffling, to prompt our curiosities and hopes and suspicions all in equal measure, so that, although ghosts and clairvoyances, and raps and messages from spirits, are always seeming to exist and can never be fully explained away, they also can never be susceptible of full corroboration [p310].

Freud, an admirer of James, experienced similar ambivalence during his own lifetime preoccupation with telepathic phenomena. He once commented to his student, Eitington, that there were two themes that always perplexed him to distraction, the Bacon-Shakespeare controversy, and occultism. At 64, Freud actually wrote to Hereward Carrington: "If I were at the beginning rather than the end of a scientific career, as I am today, I might possibly choose just this field of research, in spite of all difficulties" (E. L. Freud, 1960, letter 192). Yet eight years later a slip of memory permitted him to insist indignantly that such an assertion had never been made (Jones, 1957, v3, ch14). When 65, Freud (1922) closed his paper on "Dreams and Telepathy," in which he discussed two dreams suggestive of a telepathic factor, by saying:

> Have I given you the impression that I am secretly inclined to support the reality of telepathy in the occult sense? If so, I should very much regret that it is so difficult to avoid giving such an impression. For in reality I have been anxious to be strictly impartial. I have every reason to be so, since I have no opinion on the matter and know nothing about it [p220].

Yet, with the publication of this paper in English three years later, Freud could scold Jones for being "too unhappy about the sensation that my conversion to telepathy has made in English periodicals!" (Jones, 1957, v3, ch14).

I would suggest that Freud's ambivalence and James' sense of being perplexed to distraction by the Creator's apparent intention to keep us in a state of bafflement still haunt the scientist who conscientiously seeks to take a definitive position on the subject. It is true that in the last 50 years there has been a voluminous amount of hard experimental data subjected to "evidence handling" by the scientific community. In fact, unless one adduces systematic fraud conspired to by large numbers of otherwise honest, respectable, and competent scientists, the best of the experimental data now stands unimpeached by ordinary scientific criticism, and this despite considerable skeptical and at times hostile scrutiny of the body of evidence (Hansel, 1966). Yet most members of the scientific community steadfastly maintain a general position somewhere between simple disinterest and open disbelief (Ransom, 1971; Schmeidler, 1968).

I believe this ambivalence--though it is at times concealed by rigidly extreme positions in both directions--is nearly universal among competent scientists because it derives from unconscious sources and for that reason its effects on conscious attitudes will not be reduced until they

are simply overwhelmed by a clearly repeatable experiment.
I mean by this a demonstration of psi that may be produced
each and every time operationally defined conditions have
been met and by different experimenters who are independent
of each other.

Parapsychologists have increasingly felt such an exacting burden of proof to be unfair and inconsistent since
such branches of science as astronomy and clinical medicine
do not insist upon such elegance of demonstration.   Though
the logic of such an argument may be correct, it is nonetheless both psychologically and historically naive.   As T. S.
Kuhn (1962) has shown us, new discoveries that require basic
changes in a contemporary world-view, but which fail to offer coherent and systematic alternatives, are strenuously re-
sisted by the inertia of science almost in disregard of the
weight of the evidence.   Such conservatism maintains procedural order while testifying to the importance of the
claimed discovery.   In contrast, the easy acceptance of
trivial and expected findings simply means that occasional
undetected errors can be tolerated when no issues of consequence are involved.

This skepticism toward the unexpected deeply rein-
forces for the scientist himself the secure notion that our
chaotic universe is really an orderly place ruled by familiar
"natural laws" on whose continued operation in the future he
can safely depend.   I do not need to remind you of Hume's
reduction of this basic credo of the scientist to just another
item of faith, with roots in neither logic nor observation.
Even the heartiest critics and most prejudiced opponents of
parapsychology have acknowledged the extraordinary disorder
that the assumption of mental action at a distance would introduce to our present scientific world-view.   Freud (1921),
when writing about telepathy, made the point so vividly that
it is worth repeating:

> But consider what a momentous step beyond
> what we have hitherto believed would be involved
> in this hypothesis alone.   What the custodian of
> [the basilica of] Saint-Denis used to add to his ac-
> count of the Saint's martyrdom remains true.
> Saint-Denis is said, after his head was cut off, to
> have picked it up and to have walked quite a dis-
> tance with it under his arm.   But the custodian
> used to remark 'Dans des cas pareils, ce n'est
> que le premier pas qui coûte [in a case like that,

the beginning is the difficulty]!' The rest is easy (p193).

It seems clear that replication is an entirely legitimate demand to place upon parapsychology from the standpoint of how science really works. Epistemology aside, however, I believe all would agree that repeatability would in addition have enormous practical value in giving us the crucial leverage we need for the systematic unraveling of the many puzzles that need to be solved before the psi function will be finally understood. Here again, once there is replication, the rest is easy.

The final issue to be raised here is perhaps the most important. Upon whose shoulders should the responsibility fall for achieving repeatability? Ordinarily, when one or several scientists initially report a new discovery of potentially great importance, the rush among powerful and well-funded scientists and their institutional supporters to get in on the new discovery is great, and often the ensuing competition is bitter and ruthless. More than one Nobel prize has been unofficially contested in the back halls of science in the belief that the winner had improperly seized and exploited the basic ideas of their original discoverers. Thus, the intrinsic pressures and rewards of the free scientific market place usually see to it that the scientific community at large quickly seizes the opportunity to replicate important new discoveries in order to explore their implications. While the individual scientist may feel he has had his priority trampled by opportunistic colleagues, society itself benefits by the rapidity with which new discoveries are extended by a free science.

The exception to this general pattern seems to be those initial discoveries that are so startling as to challenge basic world views, and these, as Kuhn (1962) has shown, are handled very differently. They are frequently ignored, ridiculed, opposed, and even actively suppressed. Here, parapsychology is a modern case in point because with the amount of present evidence for its basic hypotheses, one would have expected dozens of senior scientists to have dropped nearly everything to compete for the potential gains in scientific knowledge, personal prestige, and institutional power that the replication of psi phenomena would win for its discoverers.

As we know, nothing of the sort has happened and I

do not believe it will, for the various reasons discussed earlier. Thus, paradoxically, the most exacting, difficult, and expensive scientific task--achieving reliable replication-- falls by default into the lap of organized parapsychology, rather than into the experienced hands of organized science, where it really belongs. If, as in recent years, even para- psychology itself begins to default on pursuing this crucial and essential task, then I believe its scientific support will continue to be as Spartan as it has been in the past.

It seems to me, therefore, that the few small pockets of available funding which parapsychology controls--I doubt if they number more than 10--should be devoted for the next quarter century to the funding of systematic efforts to solve the replication problem by giving the highest priority to those parapsychologists interested in pursuing it.

Perhaps, as in the case of certain dramatically suc- cessful crash programs during World War II, research groups could informally agree among themselves to parcel out particular strategies so that all the basic options would receive at least some concentrated attention.

I think it likely that such a loose cooperative enter- prise could be exciting, productive, and more coherent than present patterns of research. Nor would it, if properly exe- cuted, infringe upon the creative scientist's essential free- dom to follow his clues and his hunches. Finally, such a program would, I believe, have a much better chance of gaining more generous outside funding support, since a con- crete goal of such indisputable importance would be persua- sive evidence that parapsychologists are mature and sophisti- cated investigators who not only understand the scientific tradition, but are also willing to put it seriously into prac- tice with their own money. Though it may not be fair that we must be the ones to do it, time has shown that if we don't, no one else will.

The one loss to the individual parapsychologist that would come with replication--that of the private romance of working alone and without recognition in forbidden fields against great odds, for high and noble stakes--would surely be compensated for by the real benefits once parapsychology can tap the enormous strength, resources, and vitality of the mainstreams of the modern scientific establishment. And, after all, for the explorers among us, there will sure- ly then be another terra incognita just over the new horizon.

Inadequacies in Our Present Conceptualization of Psi

It is worth-while to consider the possibility that our
failure so far to have achieved the "promptitude of result"
that Sidgwick anticipated from this new scientific discipline
does not stem from the inherent elusiveness of psi, but rather is a consequence of our use of an inadequate theory as
our methodological guide. I will try to persuade you that
one direction to take might profitably imitate the historical
shift in clinical methodology by psychoanalysis in its long
search for evidence of unconscious processes, a search
which continues to the present.

To establish a frame of reference, let us consider
some of the basic properties of the cognitive aspects of the
psi process as commonly conceptualized. The first property
is that it involves mental action at a distance without known
intervening forces. It is this particular property that has
most stupefied the conventional scientist. Insult is added to
injury when evidence is claimed for precognition, in which
the observed precognitive effect apparently precedes its own
cause, which would seemingly reside only in the future. Some
of the emotionalism such hypotheses elicit is understandable
when one recognizes the ever-present wolf of vitalism, despite its being clothed in the sheepish language of modern
parapsychology, which still seems to threaten to retake some
of the ground gained by science since the Darwinian revolution. Distinguished efforts such as those of Whately Carington (1949) and others to banish this anachronistic issue by
the semantic wand of a radical positivism have had inconsequential influence. Yet as psychiatrist Jule Eisenbud (1956)
and physicist Henry Margenau (1966) cogently argued some
years ago, there is no sound basis for us as scientists to
be so uneasy over this property since gravitational, magnetic,
and nuclear forces all involve observable action at a distance
between two or more bodies without mediation by detectible
energies--a fact that causes us no particular discomfort and
has not interfered with the extraordinary growth of physics
in this century.

Nonetheless, the idea of mental action at a distance
remains pecularily offensive to the scientific mind. Fears
of a resurgence of naive vitalism only conceal a more basic
universal fear that has its roots in early childhood (Piaget,
1954). The infantile beliefs that the wish is father to the
event and that time and space are no barrier to magical omnipotence are eventually repressed, but such ideas are never

entirely abandoned and may reappear in consciousness in
both neurosis and psychosis, often in frightening form.   To
seriously entertain the psi hypothesis in a clinical setting
requires, in my experience, an unusually firm sense of reality if anxiety is to be avoided.   Such anxiety derives from
the human condition itself, though scientists often tend to
mask its origin by rationalizing in terms of scientific controversy.   I am not sure that much can be done about this
except to be aware of it and try to find the intellectual and
emotional resources to cope with it as one seeks or awaits
the repeatable experiment.

The second property of psi to which I would draw
your attention is the apparent rarity and unreliability of its
occurrence.   The largest collection of spontaneous cases is
that of L. E. Rhine (1967).   Using generous criteria to define presumptive psi, her lifetime collection numbers only
about 11,000 cases.   Cases so startling in their detail as to
make a chance explanation extremely unlikely are far rarer
still.

The conventional explanation for this rarity of psi
has its origins in the theoretical position of F. W. H. Myers, the extraordinary man who helped found the (British)
Society for Psychical Research, and whose little known mag-
num opus, Human Personality and Its Survival of Bodily
Death (1903), remains not only a classic but also a rich contemporary source of ideas that have never been fully explored.   Anticipating much that came later, he argued that
dreams, hypnotic trance, genius, hysteria, dissociated states,
and psychical phenomena all were a result of "subliminal
mentation" that subserved the "supraliminal stream of
thought."   The mere fact of achieving such a generalization
at that time distinguishes Myers as a founder of modern personality theory (Murphy, 1971b).

The first aspect of Myers' theory, which bears on
the rarity of psi, postulated that ideas arising in the conscious mind of the agent would penetrate to his unconscious,
and there achieve some contact with the unconscious of the
percipient.   Under various conditions the idea or feeling or
inpulse might then well up into the percipient's conscious
mind and become reportable.   As an alternative, the unconscious idea could express itself directly through motor or
sensory automatisms, thus by-passing the ordinary consciousness of the percipient, and it was this mechanism that
was felt to be operative among mediums or other gifted

sensitives. Myers shared the contemporary view of the psychiatrists of that period, reflected in the early work of Breuer and Freud (1893-1895) (whose ideas Myers was the first to introduce in England), who explained that hysterical phenomena were due to "hypnoid" states in which there is a "splitting off" from consciousness of a part of the mind, which then becomes to some degree autonomous. This theory has recently been rediscovered, dusted off, and given new life under the term "altered states of consciousness."

Myers fell short, however, in not recognizing the importance of Freud's most crucial discovery, first described in a short paper entitled "The Neuro-Psychoses of Defense," published in 1894. There Freud introduced the seminal idea of psychological "defense," postulating that ideas are kept from consciousness through a dynamic force of the mind which actively screens out of awareness ideas that are morally unacceptable, fearful, or socially unacceptable to the individual.

Gardner Murphy (1944), in considering the impediments to paranormal contact, has closely examined both these competing ideas, and notes that the theoretical literature since then accounting for the rarity of psi has followed one or the other of these two points of view. One, following Myers, attempts explanation largely on cognitive grounds where, as exemplified by Whately Carington's studies (1945/ 1972), telepathic ideas fail to emerge into the percipient's consciousness because of the difficulty these intrusive ideas have in joining the main stream of the percipient's thought. Because such ideas are unfamiliar, it is argued, they can acquire only the weakest of connections and thus by the laws of association can emerge only rarely to dominate the percipient's ordinary stream of thought. Though Carington elegantly demonstrated experimentally that psi was greater when more associations were held in common between agent and percipient, it is unlikely that this effect is a major determinant since if it were, then psi ought to occur far more actively among couples, such as twins, with widely shared ideas and experiences. Unfortunately, attempts to demonstrate this have never shown a substantial increment in psi (Kubis and Rouke, 1937).

The other major explanation bearing on the rarity of psi, largely pursued in the psychoanalytic literature following Freud's original discovery of psychological defense, has argued that the telepathic target, like an erotic or aggressive impulse that is unacceptable to the conscience, is actively held in a state of "repression" in order to defend the individual against the pain and discomfort of its appearance in consciousness. This has been thought to be a useful formulation, since it is able nicely to retain a perceptual theory of psi while at the same time accounting for its rarity by postulating an active disguising operation, functioning perhaps, as René Warcollier's observations (1938) might indicate, by fragmentation, duplication, accretion, symbolization, or as with Freud's primary process (1900), by condensation, displacement, and inversion of the manifest content. The analogy to the repressive force exerted by conscience is sometimes postulated to be an evolutionary adaptation that censors out psi in consciousness in deference to the domination of the ordinary senses, which presumably have far greater adaptive value in the ordinary struggle for survival.

Gardner Murphy (1964) tried to give a quantitative feel to the net effects of these two types of hindrances when he proposed that the penetration of psi through the barriers of personality that impede it is on the order of the electron's capacity to pass through a lead shield. We are often so startled and impressed by the occasional dramatic spontaneous case that we forget the trillions of occasions in the ordinary transactions of daily life and nightly dreams where psi plays no apparent role. Clinically, the sensitive is often thought of as having a special talent, comparable to that of an artistic or mathematical genius. Yet even among those few highly gifted sensitives the consistency and accuracy of their talent is far more erratic and elusive than that of the--may we say--ordinary genius! In fact, it is not unlikely that psi, as we presently identify it, is the rarest of all human functions.

The third property of psi, a function of its rarity and unreliability, is its apparent lack of practical importance. The funding agencies of the scientific enterprise are becoming more stridently pragmatic and even the sacrosanct disciplines of medicine and physics have been receiving decreasing support for basic research. Active concern for basic theoretical issues is simply not in the mainstream of modern science, particularly in America, as measured by dollar support. Attention to such issues is too frequently thought of as a dignified retirement occupation for distinguished scientists who have passed their productive period. It saddens me to report that the only two occasions on which I have been sought out for consultation by well-funded

federal research agencies concerned the possibility of communication with men in space and Polaris submarine crews.
The interest was momentarily high, but it was purely technological, never cosmological. Nonetheless, the present evidence does suggest that the adaptive significance of psi for
the organism is inconsequential. This is a matter of puzzle-
ment that has not been given sufficient attention. If psi is
in fact as rare and unreliable as it appears to be, then how
has the capacity survived at all? Is there precedent for
such an evolutionary survival? Or are we witnessing new
sports or mutations that quickly die out with the individual?
I would hope that such questions would be given greater
scrutiny in the future, for their answers might contain clues
of value to us.

The fourth property of psi I wish to emphasize is
that it is a primary form of communicating cognitive information. This is a most reasonable inference to draw from
the character of spontaneous cases, where the need to communicate during periods of crisis involving illness or death
is either demonstrably present or plausibly inferred on the
part of both the agent and the percipient. The trouble with
such a view is that events surrounding death and illness often become the focus of unusual attention on the part of the
participants, while the vastly complicated contents of the
ordinary dreams or the myriad hunches of everyday life are
considered trivial and receive little or no attention by the
average person. There is in fact some reason to believe
that the crisis type of spontaneous case is not typical, but
represents a skewed sample that has become available to us
more because its psi content has been emotionally important
to the people involved and thus has gained their attention
than because of anything inherent in the psi process itself.

Analytic studies of apparent psi occurrences during
therapy tend to support this view, for in this context the
content attributable to psi is rarely recognized as such by
the patient and gets reported by the patient to the analyst
only incidentally (Eisenbud, 1973). Analytic study, however,
has usually tried to show the importance of the psychodynamic constellations that furnished the context for the psi
event itself and that gave it a hidden significance. In both
the analytic and spontaneous cases, however, we are confronted with the fallacy of over-explanation, a source of considerable concern to some critics. The dynamic constellations that have been described as giving rise to psi events
are common and yet psi occurs so rarely. If psi indeed is

a form of communication, our theory must explain why it does not occur with far greater frequency than it does.

The fifth property of psi, reflected in the very term extrasensory perception, is that ESP is a perceptual process. In a paper (Kahn, 1962) some years ago I tried to show that the basic methodology that has developed over the last hundred years, and that we still use to explore the psi process, possesses a built-in circularity which may have placed us at a considerably disadvantage. The sequence goes like this. To be taken at all seriously a putative spontaneous ESP occurrence must carry with it precise and discrete information that could not be obtained by ordinary means. In designing methods to capture such spontaneous events in the laboratory, tests have almost universally used the model of the perceptual process by requiring discrete specific information, defined as the "target," to be perceived. This is well and good if psi is in fact primarily a perceptual process. If it is not, however, the very design of our experiments may serve to factor out the phenomena which we are seeking.

Group-Mind Theories, "Myers'-Problem," and Their Implications

I want now to consider the possibility that we have been very much in the position of the blind man trying to describe an elephant and that our present closely argued and seemingly experimentally supported conceptualization of psi, the major characteristics of which I have just reviewed for you, is equivalent to describing the elephant in terms of a tail, trunk, and ivory tusks. Such a description suffers the deficiency of having missed the elephant itself, that massive bulk, which to the exploring hand would seem to be almost without structure, without identifying features, and beyond description. This metaphor is a loose one, however, and is intended only to suggest that it is at least possible to propose an alternative to our present concept of psi--one which argues that psi represents a broad process through which individuals are linked in far more fundamental and perhaps presently unimagined ways than by the occasional sharing of unusual perception. If such linkages do exist, without having yet been identified, then it is possible that psi could turn out to have, like almost all other human capacities, a normal distribution in the population like intelligence, musical ability, or physical agility. Now this notion may seem bold and gratuitous but it is hardly a new idea.

To the contrary, it is essentially a return to the second aspect of the classical theory generated by Myers, and later shared by James and others. We have been far less comfortable and familiar with this aspect of Myers' theory than with the first aspect, even though the seeds of the theory are at least as old as the mystic, Plotinus, who wrote in the third century of the unknowable World-Soul.

We might refer to this as the group-mind theory, and let me quote it in James' own version (1909) which he left to us in his essay referred to above, "The Final Impressions of a Psychical Researcher," published shortly before his death in 1910:

> Out of my experience, such as it is (and it is limited enough), one fixed conclusion dogmatically emerges, and that is this, that we with our lives are like islands in the sea, or like trees in the forest. The maple and the pine may whisper to each other with their leaves, and Conanicut and Newport hear each other's fog horns. But the trees also commingle their roots in the darkness underground, and the islands also hang together through the ocean's bottom. Just so there is a continuum of cosmic consciousness, against which our individuality builds but accidental fences, and into which our several minds plunge as into a mother-sea or reservoir.... Assuming this common reservoir of consciousness to exist, this bank upon which we all draw, and in which so many of earth's memories must in some way be stored, or mediums would not get at them as they do, the question is, What is its own structure? What is its inner topography? This question, first squarely formulated by Myers, deserves to be called 'Myers' problem' by scientific men hereafter [p324].

The group-mind idea has received little attention in modern parapsychology because it has been extremely difficult to translate the various metaphors into a form where they could be experimentally tested and either accepted or rejected. A number of psychoanalysts, and Jan Ehrenwald in particular, have in fact implied support for some of the consequences that such a theory might have, though without actually adhering to the formal theory itself.

As psychoanalysts we may have been too heavily influenced by the perceptual, communicative, and quantitative
aspects of the prevailing psi model, leading us to emphasize
the narrower criteria for determining whether a putative psi
event has taken place. These issues have been pursued
most systematically by Ehrenwald (1955), who used the term
"tracer effect" to describe the requirement that names, dates,
numerals, or some combination of distinctive discrete features with a degree of uniqueness must be present. This is
in keeping with the traditional criteria for evaluating spontaneous cases and attempts to approximate, if not actually
preserve, the statistical criteria of the experimental perceptual model for the clinical case.

For example, Ullman and his colleagues (1973) have
systematically studied dreams intended to capture a "target
picture" being viewed by an agent and they indeed have reported occasions when dramatic correspondences have occurred in respect to such tracer effects, and in turn have
applied statistical techniques for evaluating the matchings of
a dream to its assigned target material. Despite the analysts' formal acceptance of these narrow criteria, perhaps
under some intimidation by the "tough-minded" experimentalists, they have nevertheless often felt that the requirement
for tracer effects allowed much to escape that was suggestive
of psi. In this context Ehrenwald (1955) has commented as
follows:

> Disregarding the operation of the psi factor in
> the making of the vast tapestry of our contempo-
> rary western civilization--and of all civilizations
> which come into our purview--would, however, be
> just as irrational as for fish to overlook the water
> in which they swim. Psi is a medium common to
> all humanity--whether or not we are aware of its
> existence [p192].

Ehrenwald acknowledges that he goes far beyond
existing data in suggesting this far reaching conclusion. The
metaphor attempts to capture the same principle as the
metaphor of James and gives an emphasis essentially different from Murphy's metaphor (1964) regarding the penetration of the lead shield by an electron. Though Murphy's
metaphor represents that aspect of Myers' theory--the idea
of "subliminal uprushes" penetrating to consciousness--which
is closer to the data, those metaphors that generate "Myers'
Problem" of testing the group-mind hypothesis can, I believe,

be usefully explored. Unfortunately, the most elegant first test of such a hypothesis is impractical. Harlow and Harlow (1962) and others have learned much about the pervasive effects of mothering merely by raising chimps in the absence of their mothers. The pervasive role of the biological environment on the organism has been easily studied merely by raising animals under sterile, germ-free conditions.

If, as Ehrenwald suggests, we are living in a sea of psi, I can think of no direct way of separating an individual from that milieu to see how he fares without it. In fact, such an experiment could only be performed by the last man on earth--and alas there would be no one left to ponder his findings! In practice, the opportunity for performing such crucial and definitive experiments is actually very rare and science has developed many methods for getting at such matters in tangential ways.

Ehrenwald (1955) has most systematically considered the possibilities for linkages beyond the tracer effects. He has described another class of criteria to evaluate psi between two individuals by which intelligible constellations of psychodynamic factors can be identified that meet the criteria of consistency and psychological significance, with psi detectable indirectly through symbolic distortions of the type commonly associated with primary process and preconscious associations.

Such a position argues that there is a psi level of function that constantly operates just as ordinary unconscious processes constantly influence the final common pathway of conscious mental activity. Ehrenwald proposes that the individual is constantly being bombarded with what he calls "heteropsychic" forces emanating from other minds, and he has made the novel suggestion that, despite the obvious distortions, the paranoid individual who believes himself under the influence of others at a distance may possess a grain of truth. Is there any advantage to a speculation that goes so far beyond observed facts? I believe that there is, for with a premise that states that psi is always actually operating-- even in those cases where the mechanism of communication has been attributed to ordinary subliminal exchanges between individuals, parents and children, or patients and therapist-- we are called upon to develop a very different kind of methodology from that to which we are accustomed.

To overcome the apparent untestability that has accounted for the relative lack of interest in group-mind theories is no small challenge. It is true that parsimony demands we seek the simpler explanations for the common reservoir shared by human culture before we assume such bold and apparently gratuitous ones as those just described. The so-called "law of parsimony," however, is actually only a procedural rule justified on the grounds that it tends to be useful. The trouble with parsimony is that nature itself is not always parsimonious. Repeatedly nature has duplicated various functions without obvious advantage and has repeatedly produced more complicated adaptive mechanisms when simpler ones were available. Thus the risk in using parsimony to judge the merits of competing hypotheses regarding nature is that it may lead--with admirable simplicity-- to the one which turns out to be incorrect. A more cogent argument against the Ehrenwald hypothesis is that one can always establish apparently meaningful connections between any two sets of verbal or pictorial data if one is allowed the freedom of translation which the rules of primary process and psychological defense mechanisms permit. It can, at its extreme, lead us to the world of Humpty-Dumpty who said, "When I use a word, it means just what I choose it to mean--neither more nor less."

Let us briefly examine what the differing operational requirements are that flow from the two aspects of Myers' theory discussed above. Murphy's metaphor (1964) emphasizes an all-or-none response--that the psi factor breaks through the barriers of personality on rare occasions and as Myers put it, achieves consciousness by a "subliminal uprush." Here the psi event tends to be taken at face value, bursting full-blown into awareness. The types of investigation that have resulted from this model have tried to define the psychological conditions under which the psi event takes place. The attitudes, personality traits, and motivational factors associated with those individuals who do and those who do not exhibit psi have received intensive attention and study (Mangan, 1958; Murphy, 1943, 1949; Schmeidler, 1960). Such studies have been our most productive source of new information during the last 30 years and some of them, particularly those of G. R. Schmeidler (Schmeidler and McConnell, 1958/1973), have come tantalizingly close to producing a degree of repeatability that would satisfy our rigorous criteria. Psychoanalytic studies similarly have looked at psi events in terms of the psychodynamics of personality and transference; indeed, there seems to be the

beginning of some agreement as to what psychodynamic constellations may generate psi, though the analysts are bur-
dened by the paucity of studied cases from which to base
their generalizations (Ullman, 1974a, 1974b).

Now let us compare this prevailing model with what
follows from the second aspect of Myers' model. Here the
emphasis is on a constantly impinging heteropsychic set of
stimuli which occasionally may break through, but which
ordinarily press on the stream of thought in such a way as
to steadily distort, modify, emphasize, and deflect the ongoing processes of consciousness. Here the occasional breakthrough is less important than the constant interaction between
the psi level and the stream of consciousness itself, which
now becomes the focus of our attention.

I alluded earlier to the fact that psychoanalysis had
developed similar models in defining the interactions of unconscious processes with consciousness. You will recall
that much of Freud's earliest work was designed to demonstrate the validity of hypothesizing "the unconscious." To
do so he depended heavily upon evidence of its direct breakthroughs into consciousness. Freud (1901) persuasively argued his case at the turn of the century on the basis of mistakes in memory, speech, reading, and writing, incorrectly
carried-out actions, and various other kinds of overt errors
traceable to unconscious wishes that momentarily seized control of the cognitive and motor systems. However, a considerable shift of emphasis has taken place since then.
Though parapraxes are still useful to us and dreams remain
of central value, we are no longer dependent upon these
overt breakthroughs to understand our patients. Our ears
have grown more sensitive, for in any stream of thought it
is possible to detect the constant operation of unconscious
processes and as we become familiar with particular psychodynamic constellations present in a patient, we begin to hear
their reflection in the ordinary stream of thought even though
their manifest content may be trivial, banal, or superficial.
What started out as the hypothesis to be demonstrated by
Freud is now taken as the premise to be assumed, even
though to many outside observers there is often skepticism
that we are really hearing what we say we hear. Let me
now suggest how such a shift may contribute to the solving
of "Myers' problem," to use William James' phrase.

The thrust of the argument is that we might let
Myers' conclusions become our premises, where we start

with the assumption that psi is an intrinsic component to the human condition and that its very pervasiveness has masked its true characteristics, leaving us only with the occasional identifiable peak or island.   The puzzle generated by "Myers' problem" is that once we give up the conventional view of psi, we no longer know what we are looking for--except in metaphorical terms that have not had much operational value.

Let me outline the idea that seems implicit in all group-mind theories.   It proposes that each mind is constantly interacting with other minds in some undefined fashion.   At the level of conscious activity, however, the impact of ideas and affects having their origins in James' "common reservoir" obviously cannot be fully intrusive except on those rare occasions when they are then identified as "spontaneous cases."   Ordinarily, the impact, insufficient for full penetration, must be soft, tangential, implicit, and potentially detectible only by the faint tracks it may leave in the ongoing processes of the ordinary stream of thought idiosyncratic to the particular personality involved.   In this model the term "psi" would refer in a strictly limited fashion to that unknown process by which the contents of minds become interactive with each other without using the ordinary channels of contact.   Nothing should be implied beyond that in the operational definition.   Considering the extreme rarity of those occasions when ideas that are totally foreign to the percipient appear, it is likely that if the psi process is constantly ongoing, then its primary effect must be limited to structural reorganizations of the ordinary intrapsychic contents of the percipient's mind.   It is to the very permutations of these structural reorganizations that the psychoanalyst has made himself so sensitive--organizations that can reveal much which is central to the personality, if psychoanalytic inferences are permitted, despite the seemingly banal and trivial ideational content that is manifest to the ordinary listener.

The Cloud Chamber Model

Let me try to condense this complex idea into a simple model, borrowed for our purposes from 19th-century physics.   In 1896 C. T. R. Wilson, working in the Cavendish Laboratory at Cambridge University, developed an ingenious method for the study of subatomic particles.   Invisible by any known method of direct observation, these charged components of the atom retained a considerable degree of obscurity. Wilson found that ions (produced by x-rays), when passed through a gas, removed some of the negatively-charged electrons from the atoms of the gas, leaving the ionized atoms positively charged and the negatively-charged electrons free of the atoms. These free negative and positive charges were found to form centers of condensation around which visible droplets formed if the gas was supersaturated with water vapor. As the particle moved through the gas, even at rates approaching the speed of light, it would leave its pathway marked by a minute cloud not only visible to the naked eye, but stable enough to be photographed and studied at leisure. The trace of the event had become independent of time and position factors. Wilson soon showed that rays from radioactive substances and ultraviolet light led to the same effects. For his work Wilson shared the Nobel Prize in 1927 and soon thereafter the positron and neutron were actually discovered with this device.

The underlying function of what has come to be known as Wilson's cloud chamber is to trap the invisible and unknown particle into leaving its trail in a substance both known and visible and thus measurable. Clearly the trail is not to be mistaken for the invisible particle itself, but inferences from the characteristics of such trails leads to precise information about the characteristics of each type of particle studied. The principle here that serves our present purpose is that the unknown particle, as it strikes a known substance, stimulates the sudden reorganization of that substance in certain ways that are characteristic of the particle but which--without any of the foreign particles' actually becoming part of the content of the chamber--continues to remain homogenous. Would there not be some advantage in thinking of psi not as a perceptual, communicatory function, but rather as an activating process that, like the subatomic particle, produces some new organizational pattern of the gases of the cloud chamber representing in our model the associational networks of the individual mind? A search for structural alterations in the ideational organization of both agent and percipient, without regard to traditional "guesses" and "targets," might reveal the presence of a psi interaction that, like subatomic particles, are universally present and active, but which remain undetected until they are allowed to act within a matrix so sensitized as to magnify their impact, thus enabling them to cross the threshold of scientific observability.

The Detection and Enhancement of the Psi "Signal"

In addition to the cloud chamber's value to us as a model of the psi process, it also may serve us in a second role--that of a physical model for what is called "signal detection." It seems clear that one of the essential operational problems with which we are confronted by "Myers' problem" is our present inability to detect the organization shifts in the mental content presumed to be occurring by the cloud chamber model. Though Wilson's ingenuity made the invisible track manifest by its trail of condensed water vapor, we have no such instrument available to us to capture psi events except the psychoanalyst's sensitive ear. This is simply not an objective enough device for establishing the weight of evidence such a momentous hypothesis as pervasive psi properly requires. Fortunately, the task of magnifying invisible signals did not die with Wilson--to the contrary, during the past several decades enormous strides have been made in developing signal detection systems by the scientific community.

In the remainder of this paper I will discuss some examples of how such problems have been dealt with successfully in other areas of science. My purpose is not to suggest designs for experiments, but rather to elicit interest in a set of alternative methods to the ones with which we are familiar in the hope that experimenters will see sufficient merit in them to devote their own thought to operational questions of how the general strategy that I am suggesting, known as signal enhancement and detection, may be applied to specific problems in parapsychology.

A variety of different tactics have been invented in the service of this task, but they all share in common the search for hidden events that are only inferred to be present, whose precise characteristics are unknown, and the evidence for whose existence is only inferable from the actual operational observations themselves. The term "signal" refers to an event or a bit of information that is to be detected through the meaningless welter of competing signals in which it is embedded and concealed and which produce "noise" through their more or less random interaction, noise that must be penetrated before the sought after signal can be isolated and identified. These techniques are designed to extract such a signal even when it is of such low magnitude as to be entirely undetectable by ordinary inspection. The methods vary considerably, but all have one requirement in common. There must be repetition of the information or event sought after. In exchange for this several extraordinary benefits accrue; the size of the signal may be extremely small in contrast to the competing signals which drown it out and one can search for it without even knowing its characteristics if one knows when or where to look.

Let me give you three examples drawn from diverse areas for illustration. The first example is well known to us and I mention it only because we do not ordinarily think of it as a signal detection technique at all. I refer to the use of the statistical techniques made familiar by the Duke Parapsychology Laboratory for establishing the presence of heteropsychic information modifying the otherwise random associations between target ESP card and the subject's guesses regarding them. Here, mathematical analysis reveals the occasional presence of small and otherwise unnoticeable psi effects (Pratt, Rhine, Smith, Stuart, and Greenwood, 1940/1966). More recently similar methods have been developed for application to free verbal material as well (e.g., Roll and Burdick, 1969).

The second example is from work done in my psychophysiology laboratory several years ago. We were interested in seeing whether we could detect the presence of an electrical event on the cortex of the brain when a subject engaged in an act of voluntary "will"--in this case, willing the discharge of a single motor neuron to produce a tiny muscle twitch. We did not know what the cortical electrical event might look like, but we did know precisely when to look for it because the tiny muscle twitch acted as a monitor for the preceding mental event of "willing" on each occasion and with an accuracy of milliseconds. Since millions of other nerve cells were firing more or less at the same time on the cortex, their signals drowned out the one small signal for which we were searching.

However, by adding cortical voltages from 100 occasions when the subject "willed" a muscle twitch and comparing them to the cumulative voltages at thousands of points in time when the subject's "willing" did not occur, we were able to generate a sizable average waveform that was inferred to be the electrical correlate of the subjective "willing" of a motor event. In theory such an analysis could be done by hand, but in fact until the advent of a computer that could make these millions of measurements automatically in a few minutes, such signal detection was highly impractical. I hope my analogy here is evident. The subtle act of sub- jective "willing" is associated with objective electrical events so small that they are undetectible by ordinary in- spection of the electroencephalograph, yet signal enhance- ment techniques makes them strikingly evident despite the noise of the millions of competing automatic events occur- ring on the cortex.

My third example illustrates the fact that such signal detection strategy can be applied to free verbal material as well. In this example, the problem was analogous to the psi problem, for the experimenters wished to settle the centuries-old controversy over whether the Epistles of St. Paul were in fact all authored by Paul, as tradition insisted, or whether some were the work of an unknown author. Or- dinary differences in literary style and subject matter had previously been used to support both positions--for apparent intrusions by a second author could as well be explained as the natural variations within one man's literary output. Morton and McLeman (1964) started by making a computer search for variables that remained constant over undisputed works of a series of Greek authors. They discovered seve- ral seemingly trivial but highly reliable factors. One, for example, was the number of times the Greek word kai-- roughly meaning and--appears in each sentence. When their test was applied to the Pauline Epistles, certain ones had kai distributions sufficiently different from the Epistles of undisputed Pauline authorship to permit the strong inference that they were produced by someone other than the man known as Paul.

Here the focus of study is form and structure rather than content. In recent years there has been the beginning of studies of free verbal material in an effort to define the structural styles that underlie verbal content. For example, such cognitive control factors as leveling-sharpening, equiva- lence range, and focusing have been identified as having a degree of intraindividual consistency (Gardner, Holzman, Klein, Linton, and Spence, 1959).

It is the thrust of group-mind theories that it is rea- sonable to expect heteropsychic stimuli, having their source in other minds, to leave their structural signatures on a percipient's stream of thought even though specific tracers do not achieve actual cognitive dominance. Such theory can even be directly applicable to survival material when suit- ably consistent structural styles are selected for comparison.

There are many permutations possible in the search for such structural characteristics and however weakly they may be presumed to impinge, signal enhancement methods can unequivocally establish their presence, given a sufficient quantity of material. The one essential requirement--redundancy of psi contact--would seem to be inherent in the idea that minds are constantly interacting in some dynamic interchange with a common reservoir, as pictured in James' metaphor quoted earlier.

As a simple example of the kind of experiment suggested by such a theory, several agents might be repetitively used in random sequence. Tracer effects would no longer be required as evidence of psi correspondences. We would merely hypothesize that some measureable shift in one or more parameters of the stream of thought would be consistently associated with the presence or absence of a particular agent. Should such shifts be obtained in a consistent fashion in a properly designed paradigm, a linkage would have been demonstrated between agent and percipient that could not easily be accounted for except by inferring a psi process. We attempt to do something like this in the analytic situation where we trust our attentive scanning to do the signal detection that allows us to track the impact of a repressed idea on the stream of thought. We can do this because we have learned the rules of primary process and the various types of cognitive transformations that may occur. Analysts and others have tended to assume, for lack of any better model, that the psi process undergoes transformation similar to that of other types of unconscious material. It may be, however, that intrusions from the psi level have their own sets of rules of which we are presently unaware and that they must be empirically determined just as Freud empirically determined the kinds of ego mechanisms that give rise to dream formation by studying the relationship of the dream to its various antecedents.

By the technique I have outlined, Myers' theory can begin to be stated in terms of the null hypothesis. If we can demonstrate that the stream of verbal material produced by a percipient is not altered in any systematic way when different agents are attempting to impinge upon the percipient's awareness, then we have produced some evidence against Myers' theory. On the other hand, if we can show some kind of systematic change, regardless of its character, it seems to me this would be some evidence in favor of the Myers hypothesis. The occasional tracer effect would then become the special case in which the inertial momentum of the ordinary intrapsychic sources of the stream of thought is momentarily broken through, as in the Murphy model (1964).

Though the two aspects of Myers' theory have been contrasted here to give each greater salience, both in fact are mutually consistent and complement each other. The first step toward repeatability, as Murphy (1971a) has summarized for us, is to seek to maximize that cluster of conditions already identified which seems to promote the penetration of the psi level into those levels of mind more accessible to awareness and report. Our best hope would be that the two aspects of Myers' theory would potentiate each other to a degree that might eventually achieve the goal we have set of rigorous replication.

Should evidence in favor of the Myers hypothesis be obtained, it would generate a model of the psi process that would have persuasive claim to high scientific priority for more intensive and serious study.

Rather than mental action at a distance being alien and psychologically unacceptable, the familiarity that results from repetitive demonstration would make psi as congenial as gravity. The rarity of psi would be seen as only epiphenomenal because its presence would be detectable now in ordinary ongoing mental processes.

Such pervasiveness of psi would now demand definition of its practical importance in all types of human relationships ranging from its role in the psychopathology of interpersonal relationships to the group affinities that underlie so many productive human endeavors.

The communicative function of psi might be brought under better voluntary control; but more importantly, the intrinsic linkages among individuals so vividly portrayed by Myers and James might finally become susceptible to operational definition.

Finally, the present definition of psi as a kind of adjunctive perceptual system might be seen as only a special case, and a minor one at that, of a much broader cognitive function that might indeed be the adaptive mechanism for a kind of knowing about which we as scientists have traditionally been skeptical, but which the poet and mystics have occasionally experienced, yet without the special kind of understanding that only science can potentially offer.

REFERENCES

Barrett, W. F. "On Some Phenomena Associated with Abnormal Conditions of Mind." Proceedings of the Society for Psychical Research, 1 (1882), 238-44.

Breuer, J., and Freud, S. "Studies on Hysteria [1893-1895]." In Freud, Standard Edition (London: Hogarth Press, 1955), v2, p1-305.

Carington, W. Matter, Mind and Meaning. New Haven, Conn.: Yale University Press, 1945.

_____. Telepathy: An Outline of Its Facts, Theory, and Implications. New York: Gordon Press, 1972 (first published in 1945).

Ehrenwald, J. New Dimensions of Deep Analysis. New York: Grune and Stratton, 1955.

Eisenbud, J. "Psi and the Problem of the Disconnections in Science." Journal of the American Society for Psychical Research, 50 (1956), 3-26.

_____. "Communication." In M. Ullman and S. Krippner, with A. Vaughan, Dream Telepathy (New York: Macmillan, 1973), p253-9.

Freud, E. L. (ed.). Letters of Sigmund Freud. New York: Basic Books, 1960.

Freud, S. "The Neuro-Psychoses of Defense [1894]." Standard Edition (London: Hogarth Press, 1962), v3, p43-61.

_____. The Interpretation of Dreams [1900]. Standard Edition (London: Hogarth Press, 1955), v4-5.

_____. "The Psychopathology of Everyday Life [1901]." Standard Edition (London: Hogarth Press, 1960), v6.

_____. "Psycho-Analysis and Telepathy [1921]." Standard Edition (London: Hogarth Press, 1955), v18, p173-93.

_____. "Dreams and Telepathy [1922]." Standard Edition (London: Hogarth Press, 1955), v18, p195-220.

Gardner, R., Holzman, T. S., Klein, G. S., Linton, H., and Spence, D. P. "Cognitive Control: A Study of Individual Consistencies in Cognitive Control." In Psychological Issues (New York: International Universities Press, 1959.

Hansel, C. E. M. ESP: A Scientific Evaluation. New York: Scribner's, 1966.

Harlow, H. F., and Harlow, M. K. "The Effect of Rearing Conditions on Behavior." Bulletin of the Menninger Clinic, 26 (1962), 213-24.

James, W. "The Final Impressions of a Psychical Researcher." The American Magazine, October 1909;

reprinted in G. Murphy and R. O. Ballou (eds.), William James on Psychical Research (New York: Viking Press, 1960), p309-25.

Jones, E. The Life and Work of Sigmund Freud. New York: Basic Books, 1957. 3 vols.

Kahn, S. D. "The Enigma of Psi: A Challenge for Scientific Method." Journal of the American Society for Psychical Research, 56 (1962), 114-24.

Kubis, J. F., and Rouke, F. L. "An Experimental Investigation of Telepathic Phenomena in Twins." Journal of Parapsychology, 1 (1937), 163-71.

Kuhn, T. S. The Structure of Scientific Revolutions. Chicago: University of Chicago Press, 1962.

Mangan, G. A Review of Published Research on the Relationship of Some Personality Variables to ESP Scoring Level. New York: Parapsychology Foundation, 1958. (Parapsychological Monographs, no. 1.)

Margenau, H. "ESP in the Framework of Modern Science." Journal of the American Society for Psychical Research, 60 (1966), 214-27.

McGraw, T. A. "On Mind-Reading and Allied Morbid Phenomena." Detroit Review of Medicine and Pharmacy, 11 (1875), 451-70.

Morton, A. Q., and McLeman, J. Christianity in the Computer Age. New York: Harper & Row, 1964.

Murphy, G. "Psychical Phenomena and Human Needs." Journal of the American Society for Psychical Research, 37 (1943), 163-91.

_____. "Removal of Impediments to the Paranormal." Journal of the American Society for Psychical Research, 38 (1944), 2-23.

_____. "Psychical Research and Personality." Proceedings of the Society for Psychical Research, 49 (1949), 1-15.

_____. Personal communication, 1964.

_____. "The Problem of Repeatability in Psychical Research." Journal of the American Society for Psychical Research, 65 (1971), 3-16. (a)

_____. "Frederic Myers and the Subliminal Self." Journal of the American Society for Psychical Research, 65 (1971), 130-43. (b)

Myers, F. W. H. Human Personality and Its Survival of Bodily Death. London: Longmans, Green, 1903. 2 vols.

Piaget, J. The Construction of Reality in the Child. New York: Basic Books, 1954.

Pratt, J. G., Rhine, J. B., Smith, B. M., Stuart, C. E.,

and Greenwood, J. A. Extrasensory Perception After Sixty Years. New York: Holt, 1940.

Ransom, C. "Recent Criticisms of Parapsychology: A Review." Journal of the American Society for Psychical Research, 65 (1971), 289-307.

Rhine, L. E. ESP in Life and Lab: Tracing Hidden Channels. New York: Macmillan, 1967.

Roll, W. G., and Burdick, D. S. "Statistical Models for the Assessment of Verbal and Other ESP Responses." Journal of the American Society for Psychical Research, 63 (1969), 287-302.

Schmeidler, G. R. ESP in Relation to Rorschach Test Evaluation. New York: Parapsychology Foundation, 1960. (Parapsychological Monographs, no. 2.)

_____. "Contemporary Psychologists View Parapsychology Today." In J. B. Rhine and R. Brier (eds.), Parapsychology Today (New York: Citadel Press, 1968), p195-206.

_____ and McConnell, R. A. ESP and Personality Patterns. Westport, Conn.: Greenwood Press, 1973 (first published in 1958).

Ullman, M. "Psi and Psychiatry." In E. D. Mitchell et al., Psychic Exploration, ed. by J. White (New York: Putnam's, 1974), p247-67. (a)

_____. "Parapsychology and Psychiatry." In A. Freedman and H. Kaplan (eds.), Comprehensive Textbook of Psychiatry, 2d ed. (Baltimore: Williams and Wilkins, 1974), v2, p2552-61. (b)

_____ and Krippner, S., with A. Vaughan. Dream Telepathy. New York: Macmillan, 1973.

Warcollier, R. Experimental Telepathy. Boston: Boston Society for Psychic Research, 1938.

Berthold E. Schwarz

PSI AND THE LIFE CYCLE

Psi occurs throughout the entire life cycle--from
birth until death and--for all that anyone knows--perhaps before and beyond. Although many people are aware of the
extensive laboratory statistical studies of ESP and of the
existence of many case reports of spontaneous psi, often re-
plete with weighty documentation, affidavits, and the like,
they may not be so well acquainted with the no less respectable and well-studied psychiatric or psychodynamic investigations of telepathy by such pioneers as Ehrenwald
(1955), Eisenbud (1970), Fodor (1959), Meerloo (1964), Ullman (1970), and others (see e. g. , Devereux, 1953). The
speculations about the psychopathological and physiological
significance of psi in everyday life illuminate all of psychical research and, if confirmed, may offer a renaissance for
mankind no less notable than the first historic reawakening.

During my psychiatric training I noted occasional
telepathic exchanges with patients during psychotherapy. Because of this and because of some personal psychic events
in my family and other experiences in treating patients, I
wondered if telepathy could have practical, everyday significance in our lives and if it could be a contributing factor in
various behavioral and psychosomatic reactions. Were
spontaneous telepathic and other psi events isolated occurrences or were they perhaps not uncommon and of intense
significance? How does one go about answering these questions?

In the course of my initial psychiatric interviews
with patients, for the past 18 years or so, I have asked
them about possible psychic events in their lives: "Have
you ever had unusual events in your life--so strange yet
true that you wondered about them and what they could be?"

As a result, I have obtained all kinds of anecdotal psychic material. These data, whatever their validity, often seemed to have a direct influence on the lives of these patients. The clinical "facts" told me that it was not right to ignore such material. I gradually came to realize that one could not fully understand a patient without taking account of this psychic material--genuine or spurious.

Psychiatric studies over the past 50 years have revealed how telepathy is related to the subconscious mind with all its propensities for symbolization, distortion, displacement, condensation, and other mental mechanisms. The dream and altered states of consciousness can also be ideal vehicles for telepathy. These pioneering researches spelled out clear-cut psychodynamic criteria for the recognition of telepathy: (a) the unique, actual or close symbolic meaning of the thoughts of two or more people happening at the same time without the aid of the usually recognized senses; (b) the "tracer thought" or word that is an allusion to the psychic nature of the event; and (c) the tendency for the telepathic event to recur when the psychodynamic constellations are similar--so called built-in controls (Ehrenwald, 1956; Schwarz, 1966).

During my extended psychiatric investigation of Jacques Romano (Schwarz, 1968), an extraordinary, jolly, youthful-appearing nonagenarian-telepathist, my wife Ardis and I noted the increased frequency and quality of telepathic events and other psychic phenomena in our family. We found that following highly exciting and interesting sessions with Romano there were clusters of psychic events within the family, between our friends and ourselves, and in my practice. The next step was to start keeping records of all possible telepathic events involving our children, Lisa, and later Eric, and ourselves (Schwarz, 1971); and concomitantly through the years, physician-patient exchanges.

The latter technique included making entries on 3" x 5" file cards of any presumed clinically creditable psi events obtained during initial consultations with a patient as well as the session number for any presumed psi episodes between the patient and physician (B. E. S.) in those instances where the patient continued with psychotherapy. Thus, from December 1955 to December 1973, 3764 patients were seen in consultation and in 3077 instances there were examples of psi or one or more physician-patient telepathic exchanges.

For the patients, most of their psi events were telepathic. There were no striking occupational, age, sex, or
religious correlations. If anything, the more intelligent patients seemed to have a better interpersonal awareness for
telepathy. The underlying personality factors, states of
consciousness, physiological, and pharmacological aspects
(e. g. , effects of tranquilizers, psychotropics, and patients
who had been under the influence of alcohol, marijuana, LSD,
mescaline, etc.)--the substrates for psi--were entirely in
accord with other published observations.

Psi and the life cycle can perhaps best be illustrated
with an assortment of examples in the form of case reports,
roughly divided according to Shakespeare's "seven ages of
man. "

I   "At first the infant, mewling
and puking in the nurse's arms"

CASE 1. IN THE BEGINNING

Barbara, a healthy newborn, was brought home by
her proud parents two weeks ago. Mrs. Love, a mother for
the first time, had had many previous telepathic experiences
and came from a family where psi was accepted as an everyday event. When being interviewed she said: "I always walk
in when something has happened. The other day the baby
was choking and gagging. The milk was coming out of her
nose. Bill [husband] and I were in the living room taking
down the Christmas tree and Barbara was in the bedroom
with the door partially closed, so that we wouldn't disturb
her. We live in a ranch house and we couldn't hear anything. We didn't intend to go in and possibly disturb her.
I usually don't go in when she's sleeping--it's usually three
and a half to four hours--and Barbara had already been fast
asleep for one hour. But I just felt I had to go in and
check her. I had a hunch. It happens a lot. I think she's
OK, and I don't want to be over-cautious, and I say, 'No,
she's all right. ' But, I still go in. On another occasion,
I kept getting the feeling that something was happening and I
started walking around. I felt that I better go in. We both
went to her room and she had the blanket completely over
her face. If something went wrong with her, I'd know it,
because I've done it so often. When I'm in there, I say,
'Gee, I'm surprised to be in here now. ' I just feel this--
that I should be there [compulsion]. "

Possibly this simple experience could be the type of telepathic event that transcends and merges with subliminal stimulation. Could this episode, where the young mother heeded her infant's needs, be the prototype of crisis telepathy which alerts us and prepares us for danger and which aids survival and which will happen again and again throughout life?

CASE 2.   MOTHER'S SECRET

Early in her psychotherapy for depression, a young mother once reported: "I was having breakfast with Tina, my three-year-old, and Frieda, our mother's helper. I was thinking about how depressed I was and that I did not want to upset my husband, for he had so much unhappiness in his previous marriage, due to the fact that his first wife was an alcoholic. While I was thinking of this first wife, whom I never knew, Tina, who was eating her breakfast, suddenly said, 'Look, I'm a ghost.' I replied, somewhat automatically, 'Caspar, the friendly ghost [her favorite TV cartoon]?' She said: 'No, Sybil!' Sybil was the name of my husband's first wife! To my knowledge Tina had never used the name nor heard it before. Frieda questioned her by asking, 'Susan? Sandy?' etc. But Tina was insistent on Sybil."

Can the child pick up sensitive areas from her parents and then amaze them by correctly synthesizing them, as in this instance, with the forbidden name; and if so, how often and how significant a clue is this to the child's emotional development?

CASE 3.   ALL IS NOT WELL

A middle-aged mother recalled how her teenage schizophrenic son would scream out horribly and inconsolably when he was a baby. At those times she and her husband would be in their bedroom and the father, who was an alcoholic, would be berating his infant son. The mother was puzzled because the baby's room was down the corridor and out of range of hearing. She was sure that her son was telepathically aware of the father's hatred for him.

She cited other instances, where, for example, she planned trips to another city as a surprise, or to visit someone and scrupulously kept the information to herself; yet her son would blurt out what she thought was a secret. She herself wondered if this process was related to her son's problems.

Perhaps these early examples are not unlike the heightened sensitivity that the schizophrenic has for heteropsychic stimuli and perhaps it becomes the nucleus for later paranoidal ideation.

II   "And then the whining schoolboy"

CASE 4. LIKE FATHER, LIKE SON

(Parent-Child Telepathy Series, #866, August 26, 1967, Saturday, 11:00 a.m.) I was working at my desk and had just read on page 26 in The Return of Russell Colvin by John Spargo (Bennington Historical Museum and Art Gallery, 1945): "Chief Justice Dudley Chase presided. He was a jurist of eminent and acknowledged ability. A graduate of Dartmouth College, he was 48 years old at the time of the trial." I thought this historic reference to a crime involving a spurious telepathic dream would be useful for my projected paper on "Crime and Telepathy." I next wondered if Daniel Webster (a Dartmouth alumnus), of a famous Dartmouth College case, was connected with this other notorious murder case of which Chase was the Judge, having to do with a false (from a legal point of view) psychic dream. At that moment, my son Eric, age eight, came into the room and said, "I thought Dartmouth was built in 1944--but this penny [in his hand] is 1946--remember when you had a penny that said when you were born?" When Eric was asked what his statement had to do with Dartmouth, he became flustered and said he didn't know. Eric picked up the central theme of (a) Dartmouth, with overdetermined telepathic tracers (psychic dream, projected paper on telepathy and crime) and also the specifically sensitized area of (b) a birthday (the age, in this case, of the justice, a mature man at the time of the famous trial; and his father's birth date). Eric also delved into the past: the founding of Dartmouth-- and the 1820 Colvin case. Eric was in positive rapport with his father.

How much love of the past and of tradition can be traced to such simple roots as this example, in which a young boy seemingly picks the thoughts out of his father's brain and almost succeeds in correctly synthesizing them? By collecting many similar cases, it is easy to see the possible role of telepathy in acquiring values for good or evil, various prejudices--or simply thoughts for the learning experience. This example also shows the mechanism of the

unconscious mind and telepathy, in which the person involved is totally unaware of his role and offers a flimsy ex-
cuse, not unlike a posthypnotic-command rationalization.

III "The lover"

Stekel, as noted by Eisenbud (1949), observed that
telepathy is often a via regia for love and sex. Unfortunately this excellent clue has not been as actively followed up
as it might have been. There are amusing cases of lovers
meeting under conditions strange indeed unless the telepathic
hypothesis be invoked; cases of possible telepathic appre-
hension of unfaithfulness causing presumed telesomatic reactions (Schwarz, 1967) in one instance and acute anxiety in
another; and examples of sexual deviations that might have
been telepathic associations.

This is a robust age, when the acme of physiological
function yields many spectacular examples in which the libido
and telepathy synchronize. There are instances of coitus
being interrupted (telepathically?) by importunate phone calls
from a jealous, unrequited lover (Schwarz, in press) and
there is the example of a patient who had an infertility problem (azoospermia) in which it seemed that on the infrequent
occasions of cohabitation, as advised by his physician, the
patient received embarrassing phone calls from his mother.

CASE 5. LOVEBIRDS

The last time I saw R. H., he and his rejected girl
friend phoned my office within minutes of each other. However, three weeks later R. H. came to my home on a surprise visit--and his former girl friend, who lived miles
away and knew nothing of these unplanned developments,
made a "spur-of-the-moment decision" for an overlapping
visit. These examples happened so often that my wife and
I had a hard time convincing R. H. that he was not being
"framed" by well-intentioned but unwanted matchmakers.

CASE 6. AN OLD FLAME

L. L. was at a reunion banquet with classmates whom
he had not seen in years. After a few cocktails he confided
to an old friend about his girl friend, whom they both knew
years ago, and he wondered how she was doing. L. L. still
had affection for his ex-girl friend but was circumspect about

it since at the time of his relationship his wife was very ill.
Shortly afterward L. L. was surprised to receive a letter
from his old flame, postmarked Japan. The dates of his
fond reminiscing and his former girl friend's writing about
herself coincided. She answered his question. There was
no other ostensible reason for her writing. Old flames
never die, they just fade away--or do they?

CASE 7. "UNWANTED" INVITATION

M. T. , a young man with bisexual conflicts, was
shocked after a very disquieting dinner conversation with his
family on "the modern subject of homosexuality. " This topic
had never been discussed in his parents' home and it precip-
itated considerable anxiety for M. T.   Later that night, when
he returned to his bachelor's apartment (in New Jersey), he
was again shocked to receive a telephone call (from Mary-
land) from a former male paramour whom he had been
thinking about during the dinner conversation, when he had
been fearful that his parents and brother would learn his
secret.

As might be surmised, the erotic is a vigorous age
of life that also provides a veritable three-ring circus for
psychic dynamics in other areas.   In addition to the possible
role of telepathy in sex, at this time there are exciting
telesomatic reactions.

IV   "Then a soldier"

CASE 8.   BURYING THE HATCHET

While at the supermarket, I debated whether to buy
a sea conch, saw off the end, and thus fashion a Polynesian
horn similar to a conch horn given to me by my great-uncle.
Dr. H. , a colleague, had always admired the heirloom horn,
which I once said I would give him, but because of differences between us the matter was dropped.   However, the
supermarket incident signaled a change in our relationship.
Within an hour of my buying the conch and recalling the un-
fulfilled promise of long ago to Dr. H. , he phoned to invite
my wife and me out to dinner.   I gave him the heirloom
horn, and since I hadn't seen or heard from him in a long
time, the only rational way to account for his (and my)
changed attitude was telepathy.   His invitation might have

symbolized the burying of the hatchet, which was recipro-
cated by my giving him the trivial but coveted gift.

V   "Then the justice"

CASE 9.   PROFESSOR FRANCESCO BASILI

Signor G. , an operatic impresario, came without appointment. Although I had not met him before, I knew from
the "grapevine" that he incorrectly thought I had been treating his late wife. When the Signor entered my reception
room, he spoke most admiringly of two mahogany chairs.
With grand gestures he said he had never seen anything else
like them. He was the only patient in all these years, or
since, to make such a fuss over the chairs. It is odd, because of the many items and other furniture in the reception
room these chairs are notable for only one reason: they
were supposedly used by Enrico Caruso. The former owner
of the chairs told me this. It can be conjectured that, under the strained circumstances of our meeting, Signor G.
telepathically unlocked this unique memory, which, with clarification of the aforementioned misinformation, formed a
sturdy bridge for the ensuing consultation. Perhaps some
objects are telepathically endowed for sentimental or highly
charged unconscious reasons, and then become suitable for
crisscrossing or spontaneous psi (psychometry?), as in this
experience.

Years later, when preparing a lecture for Quebec
City, I dashed over to my neighbor Dr. Ruggieri's house to
check his Encyclopaedia Britannica for the facts about Prof.
Francesco Basili of the Conservatorio di Milano. This man
was remembered solely for flunking an 18-year-old bumpkin
for having no musical ability. While I was going to Dr.
Ruggieri's, my peripheral thought was that it's a shame I
couldn't ethically contact Signor G. , who would undoubtedly
know about Basili. The next morning my secretary told me
that Signor G. , at the approximate time of my query, had
phoned (answering service took call) for an appointment.

VI   "Then the sixth age"

CASE 10.   TO ORDER OR NOT TO ORDER

My son and I were having dinner at Willie's Diner in
Bloomfield. Our waitress was fat, slovenly, slow, and ap-

parently stupid. It seemed to take forever to receive service. My thought was, "How nice an iced tea might be now, but she is too dumb to realize that I would ask for saccharin, and she would give me sugar and then there would be an argument." My son, who was looking straight ahead over the counter and obviously unaware of critical thoughts, might have sensed my disapproval of the waitress, as much as his own appraisal of her conduct, for he said: "What a grouchy waitress." Coincidental with our thoughts, the woman came up to the counter and asked: "You want the iced tea?" I was amazed because, although I had said nothing of the sort, and we hadn't been served, it was exactly my thought!

VII "Last scene of all"

CASE 11. "LIGHT--MORE LIGHT!"

Mrs. B. F. was an 81-year-old widow who wore thick lenses for aphakia (cataract operations) and had a florid paranoid reaction. The patient's daughter had informed me earlier that her brother, Lester, Mrs. B. F.'s son, was killed in World War II; but this is what the patient said: "He [deceased son] is a graduate of Maine University. In the Mountain Division. Notice of his death April 3, 1944, and heard nothing from him. Can't come back to life--belonged to FBI since a child, really joined at age 18, was taken into the mountains of Italy. He was really killed, but he came out of it...."

At this point the floor lamp beside my desk lit up by an intensity of one-third. There are three bulbs at the base, and a large central bulb, which was not turned on. No one touched the lamp, and there was no change in the line voltage in the house, as far as I could tell by later checking and by asking questions. Even if there were a slight increase in voltage, it should not have accounted for an extra light going on since the bulbs were all firmly screwed into the sockets; examination afterward disclosed no simple reason for this. The extra illumination was odd, because it happened so fast, and it was definite. It was "unreal."

The patient continued: "He came out of it. Found in a hospital just outside of Alaska in the Aleutians. Mentally bad but recovered physically but didn't know where he was. In the FBI since--another back injury--now I hear a voice in my head saying, don't tell you [doctor] this. I just heard someone in my daughter's room saying tell him anything you want to, etc."

This example is a fact, in so far as it was observed and written down in statu nascendi; and although it did not make sense and I didn't want to "believe" it, it happened. Since it touches on similar very sensitive areas in my own life--my younger brother was killed in General Patton's Army in World War II--it is the kind of situation that is suitable for telepathic sending or receiving in physician-patient or other interpersonal relationships.

Conclusion

We have had a possible telepathic purview of the seven ages of man. What is reported here has been greatly boiled down. The psychic nexus is actually much more extensive. This nexus, which takes in many families and age groups, is really, when reduced to its essentials, not much different from the early easy-to-understand parent-child examples. Life begins with the vital dependency of the infant on his mother, and the earliest fears are those of separation. The problem goes on in one form or another throughout all of life until the final separation.

REFERENCES

Devereaux, G. Psychoanalysis and the Occult. New York: International Universities Press, 1953.

Ehrenwald, J. New Dimensions of Deep Analysis. New York: Grune and Stratton, 1955.

_____. "Telepathy: Concepts, Criteria, and Consequences." Psychiatric Quarterly, 30 (1956), 425-49.

Eisenbud, J. "Psychiatric Contributions to Parapsychology: A Review." Journal of Parapsychology, 13 (1949), 247-62.

_____. Psi and Psychoanalysis. New York: Grune and Stratton, 1970.

Fodor, N. The Haunted Mind. New York: Garrett/Helix, 1959.

Meerloo, J. A. M. Hidden Communion: Studies in the Communication Theory of Telepathy. New York: Garrett Publications, 1964.

Schwarz, B. E. "Built-In Controls and Postulates for the Telepathic Event." Corrective Psychiatry and Journal of Social Therapy, 12 (1966), 64-82.

_____. "Possible Telesomatic Reactions." Journal of

the Medical Society of New Jersey, 64 (1967), 600-3.

_____. The Jacques Romano Story. Secaucus, N.J.: University Books, 1968.

_____. Parent-Child Telepathy. New York: Garrett/ Helix, 1971.

_____. "Telepathic Humoresque." Psychoanalytic Review, in press.

Ullman, M. "The Experimentally-Induced Telepathic Dream: Theoretical Implications." Journal of the American Society for Psychical Research, 64 (1970), 358-74.

Jan Ehrenwald

PARAPSYCHOLOGY AND THE SEVEN DRAGONS: A NEUROPSYCHIATRIC MODEL OF PSI PHENOMENA

On trying to formulate a theory of psi phenomena, one has first to proceed like the hero of a medieval mystery play: he must slay, or come to grips with, the dragons guarding the entrance to the sanctuary of science.

The first dragon is the challenge of scientific fact-finding. The data of parapsychology have to be assembled and validated by the consensus of qualified workers in the field, while doubtful or spurious evidence must be discarded. On the other hand, all the evidence that has stood the test of scientific scrutiny has to be included--regardless of the consequences. The second dragon is the paradox that although we feel duty-bound to apply the principles of the scientific method to our findings, they run counter to some of the basic propositions of science itself. The third, fourth, and fifth dragons stand for the classical Kantian categories of Time, Space, and Causality which are clearly incompatible with direct action and thought at a distance implied by telepathy, clairvoyance, and psychokinesis, while precognition seems to arrest time's arrow in its flight and to reverse the purportedly irreversible chain of causal events. The sixth dragon guards our conventional doctrine of cerebral localization, confining consciousness and other specific functions to more or less circumscribed areas of the brain cortex, or perhaps to lower echelons of the central nervous system. The seventh dragon is the picture of personality structure, suspended in splendid isolation in classical Euclidian space, functioning in Newtonian, prerelativistic time, and subject to strictly foreordained laws of cause and effect.

Clearly, coping with the seven dragons requires considerable efforts of mind-bending and mind-stretching. More than that: it requires the unlearning of some of our conventional habits of thinking and tacit theoretical presuppositions. Fortunately, modern relativistic physics, diverse non-Euclidian geometries, the probabilistic approach of quantum mechanics, and Goedel's theorem in mathematics have already done most of the job for us. We must realize, however, that our current theories of personality--the kingpin of the behavioral sciences--are still lagging some half a century behind the present stage of the natural sciences. We are still committed to the picture of human personality conceived as a walled-in medieval city instead of as an open-ended, surrealistic montage pervious to psi.

This is where our attempts to formulate a new, comprehensive theory of psi phenomena have to come in. I submit that once we get the seven dragons out of the way, it will be possible to present a set of interlacing and mutually supporting hypotheses, knit together in a coherent neuropsychiatric model, which should help toward a better understanding of psi phenomena and serve as a rationale for further experimentation.

The first hypothesis takes off from thoroughly familiar ground. It amounts to a simple linear extension of the basic cleavage between afferent and efferent neural conduction, between input and output, between sensory and motor activity characteristic of our mental organization: it can be described as the "extension hypothesis."

The Extension Hypothesis

The starting point for this hypothesis is the elementary fact that the reliability or acuity of my cutaneous perceptions or my sensitiveness to touch is at its best at, say, my finger tips; it is less at the dorsum of my hand; still less on the surface of my intestinal organs. It is zero on my fingernails; on the enamel of my teeth; on a lock of my hair clipped off by the barber. Psychologically speaking, my extracted wisdom tooth and hair and nail parings belong to the non-ego. They are no longer part of my body image, or at least only an expendable part of it.

In a similar vein, I can move my right index finger at any time at my whim; somewhat less reliably, I can raise my left eyebrow; with some practice, I can move my right ear. But only a yogi or a subject trained by special feedback techniques can influence his heart muscle voluntarily. And nobody can lift a hemianesthetic and paralyzed leg. It too has become non-ego as far as the patient's awareness and volitional control are concerned.

On the psi level of functioning the situation is vastly different both quantitatively and qualitatively. What is usually relegated to the non-ego is no longer cut off from the ego by a sharp demarcation line. A symbiotic mother may be directly aware of her baby's distress (Ehrenwald, 1971). If she is neurotic, she may be instrumental in her child's acting out her own emotionally charged, repressed, antisocial impulses (Ehrenwald, 1955). An analytic patient may produce a dream which reflects some of his therapist's emotionally charged mental content. A gifted telepathic sensitive may be able to "pick" a virtual stranger's brain. He may do so with special reference to such unique "bits" of information as names, numerals, or other "tracer elements" (Ehrenwald, 1955) in the agent's mind. Or a sensitive may function under clairvoyant conditions; that is, he may gain knowledge about objects and events that are not, at the critical moment, part of any other person's mental content. Indeed, we know that "good" percipients tend to perform just as well under clairvoyant as under telepathic conditions; some experimental subjects pile up scores giving odds of several millions to one against chance in tests for clairvoyance.

The motor counterpart of these experiments is the attempt of a subject to influence the fall of dice thrown from a cup or to deflect their path as they roll down an incline (Rhine, 1970). Results of such psychokinesis (PK) experiments are less impressive statistically than those obtained in laboratory ESP tests, but some have attained odds against chance of a thousand to one or better.

Well-documented instances of spontaneous PK incidents are few and far between. A notable exception are the semi-spontaneous phenomena of the Russian housewife, Nina Kulagina, whose ability to move such trivial objects as a pack of cigarettes, a box of matches, or a piece of bread has been investigated by a number of Russian experimenters with impeccable scientific credentials. Several qualified Western observers--e. g. , Pratt and Keil (1973)--have confirmed these observations, and films brought to this country likewise tend to bear out the genuineness of Kulagina's extraordinary feats of PK. No less striking are some of the experiments with the sensitive Ingo Swann demonstrating his ability to raise or lower temperature as recorded on thermal monitoring devices at a distance from him (Schmeidler, 1973). Thus, PK need no longer be regarded as merely a cluster of freakish incidents or as mere statistical artifacts. At the same time, the observations tend to give some support to such anecdotal accounts as Jung's "poltergeist" in Freud's bookcase (Jung, 1963) and to stories of related phenomena usually attributed to disturbed children or adolescents. More recent reports about the sensational exploits of Uri Geller (see, e.g., Cox, 1974) point in the same direction.

Even more perplexing is the occurrence of apparent precognition, both spontaneous and experimental, as reported in the literature of parapsychology. Nevertheless, it should be noted that the statistical evidence for precognition under laboratory conditions is in no way inferior to that for "simple" telepathy, clairvoyance, or PK. Yet it is needless to say that in order to account for observations of precognition, we require more than a mere extension of our traditional neurophysiological model of personality, functioning in the categories of classical Euclidian space and prerelativistic time. Keeping this proviso in mind, the extension hypothesis, as proposed here, is useful in several ways:

First, it carries the basic dichotomy of our sensory-motor organization from the ego to the non-ego; from the confines of individual personality structure to the universe at large.

Second, it is suggestive of a striking structural similarity and clinical affinity of both ESP and PK to two major manifestations of conversion hysteria: hysterical anesthesia on the one hand and motor paralysis on the other. This is particularly important in the present context. The critical point is that in conversion hysteria a part of the body image is cut off from the whole, dissociated from conscious awareness, and inaccessible to volitional control: the anesthetic or paralyzed limb is turned into non-ego as far as the patient's perceptions or motor behavior are concerned. By contrast, in telepathy, clairvoyance, or PK, a specific segment or area of the non-ego is temporarily turned into ego and becomes accessible to the subject's direct awareness or volitional control. In effect, both psi phenomena and conversion hysteria are marginal manifestations of our mental life. They are Grenzfälle or borderline cases, one representing the mirror image of the other.

A third implication of the extension hypothesis is closely related to this state of affairs. In the late 19th century Charcot, Janet, and their associates, puzzled by the discovery of glove- or stocking-shaped anesthetic zones in their hysterics or hypnotized subjects, were forced to the then revolutionary proposition that such disturbances cut across the familiar lines of neural distribution and must therefore be attributed to the power of the patient's ideas or imagination. This is how the new principle that functional disorders--of symbolic representation, of "organ language"-- transcended the familiar laws of cerebral localization was born. We shall see that the occurrence of psi phenomena forces upon us an even more revolutionary proposition--that the "power of ideas" may extend from what can be described as the autopsychic into the heteropsychic sphere without benefit of neural conduction or even anatomical contiguity. It is nevertheless in good keeping with this proposition that psi phenomena, though seemingly incompatible with causal laws, fully conform to familiar psychodynamic principles (Ehrenwald, 1955; Eisenbud, 1970).

A fourth implication of the extension hypothesis is derived from further historical considerations. There is a vast body of evidence connnecting psi phenomena with hypnosis, trance states, and conversion hysteria. There is reason to believe that some of Mesmer's and de Puységur's patients were indeed "psychic." Janet's and Gibert's experiments with Léonie involving hypnosis at a distance are a matter of historical record. Such experiments were recently revived by the Russian physiologist Vasiliev (1963) and other Soviet scientists. Moreover, many so-called "physical" mediums--from Eusapia Palladino and Rudi Schneider to Ted Serios--showed marked evidence of hysteria or other psychopathology. It should be noted, however, that such a clinical association is by no means unconditional; it is less apparent, or altogether absent, in many "mental" mediums.

The Genetic Hypothesis

This hypothesis tries to account for the origin of the newly discovered continent of the mind discussed here. It is derived from a vast number of observations on the relationship between mother and child during the symbiotic stage. I have pointed out elsewhere (Ehrenwald, 1971) that mother-child symbiosis can rightly be described as the cradle of ESP.

At the early symbiotic stage, communication is usually thought to be based on unconscious expressive movements, on "body language," on "mutual cuing" by intonation of voice, etc. However, in order to account for the flawless interaction and the delicately balanced regulatory functions operating within the mother-child unit, child psychiatrists and analysts have talked about empathy, intuition, or remnants of animal instincts otherwise lost to man (Mahler, 1968). Others suggest that "one unconscious" is able to communicate directly with "another unconscious." This, for instance, should account for the modus operandi of a symbiotic child's acting out his mother's repressed antisocial impulses, as described by Johnson and Szurek (1952) and other child analysts. I have described elsewhere (Ehrenwald, 1971) several cases in which strongly motivated mothers of mentally defective or otherwise handicapped children seemed capable of making up for their offsprings' shortcomings without the apparent aid of the usual channels of communication.

How, then, in view of the limited repertoire of conventional signaling devices used by them, do mother and child succeed in functioning together in such a harmonious way? How does mother know if baby cannot tell? How does baby respond to mother's cues if he doesn't understand? It is here that the telepathy hypothesis comes to our rescue. Telepathy, in this case, far from being a mere psychological curiosity without an apparent goal or discernible purpose, is well suited to fill whatever communication gap exists between mother and child in the symbiotic phase. Introducing the telepathy hypothesis into the symbiotic model assigns a vitally important physiological function to an otherwise seemingly superfluous or redundant mode of communication. Telepathy is a means of preverbal communication gradually lost in the course of separation/individuation.

Nevertheless, under pathological conditions--e.g., in prolonged symbiosis, in the REM state, or in the psychoanalytic situation--telepathic incidents may again make their appearance. They have frequently been reported between twins, lovers, and marriage partners, or other persons tied together by intimate bonds. This is how we arrive at the concept of a symbiotic gradient ranging from the early symbiotic phase to ESP in the family and then in society at large. In case of need, such a scheme can be extended to embrace inanimate objects, and indeed the aggregate of atoms, protons, and electrons from which both animate and inanimate matter has sprung. This would in effect amount to a vindication of some of the reports put forward by mystics of all ages and cultural backgrounds.

Personality: Open or Closed?

Our third proposition is closely linked with the genetic hypothesis. It postulates an open, non-Euclidian, post-Freudian personality structure as opposed to the traditional view of a closed, isolated, self-contained personality. I have pointed out above that more than half a century after the advent of relativistic physics and the formulation of quantum mechanics, current theories of personality are still steeped in the classical Judeo-Christian, Aristotelian, or Cartesian tradition. The classical personality structure, viewed in this light, is located in Euclidian space and pre-relativistic time, subject to the ironclad laws of cause and effect. By contrast, the open, postclassical, post-Freudian, non-Euclidian model, as conceived here, is continuous with the non-ego and with the rest of the world through the symbiotic gradient. It is potentially open to a virtually infinite range of impressions crowding in on the ego from outside. It is needless to say, however, that such an ego would be instantly swamped and disorganized by such a barrage of stimuli. It would suffer a breakdown comparable to that of an acute schizophrenic. It is to prevent such a contingency that our mental organization has erected diverse screening functions of the ego to protect it from sensory overload originating from both inside and outside--from the "autopsychic" and the "heteropsychic" spheres. This is why, except in various regressive states, the ego is relatively impervious to psi experiences.

The screening hypothesis, first proposed by Henri Bergson (1914), was originally merely a matter of speculation. However, like Freud's Reizschutz theory, it is now supported by evidence of the two-way, ascending and descending functions of the reticular formation in the brain stem, controlling sensory input and motor output, to and from the thalamic and higher cortical centers. In addition, clinical psychologists have contributed more specific information about perceptual defenses that protect the individual from sensory overload.

In these circumstances, the emergence of psi phenomena seems to be predicated on two heterogeneous sets of conditioning factors: (a) that psi phenomena arise from or are determined by flaws or inadequacies in the screening actions of neurophysiological regulatory functions--given that these functions control sensory as well as "extra"-sensory perceptions; and (b) that the phenomena are determined by psychodynamic or emotional factors involving the agent's, the percipient's, or the experimenter's needs (whether libidinal, narcissistic, or otherwise). In short, <u>psi</u> <u>phenomena</u> <u>are</u> <u>either</u> <u>flaw</u>-<u>determined</u> <u>or</u> <u>need</u>-<u>determined</u> <u>or</u> <u>both.</u>

In the case of overwhelming needs, emotional or interpersonal factors alone may suffice to bring about a given psi incident, e.g., in crisis situations. Alternatively, minor flaws or "minus functions" on the reticular, thalamic, limbic, or cortical levels of the central nervous system may be responsible for the breakthrough of occasional bursts of ESP incidents, e.g., in the traditional card-calling type of laboratory experiment. In this situation, one must assume that it is small clusters of neurons which are caught napping, or are firing at irregular intervals, before they return to their guard duty at the Doors of Perception against the intrusion of biologically irrelevant extrasensory flotsam and jetsam. On the other hand, the Maimonides experiments with telepathy in the REM state (Ullman and Krippner, with Vaughan, 1973) are examples of a combination of flaw- and need-determined psi responses. Here sleep provides the flaw-determined component, and the experimenter-subject relationship the need-determined component.

It should be noted, however, that our reference to "flaws" or minus functions at this point is culturally biased. It may rightly be argued that one man's "flaw" can be considered another man's psychic "proficiency." It is a flaw only insofar as Western man's adjustment to his standard, Euclidian world of experience is concerned.

The Psi Syndrome

Our fourth hypothesis should be mentioned in passing only. It suggests that the diverse modalities of psi phenomena form a syndrome of causal and spatio-temporal anomalies: They <u>run</u> <u>together;</u> they are mutually interchangeable, like time and space in the equation of relativistic physics or the particle versus wave theory of light. By the same token, they include such perplexing occurrences as precognition in life and in the laboratory. It should be noted that in so doing they are apt to pull the rug out from under the feet of most purely physicalistic theories of psi phenomena, including radiation, gravitational forces, or what not. A consistent theory of psi phenomena has to be a package deal: you have to take the whole syndrome on a like-it-or-lump-it basis. To change the metaphor: if you give the devil your little finger, he is apt to take your entire hand. Precognition is plainly incompatible with the Euclidian or Newtonian universe and runs equally counter to some of our ingrained habits of thinking.

The fact is that the statistical evidence of precognition in laboratory tests is by no means inferior to "ordinary" ESP or PK. Precognition occurs under virtually identical experimental conditions, is subject to the same need- and flaw-determined predisposing factors, and obeys identical psychodynamic principles. Indeed, it often makes its appearance in the same experimental subjects.

The affinity of the three modalities is also borne out by the difficulty of making a strict distinction among them under laboratory conditions. Even Schmidt's ingenious automated experiments (1969) aiming at separating PK from precognition failed to do so. Rhine has repeatedly pointed to the same difficulty of interpretation in a variety of GESP procedures.

In a similar vein, I noted that the Weird Sisters' prophecy that Macbeth would become "Thane of Glamis, Thane of Caudor and King Thereafter" can just as well be attributed to the witches' telepathic response to Macbeth's murderous impulses lying dormant in his unconscious, as to true precognition on their part. Alternatively, their prediction may be considered merely as a self-fulfilling prophecy.

Be that as it may, any theory failing to make allowance for precognition as an intrinsic aspect of psi phenomena would be incomplete. The package deal must cover the whole syndrome. Indeed, it appears that the distinction among the three modalities of psi is more a product of our discursive, analytic habits of thinking than a reflection of their intrinsic nature. It is the experimental design of the parapsychologist that tries to keep asunder what has originally been a unified phenomenon in nature.

In other respects "nature" does not seem to have taken kindly to psi phenomena. Their lack of dependability and accuracy, their incompatibility with logical, analytic reasoning, and the difficulty of their deliberate control has made them subject to repression in the life cycle of both the Western individual and his species. Psi phenomena do not seem (to a Westerner) to have been encouraged by the evolutionary process. This accounts for their affinity to dreams or psychotic disorders (Ehrenwald, in press) as well as for our stubborn tendencies toward not seeing them, denying them, and repressing them. This is, in effect, an integral part of the psi syndrome.

Listening with the Third Ear-- or, Processing with the Right Hemisphere?

The question of hemispheric processing leads us to our fifth hypothesis concerning the nature of psi phenomena. Ever since Broca, Wernicke, Hughlings-Jackson, and Pierre Marie, the right hemisphere has been considered the dumbbell in our mental organization. All higher intellectual functions, including speech, reading, writing, calculation, and analytic thinking, were relegated to the left side. Whatever the right hemisphere was able to do--for instance, in case of injury to the left hemisphere--did not measure up to the performance of the senior partner. It was deemed to be functionally inferior, lawless, disorganized.

A typical example is a case of a medical student who was admitted, many years ago, to the Neurological Department of the Vienna University, following a serious suicidal attempt. He was suffering from a gunshot wound affecting both parieto-occipital regions of the brain cortex, with the major damage on the left side.

The following is a summary of his case history, as I described it in my book, New Dimensions of Deep Analysis (1955).

The patient, aged 29, was admitted with a self-inflicted, penetrating gunshot wound of the head. The bullet had been removed by surgery, but the patient was left with serious damage both to his personality and to his intellectual functions. His speech was halting and at times he was at a loss in finding the names of objects or persons; that is, he showed evidence of amnestic aphasia. His handwriting was impaired, showing slight agraphic disturbances. He was unable to perform the simplest calculations. He lost his way in the hospital ward and was confused about spatial relations. His drawings showed the same confusion of up and down, right and left. Figure 1 shows an example of his

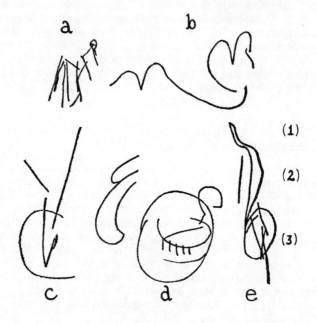

Fig. 1. Patient's drawings: (a) a French window; (b) the window latch; (c) a ship; (d) a face; (e) a tree drawn upside down, with (1) the root; (2) the trunk; (3) the crown.

drawings which he verbally described as follows: (a) a French window in his ward at the Neurologische Klinik in Vienna; (b) the window latch; (c) a ship; (d) a face, full front; (e) a tree drawn upside down with the root at the top, the crown at the bottom, and the trunk in the middle.

The most striking feature in these reproductions is the utter disorganization of the material. It seems to be broken to pieces, jumbled like meat that has passed through a chopping machine. On a diagram illustrating a compass he indicated south and west in the wrong directions. In short, displacement, inversion, and gross deviations from the horizontal were characteristic features of his spatial orientation and of his motor behavior in space.

His mistakes in temporal orientation were of the

same order. He could not tell how long he had been in the
Neurological Department, nor the length of time he had spent
waiting to be admitted to a surgical ward. He constantly
confused data referring to his stay in Vienna and to his life
prior to that in a small provincial town in Austria. "Before" and "after" in the temporal sense had lost their meaning to him much in the same way as spatial relationships
had. There was reason to believe that the patient's acalculia
was likewise due to an inability to organize ideas in a consistent system of temporo-spatial relationships.

This description is wholly in keeping with the neurological thinking current at the time, including that of my
former teacher, Otto Pötzl, author of a major (and since
then all but forgotten) study of so-called optical agnosias,
the disturbances of recognition and higher comprehension of
shapes and visual and tactile configurations. It pays exclu-
sive attention to the part played by damage to the left side
of the brain in the origin of such disturbances, and gives
little thought to the compensatory potential lying dormant in
the right hemisphere.

As it happened, I noted in 1954 that the drawings
produced by my patient are in effect the exact counterparts
of a "good" percipient trying to reproduce a drawing of a
telepathic target picture. This is illustrated, among other
points, by the now classical experiments of René Warcollier
(1948), the French parapsychologist. Figure 2 shows how

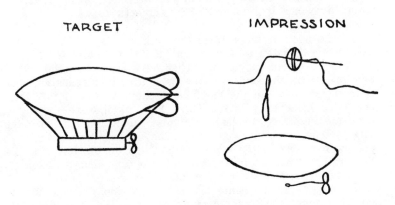

TARGET   IMPRESSION

Fig. 2. Target and percipient's impression in a telepathy
experiment by Warcollier (<u>Mind to Mind</u>, 1948).

the "normal" percipient had the same tendency to distort and disorganize the telepathically perceived target as did my brain-injured patient in trying to give a pictorial rendition of his jumbled perceptual world. More recently Ullman (1973) has called attention to the similarity of telepathic drawings and Pötzl's celebrated tachistoscopic experiments in which the subject was asked to make a drawing of his waking impressions and subsequent dream images after looking at target pictures exposed for a fraction of a second. Here, too, the resemblance between both telepathic impressions and the brain-injured patient's productions is unmistakable. The difference is that the brain-injured patient's difficulties are aggravated by the added impairment of his sensory-motor skills.

Yet what I--or for that matter, Professor Pötzl-- failed to realize at that time is that in such cases at least part of the damage caused to the left hemisphere is usually compensated for by the much maligned right hemisphere's faltering attempts to extract at least a modicum of order from the patient's disordered perceptual world. It can apparently do so only in utter disregard of spatio-temporal and casual relationships.

What, then, is the relevance of the similarity between the brain-injured patient's and the telepathic subject's perceptual world? It presents at least circumstantial evidence of the part played by the right hemisphere not only in the rudimentary drawings of patients suffering from optical agnosia, but in the telepathic drawings by "normal" ESP subjects as well.

Such an active role of the "other side" of the brain has been suggested by Gazzaniga (1967), Ornstein (1973), and others in recent years. They have found that the left hemisphere is the logician--the specialist in discursive, analytic thinking--while the right hemisphere is the artist, the poet--the Listener with the Third Ear, as it were--presiding over the intuitive, nonanalytical mode of consciousness. If this is true, we may well assign the central processing of psi impressions to the right, rather than to the left side of the brain. This would account for the conspicuous absence of the coordinates of time and space on the psi level of functioning. By the same token, it is no coincidence that psi phenomena duplicate in many respects the distortions of spatio-temporal relationships seen in my Vienna case cited above.

It is also interesting to note at this point that Freud's

primary process functioning, characteristic of the dream
level, is likewise stripped of the signposts of time and space
and also defies the laws of Aristotelian logic.

Another clue to the part played by the right hemisphere in the origin of telepathy, clairvoyance, or psychokinesis is provided by recent EEG studies. They suggest
an increase of right hemisphere activity associated with psi
phenomena.

It is needless to say, however, that even such a close
association falls short of solving the enigma of the ultimate
cerebral localization of psi. We may conjecture that it is
the right rather than the left side in which the processing of
incoming psi messages takes place or which provides the
leverage for PK activity reaching beyond the confines of the
ego. But I have pointed out (Ehrenwald, 1948) that we cannot tell how, in the last analysis, normal sensory stimuli
originating from the outside are turned into conscious awareness; how a certain wavelength of light, for example, is perceived as "red." Nor do we know how volition or an ordinary motor impulse orginating in the brain cortex is con-
verted into action. The first step from reception to perception in an extrasensory impression (or the first step in a
volitional act leading to PK) is equally mysterious. All we
know is that both take place in the "little black box" of the
skull. The difference between the two lies merely in the
fact that in one case the gap in our understanding is small
and inconspicuous and at best still baffles a few metaphysi-
cians or theologians, while the gap looms woefully large in
the case of ESP or PK and is apt to give rise to endless
debates among the experts.

Nevertheless, psychologists and behavioral scientists
in general have learned to live comfortably with the gap--or
the hiatus--in the autopsychic sphere without developing symp-
toms of an epistemological hernia. It should be only fair to
ask for the same privilege for their parapsychological con-
frères, without pressing them for ultimate answers, which
have so far eluded those engaged in more solidly established
fields of scientific inquiry.

There is, however, one more question that may le-
gitimately be asked of the student of psi phenomena: What
is responsible for the fitful emergence of occasional psi
phenomena in a person's awareness or radius of action?
What is conducive to such abrupt shifts from the standard,

Euclidian level of functioning to the non-Euclidian level?
What is the nature of the psychological quantum jump, of the
metaphysical somersault, that induces us to turn our attention from one level of consciousness to another--from Cas-
taneda's "ordinary" to "non-ordinary" psychic reality or,
put in more pedestrian, neurophysiological terms, from the
presumed dominance of the left hemisphere to that of the
right hemisphere? This question leads to what is here described as the hypothesis of the existential shift, or to what
is often more loosely labeled as an altered state of consciousness.

Psi Phenomena and the Existential Shift

Our sixth hypothesis concerns the mental state conducive to telepathic or clairvoyant perception. This state has
been described variously as "mental quietude," as relaxation, as calm alertness reminiscent of Freud's prescription
for the psychoanalyst's free-floating attention in the therapeutic situation. Its original prototype is the mother-child
symbiosis, which in turn is duplicated in diverse other
states of regression "in the service of the ego." Also related are Zen or yoga meditation and their attending alpha
states. This is why attempts at producing alpha activity in
the ESP percipient by various methods of biofeedback to promote receptiveness are now increasingly being used by experimental parapsychologists. The same is true for experiments in the REM sleep stage and other "minus functions"
of the ego. Less information is available about the EEG
concomitants and other aspects of the agent's mental state,
but suggestions concerning its psychodynamics go back to
Freud himself (1921). He drew the picture of a mind in action, of a person motivated by unconscious or preconscious
wishes, desires, and impulses--even though he might be ut-
terly unaware of his functioning as an agent.

A similar picture emerges from recent reports on
Kulagina, the Russian physical medium whose phenomena
have been referred to above. In her attempts to move by
sheer "will power" such external objects as match boxes or
ballpoint pens, she goes through a series of frantic body
movements reflecting the physical effort seemingly involved
in the PK process. Her whole behavior, as seen in the
films taken of her sittings, is strongly reminiscent of a patient's faltering attempts to move a paralyzed limb--that is,
a part of his anatomy which has virtually turned into non-ego.

Yet I have emphasized that none of our conventional principles of cerebral localization, neural conduction, etc., can account for perplexing feats of this order. We have to be ready for the literally mind-stretching conclusion that, given a proper set of beliefs, motivations, personality variables, interpersonal configurations, and otherwise favorable predisposing factors, even Western man is capable of shifting his attention, his set or Einstellung, his volitional posture and his outlook on the world from the standard, Euclidean level of adaptation to an altogether different level of functioning. It includes a shift from magic to science; from prose to poetry; from the concrete to the abstract; from left to right hemisphere dominance. Thus the change of attitudes goes beyond the narrower concept of altered states of consciousness. It covers a wide repertoire of psychomotor and motivational attitudes, conscious and unconscious; patterns of observable behavior as well as of inner-space experiences. This is what is described here as the existential shift. Yet I hinted that the existential shift is by no means confined to the field of parapsychology; it can be effected by such widely divergent experiences and interventions as religious conversion, hypnosis, catharsis in psychotherapy, transition from sleep to wakefulness, or electric shock treatment.

Despite differences, all these varieties of the existential shift have one thing in common: they consist of an abrupt, global reshuffling and reorganization of a person's physiological and psychological adaptations. In the ideal case, they affect all levels of his spiritual, cognitive, perceptual, and motivational orientation to the world and his whole repertory of behavioral responses to the environment. If a physicochemical agent is responsible for the shift, it is brought to bear on the raw nerve endings, synapses, or cortical chemoreceptors of the brain. On the other hand, such psychological influences as emotionally charged imagery, symbolic cues, radio commands, or incoming psi stimuli "home in" on the identical pharmacological or neurohumoral target areas of the brain, circumventing the familiar afferent pathways of the central nervous system. If so, they may be affected in much the same way as by a shot of norephedrin, a cortisone injection, or 200 mg. of LSD. In the last analysis, the final common pathway is the same in both instances--in the response to both somatic and psychological stimuli. But whatever be the modus operandi of the existential shift, the crucial point is that it is the fundamental reorientation of our mode of experience toward a new, or rather age-old, but culturally repressed, psychic reality that gives rise to psi phenomena.

Let me close with a passage quoted from an earlier paper (Ehrenwald, 1972):

> There can be no doubt that there are many loose ends and open questions left in the ... interlacing hypotheses proposed here. Nor is it reasonable to expect that the resulting neuropsychiatric model of psi phenomena, however comprehensive, should be capable of doing justice to the totality of man in all his existential and spiritual dimensions. But I hope that the preceding argument has made it sufficiently clear that ESP and other supposedly occult occurrences need no longer remain foreign bodies in our contemporary system of thought. Paraphrasing a famous passage from Hippocrates' On the Sacred Disease, it could be stated that 'it is thus with the manifestations called occult: they appear to me to be nowise more occult than other mental manifestations, but have natural causes from which they originate...' [p416].

REFERENCES

Bergson, H. Presidential address. Proceedings of the Society for Psychical Research, 27 (1914), 157-75.

Cox, W. E. "Notes on Some Experiments with Uri Geller." Journal of Parapsychology, 38 (1974), 408-11.

Ehrenwald, J. Telepathy and Medical Psychology. New York: Norton, 1948.

_____. New Dimensions of Deep Analysis: A Study of Telepathy in Interpersonal Relationships. New York: Grune and Stratton, 1955.

_____. "Mother-Child Symbiosis: Cradle of ESP." Psychoanalytic Review, 58 (1971), 455-66.

_____. "A Neurophysiological Model of Psi Phenomena." Journal of Nervous and Mental Disease, 154 (1972), 406-18.

_____. "The Telepathy Hypothesis and Schizophrenia." Journal of the American Academy of Psychoanalysis, in press.

Eisenbud, J. Psi and Psychoanalysis. New York: Grune and Stratton, 1970.

Freud, S. "Psycho-Analysis and Telepathy [1921]." Standard Edition (London: Hogarth Press, 1955), v18, p173-93.

Gazzaniga, M. S. "The Split Brain in Man." Scientific American, 217 (1967), 24-9.

Johnson, A. and Szurek, S. "The Genesis of Antisocial Acting Out in Children and Adults." Psychoanalysis Quarterly, 21 (1952), 323-43.

Jung, C. G. Memories, Dreams, Reflections. New York: Pantheon, 1963.

Mahler, M. On Human Symbiosis and the Vicissitudes of Individuation. New York: International Universities Press, 1968.

Ornstein, R. E. In Psychology Today, 6 (1973), 12, 87-92.

Pratt, J. G., and Keil, H. H. J. "Firsthand Observations of Nina S. Kulagina Suggestive of PK Upon Static Objects." Journal of the American Society for Psychical Research, 67 (1973), 381-90.

Rhine, L. E. Mind Over Matter. New York: Macmillan, 1970.

Schmeidler, G. R. "PK Effects Upon Continuously Recorded Temperature." Journal of the American Society for Psychical Research, 67 (1973), 325-40.

Schmidt, H. "Precognition of a Quantum Process." Journal of Parapsychology, 33 (1969), 99-108.

Ullman, M. "Bio-Communication in Dreams." Journal of the American Academy of Psychoanalysis, 1 (1973), 429-46.

_____ and Krippner, S., with A. Vaughan. Dream Telepathy. New York: Macmillan, 1973.

Vasiliev, L. L. Experiments in Mental Suggestion. Church Crookham, England: Institute for the Study of Mental Images, 1963.

Warcollier, R. Mind to Mind. New York: Creative Age Press, 1948.